North Eastern Locomotive Sheds

North Eastern Locomotive Sheds

K. Hoole

DAVID & CHARLES . NEWTON ABBOT

ISBN 0 7153 5323 3

Set in 11/13 Press Roman
and printed and reproduced in Great Britain
by Redwood Press Limited Trowbridge and London
for David & Charles (Publishers) Limited
Newton Abbot Devon

Contents

APPENDICES

List of Illustrations

Author's Note

My interest in NER sheds goes back many years and the following details have been collected from various sources, but mainly from personal visits to the sheds, and researches in the invaluable files of the British Transport Historical Records Office at York, where every assistance has been given by Mr W.J. MacDonald.

Details of some of the early sheds are scarce and in some examples the information presented is incomplete. Small scraps of information are, however, still coming to hand but if I waited until everything was complete then this work would never see the light of day. On the other hand there is a lot of information, particularly on actual locomotives stationed at the various sheds, for which there is just no space available.

Fortunately photographs of many old sheds exist, including sheds which have been out of use for over seventy-five years or more: in fact some such buildings have only recently been demolished, whilst others remain in use as warehouses etc.

If anyone can add any information, however meagre, I shall be pleased to hear from them.

CHAPTER I

Introduction

Millions of words have been written about the steam locomotive, its design, its appearance, and its performance, but how many have been written on the locomotive shed, where a steam locomotive spent about two thirds of its time, or on the staff that maintained the locomotives?

The various editions of *Locomotive Management from Cleaning to Driving* gave a survey of the technical details of the locomotive, and *The Steam Locomotive in Traffic* by E.A. Phillipson covered the equipment and staff needed to keep a locomotive in daily running order. Perhaps the most lucid exposition of steam locomotive details appeared in the *Handbook for Railway Steam Locomotive Enginemen* issued by the British Transport Commission in 1957. However, very little has been written about the sheds themselves and the people who, over the years, have toiled and sweated in primitive conditions on the filthy, dirt-producing monster we know as the steam locomotive. Certain footplate men have been venerated in print – *Bill Hoole, Engineman Extraordinary,* or *I Drove the Cheltenham Flyer* by Driver J.W. Street – but what about Bill Bloggs and his mate who took down, eased, and reassembled a big end that was tending to get warm, so that Driver X could run like the wind and get a mention in Cecil J. Allen's *Locomotive Practice & Performance* series in the *Railway Magazine*? Or Joe Soap, who clattered around in his boiler-washers' clogs, getting the scale out of the boiler to give Fireman Y a better opportunity to provide plenty of steam; or Sam Smith, who had the monotonous task of sweeping the tubes for the same reason? At the back of every footplate crew was an army of men keeping the steam locomotive in running order. Latterly, it must be admitted, they were fighting a losing battle, what with shortage of staff and materials, poor conditions, and with the shadow of redundancy hanging over them. And conditions certainly were bad, often with primitive sanitary facilities and none of the current amenity blocks. One shed I knew had a single cold water tap and a small corner washbasin for more than thirty men. It was better to get a bucketful of hot water from the injector overflow and wash on the footplate rather than use the messroom washbasin, where sand had to be used in an effort to get the grease and dirt off one's hands.

Lighting was another problem: there were usually gas lights down each road inside the shed but if work had to be done on an engine at night it often had to be carried out by the flickering light of a naked flame paraffin torch lamp, with its smoking flame going this way and that in the draughts. And draughts there were in plenty in every shed — many of the smaller sheds had large hinged wooden doors which although some 14ft high and 10ft wide were frequently damaged by engines in the hands of crews who could not see them! Another fault was that the doors were not properly secured when open and the gust of wind which caused them to swing always came just as an engine was passing. A sound of splintering timber and another door had to be laid on one side pending repair.

Carelessness also led to turntable troubles — some tables were devils to turn if a heavy engine was not balanced correctly. In some cases this required the tender tank filling with water before attempting to turn, whilst others required an empty tank and if you filled the tank first you were in trouble. When a table did stick half way round many drivers would risk moving the engine a few inches under its own steam, often with disastrous results as it ran off the end of the track and ploughed into the ballast, or worse. And how many engines have run on to a turntable, only to find too late that the table was set for another road. The engine then finished up in the turntable pit and required a crane to retrieve it!

Of course the layout of many old sheds left much to be desired, usually because of the cramped layout designed for an earlier age and smaller engines, and shed yard collisions were frequent. Fortunately usually only minor damage was done to running plates and buffers, but outside cylinders did tend to suffer in some sidelong collisions. When the three cylinders were cast in one block it was an expensive task to replace them. In at least one case a V2 at York suffered such damage but it was one of the class fitted with three separate cylinder castings and it was possible to unbolt and remove the damaged cylinder at the shed before the engine was sent to Darlington works to have a replacement fitted.

The Men

In the nineteenth century an engine driver was looked up to as a steady, hard working, reliable man but his image has declined over the years, probably because of the untimely strikes held especially in the last twenty years. Strikes by railwaymen are certainly nothing new and the North Eastern Railway suffered badly in 1867 when the footplate men demanded better conditions. They submitted a Memorial to the NER board of directors asking for a minimum wage of 5s 6d (27½p) per day for drivers, rising to 7s 6d (37½p) after six years, and firemen 3s 6d (17½p) per day to 4s 6d (22½p); ten hour day; time and a half on Sundays; a six day guaranteed week; a new top coat for each man once a year; a lodging allowance of 2s 6d (12½p) per night; one hour preparation and one hour stabling time at the start and finish of duty; and free passes for the man and his family. The directors did not see their way to granting these requests and 1,080 men came out on strike. The NER directors, not liking mutiny in the ranks dismissed the lot of them. At that time there were plenty of men waiting to step into the strikers' shoes and W.W. Tomlinson records that only 174 drivers and 67 firemen were re-employed.

The North Eastern Railway was early in the field with management and staff consultation and although discipline was very strict the North Eastern men were comparatively well off. However, the injustice of suspending a driver from duty because of alleged drunkenness in off duty hours led to a week's strike in December 1912. At other times the footplate crews went on strike in sympathy with the miners.

In the early days of railways the driver was paid a certain amount for each ton of coal per mile hauled, and out of this sum he had to provide coal and oil, and pay the fireman. The driver also carried out his own minor repairs but major repairs were done at the expense of the railway company. On the Clarence Railway in 1839 the amount was .1875d per ton per mile, and on the Stockton & Darlington Railway .1175d per ton per mile.

When hourly wages were paid different rates applied to drivers and firemen depending on the duties on which they were employed. For instance, on the NER in 1867 the crew on a shunting engine was the lowest paid and the men on the mineral and goods trains the highest, with passenger train crews coming in between:

Type of Train	*Rate per Hour*	
	Driver	Fireman
Shunting and piloting	5d	4d
Passenger	6¾d	4d
Minerals and goods	7¼d	5d

Eventually the principle was changed and all drivers of equal seniority received the same amount whether they were on a humble 0-6-0T pilot or a magnificent Gresley Pacific. However, the Pacific driver did get additional payment by way of a mileage bonus.

The rates of pay on the Stockton & Darlington section in 1872 also depended upon what type of engine a driver was working —

Type of Train	*Rate per Hour (Driver)*
General mineral, excursion, goods to Kirkby Stephen and west thereof or any similar train on NER other than the Darlington section	7½d
Goods trains on Darlington section other than to Kirkby Stephen and west thereof	6¾d
Working exclusively on the Wear & Derwent Railway with firebox engines	6d
Piloting or shunting engines, or	5d

working trains exclusively on the
Wear & Derwent Railway with
Return Tube Engines, or on the
West Durham branch
Passenger, other than excursions, or   6¾d
  when learning any new lead

In April 1874 a standard ten hour day was introduced on the
NER at the following rates of pay:

Type of Train	Rate per Day	
	Driver	Fireman
Shunting and piloting	5s 0d (25p)	3s 4d (17p)
Passenger	7s 0d (35p)	4s 0d (20p)
Mineral and goods	7s 0d (35p)	4s 2d (21p)

In a notice issued on 1 January 1883 Alexander McDonnell
modified these rates and divided the types of trains into five:

Type of Train	Rate per Day	
	Driver	Fireman
Shunting	5s 0d (25p)	3s 4d (17p)
On outlying branches and trains of minor importance	6s 0d (30p)	3s 4d (17p)
Short mineral trains and trains on short branch lines	6s 6d (32½p)	3s 8d (18½p)
Trains on main line	7s 0d (35p)	4s 0d (20p)
Express trains on main line	7s 6d (37½p)	4s 4d (22p)

Over the next thirty years wages varied little but World War I
started an upward trend. A NER booklet issued in 1918 quoted
the following rates for a 54 hour week: Driver 36s 0d (£1.80) to
45s 0d (£2.25) per week; fireman 22s 6d (£1.12½) to 30s 0d
(£1.50) per week. Increments depended solely on seniority.
However, drivers on East Coast trains could earn additional
increments to raise their pay to 47s 0d (£2.35) per week and
fireman similarly to 36s 0d (£1.80) a week.
A publication issued by the National Union of Railwaymen in
1927 gave the standard rates throughout the country as drivers

72s 0d (£3.60) to 90s 0d (£4.50) and firemen 57s 0d (£2.85) to
72s 0d (£3.60) for a week of forty-eight hours. Mileage bonus was
payable over 140 miles, with 15 miles equivalent to 1 hour above
this figure.

In 1958 a booklet on wages issued by the Associated Society of
Locomotive Engineers and Firemen quoted, drivers 198s 0d (£9.90)
to 222s 6d (£11.12½), and firemen 163s 0d (£8.15) to 198s 0d
(£9.90) for a forty-four hour week. By this time the qualifying
minimum for mileage payment had been reduced to 70 miles and
for each 10 miles between 70 and 140 miles a driver received an
additional 3d (1.25p) per shift and a fireman 2½d (1p). Above
140 miles drivers and firemen received one hour's pay for every
15 miles. Thus, for working between Newcastle and Kings Cross
a driver received a normal day's pay + 1s 9d (9p) + 45s 0d (£2.25),
which worked out at approximately two days pay for one day's
work!

An even more lucrative duty brought about by the introduction
of Deltic diesel-electric locomotives was a return trip in eight hours
between York and Kings Cross worked by York men. This gave
a total mileage of 376 — of which 306 miles qualified for mileage
bonus. This roster gave the fortunate crews *three* day's pay for one
day's work!

Crews working between 10.0pm and 6.0am on weekdays were
paid at time and a quarter, and all overtime between these hours
at time and a half. All Sunday duty, whether by night or by day,
was paid at time and three quarters additional to the basic weekly
wage.

A later award gave senior drivers a basic weekly wage of 379s 0d
(£18.95) plus improved mileage allowances, and in September
1969 a further 8% increase was announced, back dated to 4
August 1969, putting an extra 30s 0d (£1.50) a week (less tax)
into their pay packets.

Cleaners received from 10s 0d (50p) to 22s 0d (£1.10) a week
in 1918; 24s 0d (£1.20) to 42s 0d (£2.10) a week in 1927; and
72s 0d (£3.60) to 103s 6d (£5.17½) (Junior cleaner) and 149s 6d
(£7.47½) to 151s 6d (£7.57½) (Senior cleaner) in 1958. By 1968
a 15 year old cleaner started at 117s 0d (£5.85) per week and
could rise to a maximum of 260s 0d (£13.0).

To encourage footplate staff to become proficient in First Aid they were granted one or two days additional leave when certain examinations had been passed.

The Engines — Allocations

In the early days of railways an engine was allocated to a driver and fireman and they were the only persons allowed to work it. When the crew were off duty the engine was in the shed, often locked up so that no-one else could use it. With the need for greater efficiency the practice developed of having two regular crews to an engine, one set working it for the first part of the day and the other set of men for the second part. They would change over duties weekly, or at longer intervals, so that each crew got their share of early and late turns. In fact this method continued at some of the smaller steam sheds well into British Railways' days.

In the 1930s the common user method was developed, which entailed having a fleet of identical engines stationed throughout the line so that any engine could be used on almost any class of train and worked efficiently by almost any crew. Thus a locomotive could be handled by a number of crews each day and finish its day at a depot other than its own. It would normally return to its home shed on the second day, but in some cases the second day involved a further working before it returned to its home depot on the third day. With the diesel locomotive the workings or diagrams often run for six days and may take the locomotive from one end of the country to the other, with numerous changes of crew en route.

For many years engines have been 'diagrammed', that is, every train in the timetable has a particular range of locomotive types allocated to work it. The shed to supply the locomotive is specified, and also on one locomotive during its day's work.

The diagrams are prepared at the Head Office of the Company (NER), Area (LNER) or Region (BR) so that in theory each locomotive can be used to best advantage — both economically and technically. The diagrams are then issued to the respective depots prior to the introduction of a revised service so that the crews can accustom themselves to their duties. With one or two sets of men to an engine the engine and crew diagrams will correspond when they work the same engine all day, but with the modern six day cyclic rosters the engine and crew diagrams are issued separately. One crew may now handle three or four locomotives during the course of a day's work, although on an out and home turn they usually have one engine for the outward working and a different one for the return trip.

On some occasions it is necessary to change the working of a diagram from one shed to another and this may mean transferring the locomotives at the same time.

Typical NER Engine Diagram

Hull No 12 engine and men: 2 October 1922

		am
Hull	-	7-34
York	9-13	12-25
Hull	2-0*	4-25
Scarborough	7-19	8-15
Hull	9-53	10-20
Beverley	10-38	10-55
Hull	11-13	-

	1st set	2nd set
Men sign on	6-30am	3-30pm
Men sign off	2-30pm	11-30pm
Hours on duty	8-0	8-0

* = men change

Typical LNER Diagram

Blaydon No 2 engine and men: 1 May 1939
Class VI engine

			am
Shed	-		3-48 LE
Newcastle	3-55		4-10
South Shields	4-53	P	6-57 Empty
Newcastle	7-26		9-46 Empty
Heaton Carriage Sidings	9-56		- LE
Shed	-	@	10-23 LE
Heaton Carriage Sidings	-		10-33 Empty
Newcastle	10-43		11-45
Sunderland	12-25		12-47 via Wellfield
West Hartlepool	1-44	PP	3-50 via Wellfield
Sunderland	4-51		4-58
Newcastle	5-35		5-46 LE
Shed	5-56	@LD	7-48 LE
Newcastle	-		8-10
Consett	9-8		9-53 Empty
Scotswood Bridge Sidings	10-35		- LE

Newcastle		12-35	Empty
Heaton Carriage Sidings	12-45	2-0	Empty
Newcastle	2-10	2-15	LE
Shed	2-25	D	

1st set prepare engine: 3rd set locomotive duties prior to 7-48pm
P Pilot
PP Pilot until 2-45pm
@ Enginemen change
LD Locomotive duties
D Shed staff stable engine

	1st set	*2nd set*	*3rd set*
Sign on	2-48am	11-8am	7-8pm
Sign off	10-48am	6-8pm	2-35am
Hours	8-0	8-0	7-27

INSTRUCTIONS FOR PREPARING AND STABLING ENGINES 1918

Where conveniently practicable Drivers and Firemen are allowed to prepare their own engines and where this is done the following time is allowed for that purpose, calculated from booking on to leaving the shed. Also when stabling their own engines they are allowed the following time for that purpose, including coaling and booking off:

Class of Engine	*Preparing (Minutes)*	*Stabling (Minutes)*
4cc, Z, V, R, R1, S, S1, S2, Q, Q1, M, T, T1, T2	50	70
All other tender engines	40	60
Tank engines except D, W, and Y	35	50
Tank engines W	40	60
Tank engines D and Y	50	70
Shunting engines except X	30	35
Shunting engines X	50	70

Where no coaling has to be done at the finish of the day's work ten minutes are deducted from the above allowance.

Fortunately a series of *Goods Engine Workings* books have survived at York covering the years 1913 to 1926 and these give the diagrammed workings of the goods engines allocated to the various sheds. However, the GEW diagrams do not give a true picture of the freight and mineral trains which were running on any one day. This is because so many mineral trains were worked to what is now known as 'Control Order'. It is obvious that it was unnecessary to move train loads of coal to a port if the ship was not berthed ready to receive it. The ships could be delayed by storms or for many other reasons and thus the trains were run to suit the day to day position and were not ordered to run to the port of shipment until the ship concerned was ready to take aboard the coal. A similar position occurred with incoming shipments and an example may be quoted concerning pit props. Before the introduction of the modern steel variety these timber props came from the Scandinavian countries by the shipload and when a ship arrived at Hull trainloads of the props could be seen heading for the South Yorkshire coalfield. Then they would disappear until another shipload arrived in Victoria Dock.

The following table gives the number of regular freight trains worked by each shed in the summer of 1913:

Shed	Number of Daily Goods Diagrams	Shed	Number of Daily Goods Diagrams
Alnmouth	3	Malton	9
Annfield Plain	2	Masham	1*
Blaydon	20	Middlesbrough	2
Blyth	3	Newport	20
Borough Gardens	31	Normanton	5
Bridlington	1	Northallerton	4
Byers Green	1	North Blyth	2
Carlisle	18	Percy Main	2
Consett	1	Pickering	1
Darlington	39	Scarborough	2
Doncaster	2	Selby	16
Ferryhill	14	Shildon	2
Gateshead	12	Starbeck	18
Haverton Hill	1	Stockton	6
Heaton	37	Sunderland	15
Hexham	1	Thirsk	7
Hull	38	Tweedmouth	20
Kirkby Stephen	2	Tyne Dock	15
Leeds	32	Wear Valley Junction	2

West Auckland	1	Whitby	5
West Hartlepool	20	York	54

*= worked by passenger engine

By 1913 a number of Lodging Turns were being worked and typical examples were:

Hull No 30 worked Hull to Forth (Newcastle), returning from Park Lane (Gateshead), alternating with Borough Gardens engine and men.

Hull No 31 worked Hull to Monkwearmouth and return, alternating with Sunderland engine and men.

Leeds No 5 worked Leeds to Tyne Dock and return, alternating with Tyne Dock engine and men.

By 1919 in a search for economy and efficiency a number of Exchanging Turns had been introduced. On these workings the engine worked through to the destination of the train and returned the following day, whereas the men changed at some convenient point with the men on the working in the opposite direction, so that each set of men finished duty at their home shed. These turns in 1919 were:

Tweedmouth-Heaton	Gateshead-York
Tyne Dock-Starbeck (Class S engine)	Gateshead-Starbeck
Normanton-Heaton (Class S engine)	Gateshead-Selby
Hull-Darlington	Hull-Thirsk
York-Darlington	

The Grouping of 1923 enabled North Eastern engines to work further afield and in a modified list of Exchanging Turns in force from 14 July 1924 a number of Hull men exchanged with men from the Southern Area, so that the Hull engine spent alternate nights at the Southern Area shed, and the Southern Area engine spent alternate nights at Dairycoates shed:

Tweedmouth-Alnmouth	Selby-Newport

Heaton-Alnmouth
Heaton-Tweedmouth
Carlisle-Blaydon
Darlington-York
Heaton-York
Heaton-Leeds

Blaydon-York
Gateshead-York

Darlington-Kirkby Stephen
Hull-Bradford (So Area)
Hull-Bridlington
Hull-Sheffield (So Area)
Hull-Colwick (So Area)
Springhead (Hull)-Ardsley
  (So Area)
Springhead-Cudworth

TRANSFERS

A feature of railway periodicals over the last thirty or forty years has been the lists of engine transfers — details of locomotives which have been moved from one engine shed to another. Most people would say 'what does it matter where an engine is stationed, it still works on the railway' but, of course, only engines at certain sheds work certain trains and it is not just a case of hanging any train behind any locomotive. Suitability of each class of engine for a particular type of train must be considered, and also the booked speed of the train; the length of the run; number of stops; whether the duration of the main stops will allow coal and/or water to be taken; turnround time at end of run; turning facilities; weight restrictions; staffing arrangements etc. Other factors concerning the transfer of locomotives between sheds involve the state of the local trade (particularly with regard to freight engines in industrial areas); a change of loading or timing of the train; need to replace an engine withdrawn from service; allocation of new engines to a shed involving the downgrading of engines of older pattern which, in turn, can displace engines from another shed; number of engines under repair; engines with special fittings which require to be observed; staff complaints etc.

Fortunately I have been able to refer to the Register of Engine Transfers maintained in the North Eastern Area of the LNER between 1925 and 1945 and from this volume I have extracted some typical specific transfers and the reason why they were made:

17 March 1925   2228 Class Q6 0-8-0 Selby to Scarborough
1149 Class Q5 0-8-0 Scarborough to Selby
Superheated engine required at Scarborough to work 5.40am mineral
empties to Gascoigne Wood and return working with loaded mineral.

19 March 1925   1973 & 1991 Class P1 0-6-0 York to Shildon
1129 & 1195 Class A7 4-6-2T Shildon to York
1703 Class G5 0-4-4T Hull to Malton
214 Class D23 4-4-0 Malton to Hull
Tank engines required at York for working goods trains to Malton, and
tank engines required at Malton for passenger trains, all due to Malton
turntable being under repair. Engines returned May 1925.

15 June 1925   1245 Class D21 4-4-0 York to Hull
712 Class D20 4-4-0 Hull to York
Larger engine required for 8.55am Hull-Sheffield train.

9 Oct 1925   1541 Class D22 4-4-0 (dual brake) Scarborough-Starbeck
42 Class D22 4-4-0 (Westinghouse) Hull-Scarborough
Dual brake fitted engine required at Starbeck after NUR complaint
re Westinghouse brake engine being provided to assist 4.17pm ex
Newcastle from Ripon.

9 Jan 1926   2389 & 2390 Class J27 0-6-0 Shildon to Newport
410 & 2121 Class Q5 0-8-0 Newport to Shildon
Balanced wheels engines required at Newport for York change-over turn.

8 March 1928   1693 Class G5 0-4-4T Sunderland to Durham
1793 Class G5 0-4-4T Durham to Sunderland
Patches on firebox side of 1693 affected by hard water at Sunderland.

5 Nov 1928   468 Class G5 0-4-4T Darlington to Ilkley
439 Class G5 0-4-4T Starbeck to Darlington
1096 Class G5 0-4-4T Ilkley to Starbeck
Engine fitted with Raven's fog apparatus required for Darlington.

3 Dec 1928   468 Class G5 0-4-4T Ilkley to Starbeck
1096 Class G5 0-4-4T Starbeck to Ilkley
Complaint from Driver Douglas of Ilkley that his engine had been
taken off him: 1096 returned to Ilkley.

11 July 1929   684 Class D22 4-4-0 Selby to Saltburn
To work Saltburn to Leeds express passenger train.

25 July 1929   684 Class D22 4-4-0 Saltburn to Selby
Engine not strong anough for 9.14am Saltburn to Leeds express.

27 Sept 1929   6581 & 6613 Class O4 2-8-0 Dairycoates to Springhead
Experimental working on Hull & Barnsley section — in place of Class
J23 engines at Springhead to do away with double heading.

24 Oct 1934   1501 Class A8 4-6-2T Whitby to Leeds
Sunday Pullman delayed 17 minutes due to 2161 Class H1 slipping.

In May 1937 a programme of transfers was inaugurated to
concentrate engines of a class at specific sheds, and also to do

away with the practice of having a single example of a class at a shed. The first engine affected will serve as a typical example: on 31 May B16 2363 was transferred from Gateshead to York in exchange for K3 1318. This was the only B16 at Gateshead and thus by transferring it to York it could be incorporated in York's fleet of B16 engines and the stock of spares for the class held at Gateshead could be withdrawn. Gateshead had a number of K3 engines.

The scheme was implemented over a number of years until on 28 March 1943 York shed acquired all sixty-nine of the B16 engines.

Further upheavals were caused by the arrival of the WD and USA 2-8-0 engines in 1943, and also when they departed in the following year. The loan of forty J25 0-6-0 engines to the Great Western Railway from October 1939 also caused a number of transfers between sheds, including the acquisition of 0-6-0 engines from the Great Northern and North British sections. For instance, Malton shed received J36 0-6-0 9172 and 9604, which allowed J24 1821 and 1826 to be sent from Malton to North Blyth to replace J25 sent to the Great Western Railway. Details of engines transferred when a shed was closed will be found under the respective sheds.

Although most transfers were on a permanent basis it was the practice to transfer engines temporarily for a specific need.

9 Feb 1935	1223 D20 4-4-0 Gateshead to Alnmouth whilst 1877 (D17/2) under repairs
13 March 1934	864 Class N8 0-6-2T Hull to Selby to replace 861 (N8) damaged in collision
23 March 1933	1036 & 1053 Class J27 0-6-0 Sunderland to West Hartlepool
	Shortage of engines at West Hartlepool due to heating (six engines returned from York on trains hot!).
9 Feb 1933	41 and 454 Class F8 2-4-2T Blyth to Tyne Dock Engines 404 and 1582 for Darlington Works (in poor condition)

In most cases the engines were eventually returned to their own sheds but a few temporary transfers were made permanent.

Until 1925 it was the practice to transfer some passenger engines from the Northern Division to the Southern Division to help out with the summer traffic. Thus in 1925 D20 723 and D17/1 1621 were working from Scarborough and Selby sheds respectively. Normally these two engines were never seen working south of Newcastle. Just prior to the formation of the LNER the North Eastern Railway used to hire rolling stock from the Caledonian Railway to cover the demand at peak periods and assuming that 1621 came south in previous years these two factors could explain the existence of a photograph of 1621 at Bridlington on a train of Caledonian coaches.

NER DIVISIONS

For many years the Locomotive Department was divided into three divisions: Northern, Central and Southern. In June 1906 Mr Worsdell suggested that the Central Division should be abolished and the sheds divided between the Northern and Southern Divisions. This took effect from 1 January 1907:

NORTHERN	CENTRAL		SOUTHERN
Alnmouth	Byers Green*		Bridlington
Alston	Hartlepool		Hawes
Annfield Plain	Shildon	To	Hull
Blaydon	Stanhope	Northern	Leeds
Borough Gardens	Waskerley	Division	Leyburn
Bowes Bridge	Wearhead	1 January	Malton
Carlisle	Wear Valley	1907	Market Weighton
	Junction		
Consett	West Auckland		Masham
Durham	West Hartlepool		Normanton
Ferryhill*	Barnard Castle		Northallerton
Gateshead	Darlington		Pateley Bridge
Heaton	Guisborough		Pickering
Hexham	Haverton Hill		Scarborough
North Blyth	Kirkby		Selby
	Stephen**	To	
Pelton Level	Middlesbrough	Southern	Starbeck
Percy Main	Middleton in	Division	Thirsk
	Teesdale	1 January	
Seaham	Newport	1907	Whitby
South Blyth	Port Clarence		York
Sprouston	Richmond		
Sunderland	Rosedale		
Tweedmouth	Saltburn		
Tyne Dock	Stockton		

* = Transferred Northern Division to Southern Division 1921
** = Transferred Southern Division to Northern Division 1921

SHEDS IN EXISTENCE BUT OUT OF USE AT 31 DECEMBER 1922

Shed	Circular Sheds		Straight Sheds		Remarks
	Adjacent	*Separate*	*No*	*Roads*	
Battersby	-	-	1	3	demolished 1966
Boroughbridge	-	-	1	1	
Cockermouth	-	-	1	2	
Darlington (GNE)	-	-	1	2	
Darlington (North Road	-	2	-	-	In Works use: now demolished
Gateshead	-	1	-	-	now demolished
Gosforth	-	-	1	2	now demolished
Leeds (Holbeck)	-	2½	-	-	
Market Weighton	-	-	1	2	
Seaham	-	-	1	2	
Sprouston	-	-	1	1	
Sunderland (Hendon)	-	-	1	2	
Tebay	-	-	1	4	now demolished
Hensall Junction (HBR)	-	-	1	2	

PART ONE

Northern Division

NORTHERN DIVISION SHEDS IN 1914

Main Shed *Sub-shed (s)*	Engines	Men	Circular Sheds *Adjacent*	*Separate*	Straight Sheds *No*	*Roads*
Gateshead	130	562	4	-	-	-
Alnmouth	10	40	-	-	1	2
Hexham	4	20	-	-	1	2
Bowes Bridge	2	7	-	-	1	2
Borough Gardens	69	320	4	-	-	-
Tyne Dock	96	393	3	-	1	4
Annfield Plain	9	36	-	-	1	2
Pelton Level	2	10	-	-	1	1
Percy Main	33	153	-	-	2	3/3
South Blyth	25	101	-	-	1	6
North Blyth	23	97	-	1	-	-
Heaton Junction	118	565	-	-	1	8
Tweedmouth	47	182	-	1	1	4
Edinburgh	6	27	-	-	-	-
Blaydon	69	308	2	-	-	-
Carlisle	49	190	2	-	-	-
Alston	1	5	-	-	1	1
West Hartlepool	71	429	2	-	1	2
East Hartlepool	31	115	-	-	3	2/2/3
Sunderland	74	350	-	1	2	2/2
Durham	8	33	-	-	1	2
Waskerley	8	41*	-	-	2	2/2
Consett	5	14	-	-	1	1
Shildon	74	337**	3	-	-	-
West Auckland	22	102	-	1	-	-
Wear Valley Junct	4	19	-	1	-	-
Stanhope	1	5	-	-	1	3
Wearhead	1	5	-	-	1	1
Ferryhill	27	91	-	-	1	3
Byers Green	8	22	-	-	1	3
Total	**1027**	**4579**				

* Includes 6 Incline Enginemen at Weatherhill and 5 at Crawley
** Includes 7 Incline Enginemen at Stanley and 2 at Hedley Hope

CHAPTER II

Gateshead, Borough Gardens

Gateshead

The North Eastern Railway was unfortunate in that its three major constituents all chose sites for locomotive works where extensions were impossible — the York & North Midland at York, the Leeds Northern at Leeds, and the York, Newcastle & Berwick at Gateshead. The Stockton & Darlington, which joined the North Eastern fold in 1863 had, by then, taken the forward looking step of moving from Shildon to Darlington, where there was plenty of room for expansion. The works at York and Leeds were abandoned, York in 1905 and Leeds some twenty years earlier, but Gateshead continued to overhaul locomotives until 1932 and, in fact, was reopened again in World War II.

The Site at Gateshead was cramped enough with the works, but to have a large running shed on the same site made things even worse and it is a tribute to the staff that Gateshead continued as the main North Eastern shed until the end of steam and into the diesel era. Relief came in the 1870s with the opening of running sheds at Heaton and Borough Gardens (also known as Park Lane), followed by Blaydon in 1900. Heaton looked after the main line freight workings and some local passenger turns, Borough Gardens looked after local and long distance freight workings and numerous shunting turns, whilst Blaydon concentrated working trains to the west of Newcastle on the Carlisle line. Thus Gateshead developed into a shed catering mainly for the main line express passenger workings to York and Leeds in the south, and to Edinburgh in the north. Naturally the shed acquired the majority of the new express engines as they emerged from the adjacent works (together with some from private builders) and over the years its top link engines were the Fletcher Class 901 2-4-0 (1872); Tennant 2-4-0 (1885); T.W. Worsdell Class F and F1 4-4-0 (1887); Wilson Worsdell Class M and M1 4-4-0 (1892) and Class R 4-4-0 (1899); Class V 4-4-2 (1903); Raven Class Z and Z1 4-4-2 (1911) and 4-6-2 (1922).

In 1923 Gateshead shed had an allocation of sixty-two express passenger engines, made up of 24 4-4-0s, 31 4-4-2s, 5 4-6-0s and 2 4-6-2s, together with fourteen passenger tank engines and thirty-eight miscellaneous mixed traffic and shunting locomotives. In 1939 there were 24 Pacifics, in 1947 25 (+ 25 V2 2-6-2), and in 1954 35 (+ 12 V2s). Secondary express engines were 8 D49 4-4-0s in 1939; 5 B1 4-6-0s in 1947, and 8 B1s in 1954. The complete allocation for these years was:

	1923	1939	1947	1954
4-6-2				
A1/A3	-	16	16	9
A2 (ex NER)	2	-	-	-
A4	-	8	8	8
A1	-	-	-	14
A2	-	-	-	1
A2/3	-	-	1	3
4-6-0				
B1	-	-	5	8
B14	5	-	-	-
B16	10	-	-	-
4-4-2				
C6	7	2	4	-
C7	22	9	-	-
C8	2	-	-	-
C9	-	2	-	-
4-4-0				
D17/1	6	-	-	-
D17/2	3	-	-	-
D20	14	-	-	3
D22	1	-	-	-
D49	-	8	11	-
0-6-0				
J21	8	4	-	-
J25	2	-	-	-
J39	-	-	-	7

0-6-0T				
J71	4	6	8	5
J72	5	6	6	9
J77	1	-	-	-
J78	1	-	-	-
J79	1	-	-	-
MISCELLANEOUS				
A8 4-6-2T	-	3	-	-
F8 2-4-2T	2	-	-	-
G5 0-4-4T	6	2	-	1
G6 0-4-4T	1	-	-	-
H1 4-4-4T	5	-	-	-
K3 2-6-0	-	11	9	-
N8 0-6-2T	1	-	-	-
N10 0-6-2T	2	2	10	5
Q1 0-8-0T	-	-	2	-
Q5 0-8-0	-	2	-	-
V1/V3 2-6-2T	-	5	7	7
V2 2-6-2	-	-	25	12
Y1/Y3 0-4-0T	-	5	3	2
Y7 0-4-0T	3	-	-	-
TOTAL	114	91	115	94

In 1902 there was a proposal to build a new shed at Low Fell as a replacement for Gateshead, and also to accommodate engines from Heaton and Blaydon which could not be housed under cover. The position at that time was:

	Engines Allocated	*Stabling For*
Gateshead	117	75
Heaton	108	48 tender
Blaydon	58	45

However, nothing came of the scheme.

The history of the building at Gateshead is the most complicated of all NER sheds. At the date of the formation of the North Eastern Railway on 31 July 1854 extra accommodation for engines at Gateshead was already being discussed, so that on 18 August plans were ready and advertisements for tenders were authorised. The Locomotive Committee inspected the existing workshops and adjoining ground on 1 September and they approved the scheme, but on 12 October 1854 a revised plan was submitted 'with five stables under one roof'. This modified scheme was then approved and on 22 December 1854 a tender for £14,952 11s 2d was accepted. Even before construction commenced the plans were again modified and in April 1855 additional expenditure amounting to £1,000 was authorised 'for additional accommodation for future requirements'. Four turntables for the new shed were ordered in October 1855 at £450 each, and at the same time it was suggested that further extensions costing an additional £10,000 should be carried out. A decision on this matter was deferred but it was brought up again in March 1856 and although referred to the board of directors nothing seems to have been done at that time. However, Mr Fletcher brought up the matter again in February 1857, by which time the estimated cost had risen to £13,000, and Mr Harrison did the same exactly a year later but again without success.

The next move was on 4 August 1865, when plans were submitted for extra accommodation 'for about 40 engines'. The engineer was asked to prepare an estimate for a shed holding 14 engines! The revised plans were discussed on 15 September and the estimated expenditure of £6,400 was agreed to. Tenders totalling £6,874 were accepted on 27 October and construction had not progressed very far before there was another call for 'considerable extension of the engine shed accommodation at Gateshead'. This was in February 1867, and eventually a further £900 expenditure was granted for 'the enlargement of the original plan for the western extension of the engine shed'.

On 23 April 1869 the same procedure started once again, with the request for further accommodation, the submission of plans, the advertising for and acceptance of tenders (£6,130), the granting of excess expenditure, £720 5s 8d, and then 'further works required' (£3,200). A 42ft 6in turntable was also purchased for £347. This cycle was completed in 1877 and yet another commenced, this time with authorisation of a shed to hold 40 engines costing £13,522 19s 3d. In addition two turntables at £300 each delivered and erected were ordered from C. Ianson & Sons of Darlington.

Unfortunately it has proved impossible to ascertain to which portions of the present shed the various extensions listed actually refer, but a diagram of c1875 shows one large building covering six turntables and their associated radiating roads. In addition, of course, there was the roundhouse adjacent to Chaytor's Bank, usually referred to as the Newcastle & Carlisle shed but actually not as old as that may suggest. It was built to house the engines working on the Newcastle & Carlisle line after that company had been taken over in 1862 and eventually it was used as the paint shop for engines overhauled at Gateshead Works. The six turntables shown on the c1875 plan were situated so that four were in line parallel to the tracks leading from the Team Valley to Gateshead West station, with the other two between these four and the River Tyne. By 1902 the latter two turntables had disappeared, their pits filled in, and the space available included in the Works.

Of the four turntables existing in 1902 the most easterly was 42ft 5in diameter and the remaining three were 50ft diameter: the latter were replaced by three 60ft 'tables in 1910/11, when a further £12,466 was authorised for extensions. The large turntables were required for the Atlantic engines, ten of which were built in 1903-4, two in 1906, and thirty in 1910-11. Lengthening of the stalls on the south side was achieved by filling in the cutting carrying the closed Redheugh branch and then building on the site a lean-to extension made of wood. Arches were cut through the original south wall of the building and thus the engines stood partly in the old building and partly in the extension.

A similar problem due to the increase in length of locomotives cropped up again in the 1920s when accommodation had to be found, first for the Raven Pacifics and later for the Gresley Pacifics, of which five and ten respectively were stationed at Gateshead. This was solved by converting for their use the remaining portion of the tender shop of the works-part of the building at the western end had been demolished in 1905 to make way for the new north to east curve off the King Edward Bridge, and in 1924 it was decided to extend the building at the eastern end. This arrangement sufficed for thirty years and although the Pacific engines could not be turned in the shed they could be dealt with on the King Edward Bridge triangle at the western end of the shed, or on the Gateshead triangle at the eastern end. In 1956 two of the roundhouses were abandoned and the remaining two, at the eastern end, were reroofed using pre-stressed concrete beams. At the same time the turntable in No 1 shed, the easternmost stable, was replaced by a 70ft 'table, allowing Pacifics to be stabled in the main shed for the first time. However, by this time the days of the steam Pacific locomotive were numbered and by the end of 1964 the turntables had been removed and the building had been converted to a five-road straight shed for the maintenance of diesel locomotives. The extension on the east end of the one-time tender shop (later Pacific shed) was demolished about the same time and the original portion of the same building was demolished in October 1969.

The roundhouse adjacent to Chaytor's Bank was demolished in the 1960s.

Gateshead shed has been responsible for most of the workings between Newcastle and Edinburgh for exactly a century, except for the period between 14 January 1897 and 1 March 1898 when a dispute between the North Eastern and the North British necessitated engines being changed at Berwick. The disagreement between the two East Coast companies came to a head when the North British, on 18 January 1894, gave notice to the North Eastern to terminate their through locomotive workings from 30 April 1894. The matter was referred to the House of Lords and then to the Railway Commissioners who, in their decision announced on 9 February 1898, said that the North Eastern should work five East Coast through trains in each direction between Berwick and Edinburgh — the 10.0am, 6.25pm, 7.35pm, 10.50pm and 11.15pm from Edinburgh, and those arriving in Edinburgh at 4.0am, 7.15am, 3.40pm, 6.30pm and 8.45pm. Four other through trains between London and Edinburgh were to be worked by the North British between Berwick and Edinburgh. This arrangement commenced on 1 March 1898 and continued until 1 September 1904 when, at the request of the North British, the North Eastern resumed working all East Coast through trains between Newcastle and Edinburgh. In the period between 14 January 1897 and 1 March 1898 the engines of all through trains had to be changed at Berwick as the North British would not allow North Eastern engines north of that station.

In 1923, with the formation of the LNER, Gateshead engines commenced working through to Grantham, taking over the heavy

5.30pm from Kings Cross for their return working and running non-stop between Grantham and Darlington. This turn was worked mainly by Class Z Atlantics but the two new Raven Pacifics also appeared occasionally.

Gateshead men were, of course, chosen to work the Raven Pacific 2400 when it was tried against a Gresley Pacific between London and Doncaster in 1923. The driver was Tom Blades, renowned for his firing ability to Bob Nicholson in the 1895 Races to Aberdeen, and his fireman was Charlie Fisher, who retired only a few years ago from the post of Head Office Locomotive Inspector at York.

The 'Hush-Hush' — Gresley's experimental locomotive with a water tube boiler, officially known as No 10000, was stationed for many years at Gateshead until it was transferred to Neville Hill in 1935 for a final (unsuccessful) attempt to make it work.

When the non-stop Flying Scotsman was introduced on 1 May 1928 six Gateshead crews were chosen to work the train, together with four from Kings Cross and four from Haymarket (Edinburgh). For the London and Edinburgh men it was a straight out and home lodging turn, with the Edinburgh men in charge north of Tollerton and the London men thence to Kings Cross, using a Haymarket engine up and down on alternate days.

For the Gateshead men, sharing the Kings Cross engine with Kings Cross men, it was a very involved roster of seven turns spread over fifteen days. Two of these turns meant spending two nights away from home, lodging one night at London and one at Edinburgh, whilst the other five turns involved three nights away, lodging at Edinburgh, London and Edinburgh before returning home on the fourth day. On these turns the men worked a train from Newcastle to Edinburgh — lodged — up to London non-stop — lodged — down to Edinburgh non-stop — lodged — Edinburgh to Newcastle train. Thus Gateshead crews worked the non-stop north of Tollerton, down on Monday, Wednesdays and Fridays, of the first week, Tuesdays, Thursdays and Saturdays of the second week: up on Tuesdays, Thursdays and Saturdays of the first week and on Mondays, Wednesdays and Fridays of the second week; riding as passengers in the specially reserved compartment south of Tollerton in both directions.

The six sets of men originally chosen were:

Drivers	Firemen
T. Blades	W. Morris
H. Pennington	J. Ridley
J. Gascoigne	J.J. Williams
J.W. Halford	J.F. Cairn
J.G. Smith	J. Bambra
J.G. Eltringham	J. Slinger

By 1932, due to retirements and promotions these had changed to:

Drivers	Firemen
J.G. Eltringham	J. Slinger
H. Pennington	J. Ridley
J. Gascoigne	R.R. Silson
R.J. Knights	J.G. Major
T. Dron	D.A. Thompson
W.J. Walker	F.J. Cairn

The non-stop working involved a 10 hour 25 minute duty each day for the crews, of which only just over four hours were occupied in actual driving and firing. For this they received payment for 20hr 36mins and the Gateshead crews received per fortnight a wage of £27 2s 7d (£27.12½) for a driver and £21 13s 6d (£21.67½) for a fireman plus £3 15s 11d (£3.80) each lodging allowance. A high wage for the 1930s placing these six crews well above their fellow men at Gateshead shed. However, on one occasion in 1932 the Gateshead crew were relieved on arrival at the turntable at Haymarket shed and the driver claimed fifteen minutes for walking to the drivers' lobby and making out his report. This was passed by the Gateshead shed master but the Head Office at York took exception and instituted a series of letters querying the time claimed, saying that ten minutes was quite sufficient. Eventually the driver's claim was reduced by five minutes to save a few coppers — at what cost in correspondence?

Drivers running trains in front of the Scotsman were reminded that they should adhere strictly to their booked times so that there would be no delays and that the non-stop really would be non-stop! Drivers of the preceding train were also instructed not to take water at Wiskê Moor troughs, so that the non-stop could take up the maximum amount of water. A spare firing shovel had to be carried in the cab of each Pacific engine working the train.

Emergency replacement engines were available in the North Eastern Area as follows:

Down Journey		*Up Journey*	
York	Pacific engine	*Tweedmouth*	Atlantic engine
Darlington	Atlantic engine	*Newcastle*	Pacific engine
Newcastle	Pacific engine	*Darlington*	Atlantic engine
Tweedmouth	Atlantic engine	*York*	Atlantic engine

In the event of the emergency engine being utilised before the enginemen's change-over point at Tollerton was reached both sets of men had to travel on the footplate through to Kings Cross or Edinburgh.

Gateshead men were also responsible, at first, for a major part of the Coronation working, when this high-speed train was introduced on 5 July 1937. This new train was timed to cover the 393 miles between London and Edinburgh in six hours, with a stop at York in the down direction and at Newcastle in the up.

On Mondays, Wednesdays and Fridays one set of Gateshead men worked the down train to York and there handed over to another set of Gateshead men who had travelled as passengers on the 4.14pm up from Newcastle. This second set worked through to Edinburgh, whilst the first set travelled home to Newcastle as passengers on the 6.45pm ex York. The second set of men lodged overnight at Edinburgh and worked the up Coronation to Newcastle the following day (Tuesdays and Thursdays), where they were relieved by another set of Gateshead men for the journey on to Kings Cross. In both directions the Gateshead crews used a Haymarket A4 engine.

On Mondays, Wednesdays and Fridays the up train was worked by Haymarket men (with a Kings Cross A4 engine) from Edinburgh to Newcastle, and forward to London by Kings Cross men. The Edinburgh men then travelled as passengers on the 7.10pm to York, where they lodged overnight in readiness for working the down train from York to Edinburgh the following day (Tuesdays and Thursdays). On Fridays, however, they lodged overnight at Newcastle and then worked the 9.32am Newcastle to Edinburgh on the Saturday morning.

On Tuesdays and Thursdays Kings Cross men worked the down

Coronation as far as York, where they handed over to the
Haymarket men, and then travelled as passengers on the 6.45pm
ex York to lodge at Newcastle for the up train next day (Mondays,
Wednesdays and Fridays).

To commence the week Gateshead men worked up on Sunday,
the 5.20pm ex Newcastle (Kings Cross arrive 10.45pm), and Kings
Cross men worked down on the Sunday, 6.0pm Kings Cross to
Newcastle (arrive 11.25pm).

The above working was complicated by the fact that the down
train stopped at York and the up train at Newcastle. However,
with the introduction on 7 March 1938 of a Newcastle stop
for the down train the working was simplified and it was possible
to cut out the need for Edinburgh men to lodge at York on two
nights a week. The revised diagrams also required only one set of
Gateshead men instead of two. Thus on Mondays, Wednesdays
and Fridays Gateshead crews worked the down train between
Kings Cross and Newcastle and Kings Cross men worked the
up. On Tuesdays and Thursdays the position was reversed and the
Gateshead men worked the up train to Kings Cross and lodged,
and the Kings Cross men worked the down train to Newcastle and
lodged. Each day, Mondays to Fridays, the Haymarket men
worked the up train to Newcastle and returned the same evening
on the down train.

Non-stop working between London and Edinburgh was resumed
when the Flying Scotsman left Kings Cross and Waverley
simultaneously at 10.0am on 31 May 1948. The following year
the historic time of 10.0am was still used by the Flying Scotsman
but a new non-stop was introduced to leave Kings Cross at 9.30am
and Edinburgh at 9.45am carrying the name The Capitals Limited-
this was renamed The Elizabethan in 1953. Unfortunately
Gateshead crews did not participate in any of these post-war turns,
which were worked by Kings Cross and Haymarket depots.

With the introduction in 1961 of the Deltic diesel-electric locomotives Nos D9002/5/8/11/4/7 were allocated to Gateshead for
Kings Cross-Edinburgh workings in which Gateshead men played a
large part although, of course, their engines were worked by many
other crews. The practice of one engine per man had died long since,
but the practice of two sets of men to one engine survived at some
sheds until the diesel era.

The timetables for the summer of 1962 showed the Elizabethan to be non-stop once again between London and Edinburgh but, in fact, a stop had to be made at Newcastle to change crews.

ALNMOUTH

The first reference to this shed - known as Bilton Junction until 1892 - was made on 8 October 1874, when it was suggested that a shed and cottages be erected. On 14 January 1875 authority was given to build the shed and cottages at an estimated cost of £1,610 and £410 respectively. On 18 April 1875 a tender of £2,090 1s 3d was accepted for the shed and three cottages and presumably the shed was opened at the end of 1875 or early 1876.

On 5 May 1887 it was proposed that the shed be extended to accommodate the two engines working the Alnwick-Cornhill branch, the estimated cost being £900. On 30 June 1887 a tender of £1,029 7s 3d was accepted but three weeks later the contractor advised the North Eastern Railway that he had made an error and he wished to submit a revised figure. Thereupon the NER cancelled the contract and accepted the next lowest tender of £1,043 17s 3d. This business of amending tenders was rife as far as the NER was concerned and usually they allowed the contractor to amend his figures and retain the contract.

Alnmouth turns covered trips to Newcastle and Berwick on the main line and the engines also worked trains between Alnwick and Berwick via Coldstream, and west of Coldstream as far as Kelso. The shed also supplied an engine for the passenger service on the Amble branch and this spent the whole day running between Chevington and Amble: the men were changed at Chevington at 2.0pm, the early turn men being relieved by the second set who had travelled as passengers from Alnmouth.

Alnmouth shed was the last home of many of the small old passenger engines, which did not need to exert themselves on the slow workings on the main line or on the Coldstream services. Class F No 18 was there, and for years some of the famous Class M 4-4-0s were allocated to the depot — Nos 1621, 1624, 1625 and 1627. As these were withdrawn for scrapping they were replaced by some of the very similar Class Q engines, and later by Class R locomotives (LNER D20.) In BR days the shed acquired V1 2-6-2T but finished its days with K1 2-6-0 62006, 62011, 62021,

62022, 62025 and 62050. It was closed on 19 June 1966.

HEXHAM

Here again is a shed whose origin is lost in official records and the earliest mention so far discovered is one dated January 1869, when a small extension was made at a cost of £65. A tender of £267 2s 9d for further extensions was accepted in January 1878.

The shed was seriously damaged by fire in 1929 and although consideration was given to closing the shed, rather than repair it, it was decided that it would be uneconomic to close it. The shed was again damaged by fire, caused by an incendiary bomb, in World War II and it was again rebuilt after the war.

In the *1923 Passenger Engine Working Book* Hexham's duties covered four diagrams, each engine requiring two sets of men daily and they worked solely to Newcastle and on the Allendale branch. By 1939 the number of turns had been reduced to three, although all worked by two sets of men. In addition there was a Sentinel shunting engine for working the yard at Hexham. After World War II Hexham worked four turns, three of which required three sets of men, whilst the fourth required three sets. All were rostered for G5 engines and the duties were solely between Newcastle and Haltwhistle.

The engine allocation was:

	1923	1939	1954
G5 0–4–4T	4	4	6
J21 0–6–0	-	-	1
J36 0–6–0	-	1	-
Y1 0–4–0T	-	1	-
	4	6	7

The shed closed on 6 April 1959 but the last steam engine had been transferred away on 25 January 1959—this was V3 2–6–2T 67682, which went to Botanic Gardens shed at Hull.

BOWES BRIDGE

The origins of this shed are unknown but it seems likely that there was a shed in the vicinity ever since the earliest days of steam worked railways as the Tanfield Wagonway is one of the oldest lines on Tyneside. The first mention of a shed appears in a Minute dated 6 January 1885, when the NER agreed to pay £5 per annum for the tenancy of the Engine Shed at Bowes Bridge. Who this amount was to be paid to is not stated but it seems probable that it was to the firm of John Bowes & Partners, owners of the nearby Marley Hill colliery and engine shed.

In 1890 it was decided that a spare 42ft turntable should be installed at Bowes Bridge 'and the two tank engines replaced by one tender engine'. However, Class L 0—6—0T 548 is known to have been working from the shed in 1895 and for many years in LNER days the allocation was two N10 0—6—2Ts outstationed from Gateshead shed. In 1939, for instance, 1109 and 1138 were the two tank engines. Tender engines did get to Bowes Bridge at times and in 1961 the two locomotives there were N10 0—6—2T 69101 and J25 0—6—0 65728. On 16 January 1943 two N10 engines, 1138 and 1321, were noted at Darlington Works after having been damaged when Bowes Bridge shed was destroyed by fire. For a number of years the engines were stabled in the remains of the shed, open to the elements, until a new shed was erected in 1954/5.

The earlier shed had been converted from a winding house, and the chimney serving the boilers was not demolished until 1935 and the base converted into a sand-drying furnace, but even this disappeared when the new shed was demolished about 1966. The shed had ceased to house locomotives from September 1962.

Borough Gardens

This shed, originally known as Park Lane, was first authorised in 1873 and in the following year a tender of £20,035 was accepted for the building, which consisted of one large shed containing four turntables and radiating stalls. It was predominantly a freight shed, stabling the engines working to the east of Gateshead on the south bank of the River Tyne, and also providing the engines for some long distance goods workings. For instance an engine from this shed worked to and from Hull, alternating with a Dairycoates engine, and in BR days a number of B1 4—6—0s were allocated to Borough Gardens for working fitted freight trains.

The four turntables were of three different sizes—there were two of 42ft 6in diameter, one of 45ft, and one of 50ft, but the 45ft turntable fell into disuse in the 1950s and was, in fact, deleted from the WTT Appendix in August 1955. An 1877 reference mentions that the shed provided accommodation for forty engines and in conjunction with the fact that there were two 'tables of 42ft 6in it seems probable that originally the shed consisted of only two roundhouses, and that the sections containing the larger 'tables were added at later dates. However, no definite proof of this has so far been located.

The shed was closed on 13 June 1959 and after standing derelict for a couple of years the site was cleared to make way for a new Central Freight Depot serving Gateshead and Newcastle.

The engines stationed at Borough Gardens between 1923 and 1959 were:

	1923	1939	1959	*(Engines at Closure)*
398 0–6–0	11	-	-	
J22 0–6–0	2	-	-	
J24 0–6–0	6	8	-	
J25 0–6–0	4	1	3(65702/12/28)	
J26 0–6–0	2	-	-	
J27 0–6–0	3	5	4(65785,65823/47/93)	
J39 0–6–0	-	-	8(64700/7/10, 64846/51/4, 64921/36)	
J71 0–6–0T	12	-	2(68278,68316)	
J72 0–6–0T	5	7	8(68694/5/7, 68705/28/30/7, 69017)	
Q5 0–8–0	1	-	-	
Q6 0–8–0	15	23	17(63342/6/50/4/8/ 66/77/84/6, 63400/2/8/31/4/ 44/56/8)	
N8 0–6–2T	-	4	-	
K1 2–6–0	-	-	1(62060)	
	61	48	43	

The forty-three engines remaining at Borough Gardens at closure were dispersed to Blaydon, Consett, Gateshead, North Blyth, South Blyth, Sunderland, Tyne Dock, Thornaby, West Hartlepool and York.

CHAPTER III

Percy Main, Heaton Junction, Tweedmouth

Percy Main

The buildings here were the works and shed of the Blyth & Tyne Railway, taken over by the NER in 1874. They were little changed over the years and two adjacent buildings in good repair were in use until the end while the third building had lost its roof but had received a covering over a small part of the area to allow engines to be prepared and stabled under cover.

The Blyth & Tyne Railway was predominantly a coal carrying line and, in fact, considered passengers a nuisance. Thus in NER, LNER and BR days the locomotives stationed there were mineral engines: latterly these were invariably six coupled engines, although eight coupled engines were at Percy Main in North Eastern days.

During the latter years of the NER the shed yard was used for breaking up withdrawn locomotives and fortunately some excellent pictures of this taking place have survived. In 1923 one of the NER crane tank locomotives was stationed at Percy Main presumably to help in the breaking up of engines, but it did not stay long.

The allocation over the years was:

	1923	1931	1939	1950
398 0-6-0	3	-	-	-
J24 0-6-0	3	2	-	-
J25 0-6-0	3	3	3	-
J26 0-6-0	1	1	-	-
J27 0-6-0	20	19	14	24

J77 0-6-0T	1	-	-	-
J78 0-6-0T	1	-	-	-
	32	25	17	24

On 28 February 1965 the shed was closed to steam and the fourteen J27 remaining were transferred away:

To South Blyth: 65790/5, 65805/9/12/3/4/21/5/42

To North Blyth: 65796, 65802/58

To Sunderland : 65817

Thenceforward Percy Main housed only the diesel shunting engines for the area but even this practice ceased from 27 February 1966 when they were all transferred to Gateshead and the depot then closed completely. The engines concerned were:

D2045/8/50/5, D2104/5/6/65/6, D2310/3/5/21/2/6-9/32/3/5/9 D3072, D3241/2/4, D3316/21/4, D3455, D3673/8/9, D3875. D3938/9/40/2.

Demolition of the buildings commenced in October 1966.

The Percy Main district sheds came under the supervision of Heaton from 20 June 1932.

SOUTH BLYTH

A shed at Newsham or Blyth was suggested in 1877 but a suitable site was not found until 1879. On 5 June of that year a shed was authorised at an estimated cost £2,795 and in the following month a tender of £2,365 10s 1d was accepted. On 25 June 1894 general extensions at Blyth were authorised and a tender of £11,700 was accepted, but only an unknown proportion of this amount was for actual extensions to the shed. However, as the shed was originally specified to hold nine engines it is probable that the shed was extended from three roads to six at this time. This is supported by an examination of the building, which shows differences in the brickwork between the two halves, suggesting that they were built at different times. However, great care has obviously been taken in matching the extensions to the original building, even to perpetuating the round-topped doors.

Although mainly a shed supplying mineral engines for the haulage of coal in the area it did in 1923 have four passenger duties, all of which were double-manned, and involved workings between Blyth, Morpeth, Newbiggin, Manors North and Monkseaton, the locomotives used being Class BTP 0-4-4Ts and Class F8 2-4-2Ts, of which five of each were stationed at Blyth. Why ten engines were provided for four duties is unknown. However, as the duties involved running for between thirteen and seventeen hours a day it seems probable that engines were changed during the day.

Latterly the passenger workings were handled by G5 0-4-4Ts, until the class became extinct in December 1958, when Blyth lost 67281,67305,67311 and 67323.

Blyth was closed to steam locomotives on 28 May 1967 when its remaining J27 0-6-0, 65789, 65795, 65812, 65855 and 65879 were transferred to Sunderland to end their days. The depot remained open for diesel locomotives until 29 January 1968, when they were transferred to a new diesel depot at Cambois, and Blyth shed finally closed. It has since been demolished.

BLYTH ALLOCATION 1923—1947

	1923	1933	1939	1947
BTP 0-4-4T	5	-	-	-
F8 2-4-2T	5	8	-	-
G5 0-4-4T	-	-	5	10
398 0-6-0	2	-	-	-
J21 0-6-0	1	1	-	3
J22 0-6-0	3	-	-	-
J24 0-6-0	5	4	3	-
J25 0-6-0	5	4	4	-
J27 0-6-0	-	-	3	4
J77 0-6-0T	4	2	2	2
	30	19	17	19

NORTH BLYTH

Because of the coal staiths on both sides of the River Blyth it was necessary to have a locomotive shed on each bank to avoid the long detour via Newsham and West Sleekburn Junction to get from one side of the river to the other. Thus North Blyth was yet another North Eastern shed where mineral traffic was the life-blood of the duties. As the fortunes of the pits rose and fell so did the traffic handled by the railway, although in this case the collieries in the area were more modern than those further south and thus did not fluctuate so greatly.

However, North Blyth did have three passenger turns in North Eastern and LNER days and the engines used thereon followed the same pattern as at many other sheds, namely Fletcher BTP 0-4-4Ts from the 1870s, followed by the Class A (LNER F8) 2-4-2T, although in this case North Blyth does not appear to have progressed to G5 0-4-4Ts as almost all the other sheds did. In fact North Blyth must have lost its passenger duties in the 1930s, most probably to South Blyth.

The three turns in the *1922/23 Passenger Engine Working Book* comprised three single manned turns, two of which operated between Bedlington and Newbiggin, and the other between Newcastle-Manors North and Morpeth.

Towards the end of steam traction on British Railways North Blyth became one of the last homes of the ex North Eastern P3 0-6-0s — LNER J27s, and at one time there were as many as twenty-three shedded there. As these were withdrawn they were replaced by K1s and 4MT 2-6-0s, until steam finally disappeared on 9 September 1967.

The engines at closure were 4MT 43000/50/63/70 and 43137. The shed continued in use by diesel locomotives until the new diesel depot at Cambois was opened on 29 January 1968. The allocation over the years was:

	1923	1933	1947	1954	1965
F8 2-4-2T	1	2	-	-	-
G6 0-4-4T	1	-	-	-	-
J21 0-6-0	4	3	-	-	-
J22 0-6-0	2	-	-	-	-
J24 0-6-0	3	4	-	-	-
J25 0-6-0	6	10	-	1	-
J27 0-6-0	-	-	15	23	15
J77 0-6-0T	3	6	5	6	-
K1 2-6-0	-	-	-	-	2
Q5 0-8-0	4	3	-	-	-
Q6 0-8-0	-	-	-	-	7
	24	28	20	30	24

The first mention of the shed was on 30 May 1895 when plans were submitted for a building to house 36 engines, together with 95 cottages for workpeople, but approval was given for a shed for 20 engines and 70 to 75 cottages, Work commenced early in 1896 and it is thought the shed was opened in the following year.

From 1904 the NER obtained sand for locomotive purposes from the beach at North Blyth and for this privilege they paid Lord Ridley £100 per acre worked. The sand was excavated by steam navvy and loaded into NER wagons standing on a siding which crossed the Cowpen Coal Company's line on the level. In exchange for the use of the level crossing the coal company obtained facilities for occasionally turning their engines on the North Eastern turntable.

Heaton Junction

In December 1872 it was reported that 'additional facilities are required to handle increased goods and other traffic, necessitating an engine shed and cottages at Heaton, at an estimated cost of £23,000'. The shed itself was authorised in February 1874 at a cost of £9,270 18s 6d. In 1889 extensions costing £20,300 were authorised but this included the provision of 'a shed for varnishing engines and coaches'. Later in the year plans were submitted for proposed carriage storing and washing sheds, engine and carriage painting shop, and extension of engine shed at Heaton Junction' and this scheme was approved. On 8 January 1891 a tender of £14,500 was accepted for the shed building, with the engineer authorised to spend a further £5,800 on a 50ft turntable and sidings.

It has not been possible to identify to which buildings the above authorisations actually apply, but it is considered that those included were the actual locomotive depot, the carriage sheds latterly used for Tyneside electric stock and destroyed by fire on 11 August 1918, and probably some of the Walker Gate carriage and wagon shops.

The first engine shed was opened on 31 August 1875 and one account states that there was accomodation for thirteen engines. It seems probable that this building was the section nearest the Tynemouth lines, with three roads. Over the years the extensions brought the shed up to an eight road building and until 1930 these were all dead-end roads. In 1930 the five roads on the main line side of the building, at the south end, were extended through and although two terminated adjacent to the offices and stores block, the other three roads gave entry and exit from the south.

In 1894 plans and estimates were prepared for a shed to hold 132 and 154 engines and if it had been proceeded with this would have been the largest shed on the NER.

In 1923 Heaton engines and men worked 1 return trip to Edinburgh and 5 to York and there were 17 rostered local workings, of which 4 engines were operated by one set of men and 13 by two sets. Their duties took them to Bishop Auckland, Waterhouses,West Hartlepool,South Shields,Chevington, Blyth and Newbiggin, Blackhill, Darras Hall, and on the Tynemouth branches.

In 1939 there were 14 local turns rostered to be worked by the following classes of engines:

CLASS OF ENGINE	TURNS
G5 0-4-4T	2
G5 or J21 0-6-0	1
V1 2-6-2T	6
V1 or A8 4-6-2T	3
Not specified	2

Of these, 12 engines were manned daily by two sets of men, and 2 engines by two sets. In addition there was one Sentinel steam railcar single manned, and two Sentinel cars each manned by two sets. Heaton men also manned the two electric locomotives used between Trafalgar Yard and Newcastle Quayside.

Engine allocations were as follows:

	1923	1939	1954
A1 4-6-2 (Gresley)	-	3	-
A1 4-6-2 (Peppercorn)	-	-	3
A2 4-6-2 (Thompson & Peppercorn)	-	-	3
A3 4-6-2	-	3	10
A4 4-6-2	-	1	-
B13 4-6-0	8	-	-
B15 4-6-0	8	4	-
B16 4-6-0	17	-	-
C6 4-4-2	6	-	-
C7 4-4-2	7	5	-
D20 4-4-0	3	-	1

G5 0-4-4 T	17	8	-
G6 0-4-4T	3	-	-
H1 4-4-4T	9	-	-
J21 0-6-0	31	12	3
J26 0-6-0	1	-	-
J27 0-6-0	1	6	4
J39 0-6-0	-	4	7
44 0-6-0T	1	-	-
J71 0-6-0T	10	7	6
J72 0-6-0T	6	6	9
J73 0-6-0T	1	-	-
J76 0-6-0T	1	-	-
J77 0-6-0T	-	-	1
J94 0-6-0T	-	-	2
K3 2-6-0	-	14	9
N8 0-6-2T	3	-	1
N10 0-6-2T	-	4	-
Q5 0-8-0	-	2	-
T1 4-8-0T	1	-	-
V1 and V3 2-6-2T	-	12	12
V2 2-6-2	-	5	17
Y7 0-4-0T	2	-	-
4MT 2-6-0	-	-	5
ELECTRIC	3	2	2
	139	98	95

All the steam locomotives at Heaton were transferred to other sheds on 16 June 1963 but the shed continued to be used for repairs and storage of locomotives and, in fact, some workings continued to operate from Heaton although nominally under the control of Gateshead. The steam engines remaining at closure were:

```
A3 4-6-2: 60040/5/52/60/71/3/82/3/5/8/91        (All to Gateshead)
B1 4-6-0: 61019/22/35/8, 61216,61322            (      do       )
J27 0-6-0:65796,65869 (To Percy Main); 65864/70/4/82(To Sunderland )
J72 0-6-0T: 69008/24/8                          (To Gateshead  )
V2 2-6-2: 60812/35/65/8/91, 60904/10/3/22/40/4/62/76(To Gateshead )
V3 2-6-2T: 67620/42/6/51/2/6/8/83/90/1          (To Gateshead  )
```

A3 4-6-2 60058(allocated to Heaton) was withdrawn at Doncaster Works on 19 June 1963. The fourteen diesel shunting locomotives had departed on 2 June 1963, ten to Percy Main and four to Gateshead. The two electric locomotives 26500 and 26501 remained at Heaton until 14 September 1964, when they were both condemned at South Gosforth car sheds.

Tweedmouth

Little is known of the first shed at Tweedmouth and presumably it was opened with the line from the south on 1 July 1847. However, by November 1857 the roof of the building was in need of re-slating at a cost of £208 10s 0d. In 1877 a new circular shed for twenty engines was authorised and tenders totalling £8,465 5s 3d were accepted for the building, plus £305 for a turntable from C.Ianson & Sons of Darlington.

In April 1881 a new roof was authorised for the engine shed at a cost of £1,570 1s 6d and presumably this refers to the straight shed, although it is considered unlikely that it is the same building referred to in the Minute of 6 November 1857 mentioned above. However, no date for the construction of the three-road straight shed has been located, although it is known to have been opened some years before the roundhouse.

In 1907 the goods shed of the adjacent station was appropriated for locomotive use and converted into a repair shop at a cost of £1,833 and this building also served to house the breakdown crane.

Although a frontier town between the North Eastern and the North British, Tweedmouth was not responsible for the main East Coast passenger workings as these (except for the period of the dispute between the two companies)were always worked by Newcastle (Gateshead or Heaton) and Edinburgh engines. As the through working did not apply to freight traffic a number of heavy goods engines were stationed at Tweedmouth, together with some North Eastern Atlantics. However, the main duty of the latter was to act as stand-by engines for East Coast passenger trains in the event of a locomotive failure.

The allocation was as follows:

	1923	1933	1947	1954
B1 4-6-0	-	-	-	4
B13 4-6-0	8	2	-	-
B16 4-6-0	7	4	1	-
C6 4-4-2	3	-	-	-
C7 4-4-2	-	8	4	-
D17/1 4-4-0	3	-	-	-
D20 4-4-0	8	6	3	-
D32 4-4-0	-	3	-	-
1440 2-4-0	1	-	-	-
F8 2-4-2T	5	4	-	-

G5 0-4-4T	-	-	1	1
J21 0-6-0	3	4	4	1
J22 0-6-0	1	-	-	-
J27 0-6-0	-	1	2	-
J33 0-6-0	-	1	-	-
J35 0-6-0	-	1	-	-
J37 0-6-0	-	11	-	-
J39 0-6-0	-	-	-	7
J25 0-6-0	-	-	-	1
J77 0-6-0T	3	3	4	3
K3 2-6-0	-	9	-	8
N8 0-6-2T	2	3	-	-
N10 0-6-2T	-	2	-	-
V2 2-6-2	-	-	-	6
	44	62	19	31

From 1 August 1924 Tweedmouth became responsible for the engines at the former North British shed at Berwick, at the other end of the Royal Border Bridge, and twenty-one engines were transferred:

D31 4-4-0	1		J35 0-6-0	1
D32 4-4-0	3		J37 0-6-0	11
E7 2-4-0	2		J82 0-6-0T	1
J31 0-6-0	1		N15 0-6-2T	1

At the same time Tweedmouth became the parent shed for the former NBR shed at Duns.

Major changes in motive power at Tweedmouth took place in 1928 when a number of North Eastern Atlantics were displaced from other sheds and found their way to Tweedmouth. Thus in February 1928 2207 was transferred from Leeds, followed in March by 718 while Leeds engine 2206 was transferred to Gateshead and displaced 720 to Tweedmouth in the same month. In April 1928 729 arrived from Leeds and 736 from Gateshead, allowing C6 4-4-2 697 and 703 to be transferred to Darlington to act as stand-by pilot engines for the non-stop Flying Scotsman which commenced running on 1 May. Further C7 engines arrived at Tweedmouth in June 1930 when 2165,2202,2203 and 2205 from Gateshead were exchanged for C6 295,696,699 and 700.

In July and August 1929 B16 4-6-0 909,928,933,1375,1376 and 1378 were sent to Hull Dairycoates, and 921 and 926 to

York, on being replaced by eight K3 2-6-0 engines. However, B16 engines returned to Tweedmouth two years later when 911, 921, 1372 and 1379 arrived.

The next great change in the situation came in March 1939 when Berwick Marshalling Yard was closed. Henceforward engines on goods trains worked through between Newcastle and Edinburgh, although men were changed at Tweedmouth. Tweedmouth immediately lost half its allocation, which at that time was:

C7	4-4-2	718/20/9,2165,2202/3/5
D20	4-4-0	592,723,1210,2015/25/9
D32	4-4-0	9882/7/8
K3	2-6-0	1306/7/8/10/24/31/45/64/5/7/8/86/7/8,3823/8/9
J21	0-6-0	570,1562
N8	0-6-2T	1072/91,1165
J77	0-6-0T	37,57,1347
J35	0-6-0	9191
J37	0-6-0	9046,9123,9274,9301/5/13/4,9435/62/80/91

Transferred away were:

C7	2	J77	1
D32	1	K3	15
J35	1	N8	1
J37	5		

In exchange two J39 0-6-0s, 2735 and 2736, from the Scottish Area, were sent to Tweedmouth.

After World War II, with a surplus of large engines, Tweedmouth housed V2 2-6-2s and eventually Pacifics: for instance A1 4-6-2 60116/27/9/32/7/42/3/7/51/5 were transferred there on 9 September 1962 to end their days on stand-by and goods turns.

In January 1939 D32 9887 and 9888 were transferred from Tweedmouth to Blaydon in exchange for D20 2027 and 2028 since the D32s were required at Blaydon for the Border Counties line working.

On 19 August 1939 C9 727 was transferred from Gateshead to Tweedmouth. This was one of the pair of North Eastern Atlantics rebuilt with a booster bogie under the cab and the leading end of the tender.

The other engine, 2171, appears to have followed later but the transfer was not recorded offically. However, on 2 November 1940 D49 211 'The York & Ainsty' and 362 'The Goathland' were transferred to Tweedmouth from Alston (where they had been stationed under the wartime Evacuation Scheme) specifically to replace 727 and 2171, which are then shown as transferred to Gateshead, from where they were withdrawn in 1943 and 1942 respectively.

In 1922/3 Tweedmouth had two main line turns. One started off on the 9.11am Berwick to Newcastle and the 4.8pm return, arriving at Berwick at 6.1pm, with the men being relieved as the train called at Tweedmouth at 5.54pm, giving them a working day of 9hrs 48mins. The second involved assisting the 11.13am Berwick to Edinburgh, then working the 2.12pm fish train from Edinburgh to Newcastle, returning home assisting the 8.30pm Newcastle-Berwick, giving a 10hr 22min day.

There were four full turns, and one part-time turn worked by a relief set:

1. Berwick-Alnwick and return via Coldstream (first set)
   Berwick-Alnmouth (via Belford) and return via Coldstream (second set)
2. Berwick-Alnmouth (via Belford) and return to Tweedmouth (first set)
   Tweedmouth-Coldstream-Alnwick-Alnmouth, returning via Belford (second set)
3. Tweedmouth-Coldstream(empty)-Berwick-Alnmouth(via Belford) Alnwick-Coldstream-Tweedmouth
4. Two trips Berwick-Kelso and return.

The relief set worked from Berwick to Alnmouth and back via the main line. The main line standing pilot was also responsible for working two Berwick-Kelso trains across the Royal Border Bridge so that the train engine could couple on at the opposite end in Tweedmouth station.

In 1939 Tweedmouth still had four local turns — No 1 worked between Berwick,Burnmouth, and the former North British terminus at Eyemouth, going out light engine from Tweedmouth each morning to work the first train from Eyemouth at 7.10am. The last train terminated at Eyemouth at 6.37pm, except on Saturdays, and the engine then returned light to Tweedmouth. On

Saturdays a relief set worked a late train from Eyemouth to
Burnmouth and back before running light engine back to
Tweedmouth. Although worked by a North Eastern Area engine
and men this branch was actually in the Scottish Area. From 1
August 1924, when Tweedmouth became responsible for the
workings formerly taken by the North British shed at Berwick,
former North Eastern engines began to work the service and the
favourite class appears to have been the J21 0-6-0. In fact these
engines were still working the branch in 1940 but to liberate an
engine for other duties two former Great Eastern Class E4 2-4-0
were transferred to Tweedmouth on 8 January 1940, No 7463
from Darlington and 7496 from Kirkby Stephen. They remained
at Tweedmouth until returned to the Southern Area on 9
April 1942.

Duty No 2 was rostered for a G5 0-4-4T with one set of men.
The first set worked the 7.22am from Berwick to Alnmouth, and
then after working three return trips to Alnwick, worked the 1.15pm
Alnmouth-Berwick as far as Tweedmouth, where they were
relieved by a relief set for the trip to Berwick and light engine
back to shed.

No 3, with an unspecified class of engine, also worked Berwick
to Alnmouth and back, with one return trip Alnmouth-Alnwick.
No 4 worked from Berwick to St Boswells and back during the
afternoon and evening. There was also one Sentinel steam railcar duty to Coldstream and back with one set of men, but on
Saturdays, with two sets, the car worked a much longer day and
travelled as far afield as Kelso and Alnmouth.

With dieselisation Tweedmouth lost its importance as a
half-way stage main line shed. Until then, of course, it was the
only shed between Newcastle and Edinburgh capable of supplying large engines to replace any failures on east coast expresses.
Gradually the number of engines at the shed was run down
until there were only two steam locomotives — 3MT 2-6-0
77002 and 77004, and even these were transferred away on
19 June 1966. Henceforward the only locomotive provided
was a 204hp diesel shunter for goods yard work. The
straight shed was demolished in April 1968 and the roundhouse
let or sold to a private firm.

North Eastern Railway engines appear to have worked to
Edinburgh from Berwick, via Kelso, in the 1850s but it was
not until 1869 that the company reached agreement with the
North British Railway with regard to North Eastern engines
working direct, via Dunbar. On 7 August 1869 the NBR agreed
to provide a shed for NER engines at St Margarets, with the
NER agreeing to pay 6½% on the capital for a minimum of
seven years, plus £25 per engine per annum, with free water. The
building was completed in 1871 at a cost of £9,474 3s 11d.

Soon after the shed was opened the NBR cast envious eyes on
the space available in the new building and they agreed to forego a
quarter of the interest if they could stable up to six engines there.
If, however, the NER required space for more than twelve engines
the NB locos were to be withdrawn from the shed, the NER then
being responsible for the full interest again. This arrangement
continued for just over thirty years, although it was no doubt in
abeyance during the dispute between the two companies when
the North British gave notice that their locomotives should work
the east coast trains north of Berwick.

North Eastern engines ceased to work through to Edinburgh on
14 January 1897 and in the years during which the dispute
dragged on the NBR must have found the NER shed at St
Margarets to be invaluable, so that when North Eastern engines
resumed full working of east coast trains in 1904 they were housed
at Haymarket shed.

At Haymarket a mess-room and store was built for NER use and
other conditions were:

> £25 per annum for every engine stabled regularly
> £2 1s 8d for thirty irregular stablings
> Water 1s per tender and 6d for boiler wash-out
> Lighting-up from NBR furnace 1s per engine
> Turning free!

At Grouping the four Class Z Atlantics were responsible for only
two regular turns, plus one which ran Mondays only. One engine
worked the 1.45pm Edinburgh-Newcastle and returned with the
7.7pm from Newcastle, and another the 7.40pm to Newcastle
and 1.17am return. The Mondays only working was on the 1.22pm
ex the Waverley, returning 'as required'. Thus there were two spare
engines throughout the week, obviously in case of failure of a

Newcastle engine at Edinburgh. With the Grouping a former North British engine could be used in an emergency and one Atlantic was removed, leaving 714, 2193 and 2194.

Eventually the North Eastern engines and men were integrated into the Southern Scottish Area of the LNER and took their place in Haymarket links, so that a North Eastern Atlantic could be seen working to Glasgow (Queen Street), although their primary duty involved fish trains and emergency duties southwards to Newcastle. As a reminder of North Eastern workings the successor to the 1.45pm Edinburgh to Newcastle eventually became a Pacific worked Haymarket turn.

The three North Eastern Atlantics remained at Haymarket for many years, and, in fact, until 2194 was transferred to the North Eastern Area on 16 March 1939, and 714 and 2193 followed on 2 June 1943 after a spell at St Margarets.

CHAPTER IV

Blaydon, Carlisle, West Hartlepool, Sunderland, Tyne Dock

Blaydon

After some discussion a shed at Blaydon was approved on 18 June 1897 and it was decided that it should accommodate 48 engines in two round sheds with 50ft turntables. The estimated cost was given as £30,247, with an estimated saving on light engine workings of £4,000 a year. Plans were approved in November 1897 and on 3 March 1898 a tender of £24,000 was accepted, together with a figure of £1,045 for water and gas mains work by the NER engineer. The shed was opened in 1900 and catered mainly for workings on the local lines to the west of Newcastle, and shunting the yards in the same area.

The number of engines stationed at Blaydon in 1923 was 71, and although the total fell to 59 in 1939 it was back to 71 again in 1950.

	1923	1939	1950
A8 4-6-2T	-	-	1
B13 4-6-0	3	-	-
D20 4-4-0	1	2	-
D49 4-4-0	-	-	2
G5 0-4-4T	7	3	7
H1 4-4-4T	5	-	-
J21 0-6-0	17	10	3
J24 0-6-0	3	-	-
J25 0-6-0	2	-	-
J26 0-6-0	2	-	-
J27 0-6-0	3	-	-
J36 0-6-0	-	-	1
J39 0-6-0	-	10	13
J71 0-6-0T	9	5	1

J72 0-6-0T	4	2	-
J77 0-6-0T	1	2	-
J94 0-6-0T	-	-	11
K1 2-6-0	-	-	10
K3 2-6-0	-	3	-
N8 0-6-2T	2	-	-
N9 0-6-2T	1	-	-
N10 0-6-2T	1	-	1
Q6 0-8-0	9	14	17
V1 2-6-2T	-	8	4
Y7 0-4-0T	1	-	-
TOTAL	71	59	71

In the 1930s Blaydon had two ex North British D31 4-4-0s for working the Border Counties line trains between Newcastle and Riccarton Junction. When these were withdrawn — 9766 in June 1937 and 9312 in December 1938 — their duties devolved upon two ex North Eastern D20 4-4-0s, 2027 and 2028. However, the North Eastern engines were not satisfactory and on 23 January 1939 they were exchanged for D32 9887 and 9888 from Tweedmouth — bringing North British engines back to the North British Border Counties line. The official reason given for this transfer was 'Class D32 engines required at Blaydon in connection with Newcastle-Hawick working, with a view to avoiding loss of time and emission of sparks in re-afforestation on this route.' The D32s remained at Blaydon until 1948 when they departed, one to Duns and the other to Tweedmouth. After an interval D49 62747 'The Percy' and 62771 'The Rufford' were transferred to Blaydon to take up the Border Counties line workings from the Newcastle end.

By 1939 the ten mineral 0-6-0s of classes J24, J25, J26 and J27 had been replaced at Blaydon by ten J39 0-6-0s, and the three B13 4-6-0s by three K3 2-6-0s for express goods work. For local passenger workings eight V1 2-6-2Ts replaced the five H1 4-4-4Ts and some of the G5 0-4-4Ts. Actually Blaydon received ten V1s new from Doncaster Works in 1935: 414, 419, 423, 446, 465, 477, 479, 481, 484 and 486, but subsequently lost 477 and 486 to Heaton and 414, 446 and 481 to Gateshead, leaving five of the class to be exchanged for a similar number of A8 4-6-2Ts from Middlesbrough in January 1939. The V1 engines were required at Middlesbrough to work the expresses to Newcastle, which were changed over to corridor stock about this time.

On 7 November 1931 Blaydon lost two J21s and a Q6 to Gateshead, three Q6s, one N9 and one J71 to Borough Gardens and a J21 to Heaton due to the closure of Blaydon Marshalling Yard, and the consequent reduction in work. Three weeks later they were all transferred back again with the re-opening of the Yard!

In late NER days Blaydon's passenger workings were all in the immediate vicinity of Newcastle, the furthest being to Durham via Blackhill and the Lanchester Valley line. Even by 1939 the weekday rosters took the engines and men no further than Darlington, and that on only one duty – the others, as before, were chiefly on the Blackhill line, calling for three A8s and three G5s each double manned, and one G5 single manned. There was in addition, of course, the Riccarton working at 6.7am from Newcastle and 10.13am return. In the afternoon the engine went through to Hawick and spent the night there, but the crews changed footplates at Reedsmouth so that the Blaydon men returned with a Hawick engine on Mondays, Wednesdays and Fridays and a Blaydon engine on Tuesdays, Thursdays and Saturdays. Saturday workings called for seven A8s, three G5s and one J39, in addition to the D32 on the Border Counties turn, and in the summer months there was a Saturday working as far as Kirkby Stephen although the engine went through to Tebay. The train worked was the 9.20am Newcastle-Blackpool, which arrived at Kirkby Stephen at 11.30am; at 12 noon the same men relieved a Kirkby Stephen set on a Blackpool-Newcastle, arriving back in Newcastle at 2.12pm. The empty stock was worked to Scotswood Bridge Sidings (via Dunston) and the engine was due on Blaydon shed at 3.0pm, in time for the men to book off at 3.20 after an eight-hour day. The Kirkby Stephen engine (a J21) spent the week at Blaydon and the Blaydon engine spent a week at Kirkby and they were then exchanged back again the following Saturday.

In the 1950s Blaydon men worked as far as Scarborough on summer Saturdays with Edinburgh-Scarborough trains via Gilling and Malton, and it was a Blaydon driver who came to grief with A3 'Colombo' at York on 4 August 1958, when the engines overshot one of the bay platforms and finished up with the front buffers touching the footbridge.

The steam locomotive allocation was terminated on 16 June 1963 and the shed closed completely on 15 March 1965. The buildings were demolished in April and May 1966.

Carlisle (London Road)

There must have been a shed here from the very early days of the Newcastle & Carlisle Railway and the earliest NER reference is dated 6 May 1864, when Mr Fletcher reported that the engine shed at Carlisle had been destroyed by fire on 30 April. A fortnight later it was stated that the cost of restoring the shed would be £700, and of repairing the four engines damaged in the fire £254 6s 5d. However, it was decided to build 'a larger shed with considerable improvements, at an estimated cost of £2,000'. A tender of £1,822 12s 0d was accepted on 1 July 1864 and presumably the new shed was opened in the following year.

In November 1880 plans for another new shed were submitted and this was built as an extension to the earlier building, providing accommodation for a further twenty locomotives. One of the turntables noted on a visit to the building in 1961 carried a plate giving the date as 1881.

In June 1899 the 'old shed' (the 1865 building?) was reported unsafe and inconvenient as it would only accommodate ten engines. A new shed was authorised and a tender of £12,439 11s 4d was accepted on 19 December when it was noted that two turntables would also be required. This building was apparently erected on the site of the 1865 shed, to the north of the 1881 extension. The turntable disappeared before it was possible to check the date it carried, but the second turntable ordered was placed in the shed yard and carried the date 1890. The completed building, therefore, consisted of two adjoining roundhouses and as usual in NER practice an alternative way out of the shed was provided in case of blockage of one of the interior turntables. However, an unusual feature here was that from the rear (1890) shed the turntable in the yard had to be used to turn the engine through 90 degrees before it could get on to an outgoing road.

In 1923 the allocation comprised forty engines of NER designs but on 1 June 1925 the shed was transferred to the Southern Scottish Area of the LNER and it began to decline in importance.

	1923	1 June 1925	1933
D17/2 4-4-0	8	5(1876,1901/21/4/6)	4
D22 4-4-0	3	2(154 & 1324)	-
D29 4-4-0	-	-	2
D30 4-4-0	-	-	1
G5 0-4-4T	1	-	-
G6 0-4-4T	2	-	-
398 0-6-0	2	1(45)	-
J21 0-6-0	8	2(104 & 511)	1
J24 0-6-0	-	-	1
J25 0-6-0	2	-	-
J27 0-6-0	4	3(790,839,1067)	-
J71 0-6-0T	2	2(285 & 453)	-
N8 0-6-2T	2	-	1
Q6 0-8-0	6	3(2254/7/9)	1
J22 0-6-0	-	2(388 & 502)	-
	40	20	11

In 1933 the shed was closed and the engines transferred to the former North British shed to join J21 104, J24 1841 and 1944, J27 790, 839 and 1067, and Q6 2257 and 2259, which had been transferred there earlier. London Road continued out of use for some years, except for accommodating a few stored engines in the 1930s. In the 1950s part of the building was in use for repairing wagons and another part was boarded off to provide a store for a coal merchant. Until the 1960s locomotives from Tyneside shed used the yard and turntable before returning eastwards.

In 1923 London Road engines had six workings to Newcastle and back with their fleet of D17/2 engines, and another engine worked an early morning return trip to Gilsland, followed by a mid-morning return trip to Haltwhistle. The second set worked the same engine on two return trips to Brampton Junction in addition to acting as pilot at Citadel station. Carlisle also provided a BTP 0-4-4T for the autocar service between Brampton Junction and Brampton Town and this left London Road at 7.10am and did not arrive back until 8.10pm. The crews were changed at 2.5pm after the second set had travelled out as passengers to Brampton Junction on the 1.30pm ex Citadel station. However, as the Brampton autocar service did not run between 12.18pm and 2.10pm the early turn fireman was allowed to return to Carlisle on the

12.24pm from Brampton Junction on Mondays,Wednesdays and Fridays, and the driver did the same on Tuesdays,Thursdays and Saturdays, leaving one man on the engine to await the arrival of the late turn crew. He then returned to Carlisle on the 2.10pm from Brampton Junction and was allowed 35 minutes to reach the shed and book off, giving each man 27 minutes overtime on three days per week.

On the freight side London Road had eighteen booked turns prior to World War I, one of which was a lodging turn to Newport (Middlesbrough). It was on this turn that P3 1067 ran through some trap points and finished up with the front wheels in the River Tees at Thornaby in May 1914. Class 398 0-6-0 991, another Carlisle engine, withdrawn in May 1925, was to have been restored and placed in York Railway Museum but instead it was decided to place in the Museum the Stirling 'single' No 1 and so 991 was scrapped.

ALSTON

The only reference regarding this shed concerns repairs to the roof in 1872 at a cost of £446 13s 4d. It is considered, however, that the shed was erected at approximately the same time as the branch to Alston was opened in 1852.

The locomotives stationed there in the early days are unknown, but from about the turn of the century there was usually a Class A 2-4-2T or a Class O 0-4-4T there for passenger workings, and a P1 or C 0-6-0 for the goods, although at some periods there was only one engine, which was used for both the passenger and goods traffic: for instance in 1933 N8 0-6-2T 863; in 1939 J21 0-6-0 51; in 1950 G5 67315 and J39 0-6-0 64851; and in 1954 4MT 2-6-0 43128 and 76024. The engine allocated at closure on 27 September 1959 was 3MT 2-6-0 77011.

As a precaution against possible bombing raids various engines from more vulnerable sheds were dispersed under a locomotive evacuation scheme introduced in May 1940. This involved the transfer to Alston of D49 4-4-0 211'The York & Ainsty' and 361 'The Garth'; G5 1755, 1795 and 2086; and C7 4-4-2 2211. After six months 2211 was returned to Gateshead and the two D49s were sent to Tweedmouth to replace the two C9

booster engines 727 and 2171. G5 1755 and 1795 departed for
Hexham and Blaydon respectively in 1941, leaving 2086 to uphold
the G5 tradition at Alston until 1953.

The shed was a single-road building, one wall of which was the
outer wall of the station — an unusual feature in the north-east.
The depot was closed on 27 September 1959 when diesel railcars
took over the service on the branch which, at the time of writing, is
still open.

West Hartlepool

The West Hartlepool Harbour & Railway was taken over by the
North Eastern Railway in 1865 and the first North Eastern
reference to an engine shed is dated 17 August 1866, when
Mr T.E.Harrison reported that additional accommodation was
required at West Hartlepool and recommended that a shed similar
to that at Hull Dairycoates be erected. This scheme was generally
approved in February 1867, but in August there is a Minute dealing
with a refusal of the contractors to carry out the conversion of the
wagon shop into an engine shed because the prices for the
masonwork were too low. The connection between this conversion
and the provision of a new shed is undetermined.

In December 1869 Mr Fletcher reported that an engine shed was
required at West Hartlepool and six months later a tender of
£6,093 16s 9d was accepted. This building was completed at the
end of 1871. On 9 January 1874 Mr Fletcher reported that the
north end of the old West Hartlepool shed had blown down and
that the south end would have to be taken down and two months
later it was decided to erect a new shed and to re-erect the shed
which had been blown down. A tender amounting to £2,616 6s 8d
was accepted for the rebuilding of the shed and another of £9,993
for the building of the new shed. No further sheds appear to have
been authorised at West Hartlepool since that date and it is
suggested that the two buildings sanctioned in 1870 and 1874 are
the two adjoining roundhouses at the south end of the yard.
Could the three-road double-ended straight shed at the north end
of the yard be the reconstructed building? Or was this building
at one time the Wagon Shop, but converted to locomotive use when

new Wagon Shops were built on the east side of the passenger lines? Unfortunately it has been found impossible to reconcile the buildings as authorised with the buildings in situ in the present century.

West Hartlepool's main turns in 1922/3 were three to Harrogate worked by 4-4-0 engines: one of these was manned by two sets of men and the other two by one set. Seven other duties requiring twelve sets of men operated mainly between Newcastle, South Shields, Middlesbrough and Ferryhill, but one turn reached as far as Whitby and another to Thirsk. There were also two minor turns worked by reliefmen which worked only as far as Stockton and Hartlepool. An autocar — a BTP (G6) 0-4-4 with a driving coach at either end — worked between West Hartlepool and Hartlepool from 8.35am to 11.31pm each weekday. The local turns were, of course, worked by G5 0-4-4T.

In 1939 the G5 engine were still busy on the local turns, of which one was worked as a push-and-pull unit. This differed from the North Eastern version in that coaches could be attached only at one end of the engine and thus it was either hauling or propelling. Altogether there were eight duties necessitating sixteen sets of men — exactly the same as in 1922. The autocar service of 1922 between the Hartlepools was by this time worked by a Sentinel steam railcar.

When Hartlepool shed was closed on 17 April 1939 the whole fleet of thirty engines was transferred to West Hartlepool and the duties worked from there. For details of these engines see Hartlepool.

	1923	1933	1939	1954
A7 4-6-2T	2	2	4	-
A8 4-6-2T	-	-	-	3
D17/2 4-4-0	7	6	-	-
D20 4-4-0	-	-	3	1
E5 2-4-0	1	-	-	-
G5 0-4-4T	10	11	10	6
G6 0-4-4T	2	-	-	-
398 0-6-0	1	-	-	-
J21 0-6-0	14	11	3	-
J22 0-6-0	1	-	-	-
J26 0-6-0	9	10	10	2
J27 0-6-0	7	7	8	8
J39 0-6-0	-	3	5	1

J71 0-6-0T	9	11	10	9
J72 0-6-0T	8	7	7	8
J73 0-6-0T	-	-	-	3
J77 0-6-0T	5	6	-	-
J94 0-6-0T	-	-	-	5
N8 0-6-2T	-	1	2	-
N9 0-6-2T	-	3	-	-
N10 0-6-2T	-	1	-	-
N11 0-6-2T	-	1	-	-
Q5 0-8-0	1	-	-	-
Q6 0-8-0	-	-	3	14
4MT 2-6-0	-	-	-	1
Diesel Shunters	-	-	-	6
	77	80	65	67

West Hartlepool was the first shed in the Region to receive an allocation of small diesel shunters and in 1953/4 two types were delivered — 11105/6/7, 204hp diesel-mechanical, and 11700/1/2, 200hp diesel-hydraulic. These were for use in the extensive timber yards in the dock area and they superseded some of the J71s, J72s and J73 0-6-0Ts.

The shed continued to serve the area in an unspectacular way until the end of steam in the north east, maintaining a strong North Eastern flavour until the very end. West Hartlepool never housed any Pacifics or other engines which hit the headlines — only a stud of old faithfuls which went about their daily task unsung and, latterly, uncared for.

When closure finally did come on 17 September 1967 there were nine steam locomotives to go for scrap and fourteen diesels to go to Thornaby:

Q6 0-8-0 63344/87
WD 2-8-0 90074/6, 90360, 90478, 90627/77/95
204hp shunters D2067/8/70/6/7/8/99, D2149/53, D2204/5, D2340,
350hp shunters D3137, D3672

The two sheds at Hartlepool were transferred into the Middlesbrough district on 1 April 1933.

HARTLEPOOL (or EAST HARTLEPOOL)

Little information on the actual shed buildings has been located but on examination they all appeared to be of considerable age. There were in fact, three separate buildings — two single-ended straight sheds, one with two and the other with three roads, and a double-ended shed also with three roads. The only reference located mentions an additional shed for twelve engines, authorised in 1861 at an estimated cost of £2,000 which was completed in the following year.

The shed housed freight and shunting engines and in 1923 had only one passenger working, Mondays to Fridays, and that by a set of reliefmen who worked a train for workmen from Hartlepool to Graythorpe Halt on the Seaton Snook branch. On Saturdays there were two rostered passenger duties, each covered by two sets of men — one worked between West Hartlepool and Ferryhill and the other between Hartlepool-West Hartlepool-Sunderland-Newcastle. These were worked by the N8 0-6-2Ts, of which the shed had four. The full allocation was:

	1923	17 April 1939 and Closure
J24 0-6-0	-	1 (1826)
J26 0-6-0	2	4 (67, 1139, 1670/98)
44 0-6-0T	1	-
J71 0-6-0T	12	8 (77, 137, 176, 260, 541, 980, 1143, 1832)
J72 0-6-0T	6	7 (1736/61/3, 2185, 2309/24/7)
J73 0-6-0T	-	4 (547/8/52/3)
J77 0-6-0T	2	1 (953)
N8 0-6-2T	4	-
N9 0-6-2T	6	-
Q5 0-8-0	2	1 (1215)
Q6 0-8-0	-	4 (1284, 2230/9/62)
	35	30

When the shed was closed all thirty engines were transferred to West Hartlepool shed and the duties worked from there. The three shed buildings have now been demolished.

Sunderland

The Durham & Sunderland Railway was a rope-worked line until the mid-1850s and the Minute of 20 June 1856 proposing the conversion of 'the Old Engine House at Sunderland Moor' into an engine shed refers, most probably, to the building which housed the winding engine and referred to by W.W. Tomlinson in his *History of the NER.* However, the building must have proved unsuitable because on 13 March 1857 plans were submitted for a new shed for six engines, at an estimated cost of £600, and the building was completed later the same year.

In January 1861 a plan for additional accommodation was ordered to be prepared and when submitted in March the cost of the proposed shed was estimated at £1,000. On 7 June 1861 a tender of £1,673 15s 7d was accepted for the construction of the shed, together with a goods warehouse and offices. This development was on the site of the original passenger station at Sunderland Moor, which had been replaced by a new station at Hendon from 1 May 1858.

The first mention of a shed at South Dock, slightly to the east of the previous site, comes in September 1874, when an instruction was issued that trial borings should be made. Plans for the new shed were submitted in November and a month later a tender of £11,320 8s 4d was accepted, plus a turntable at £410. Presumably these details refer to the roundhouse but nothing is known of the two small two-road straight sheds on the west side of the roundhouse, both of which were extensively rebuilt and fitted with flat roofs by British Railways.

Sunderland, as the centre of many small mining communities in north east Durham, was responsible for an intensive local service,for which twenty-four passenger tank engines were provided in 1923. In addition the automatic brake fitted J21 0-6-0 and N8 0-6-2T could be used on passenger trains at times of pressure. Fourteen engines were required daily during the winter of 1922-3, necessitating a total of twenty-three sets of men, nine engines being double manned and the other five single manned. All the turns were in the area bounded by Hartlepool, Ferryhill,Bishop Auckland and Durham, the longest run being the twenty-seven miles to Bishop Auckland. The 2-4-2Ts and 0-4-4Ts were ideally suited for these short distances with many intermediate stops.

By 1939 the number of locomotive turns had been reduced to twelve (requiring twenty-five sets of men)but as there were four

Sentinel car turns (requiring eight sets of men) the shed was busier. Of the twelve locomotive turns ten were specified to be worked by G5 0-4-4Ts and the other two turns had no particular type of engine rostered to them.

Ten years later, in the winter 1949-50 service, the ageing G5 engines were still playing an important part in the workings around Sunderland and of the twelve rostered duties eight were booked to be worked by G5 engines (one of which was push-and-pull fitted) and the other four by A8 4-6-2T engines. All were manned by two sets of men except for one G5 working which required three sets each day, so that there were twenty-five sets of men employed each day on passenger turns. Even by this time the workings had changed little over the years and the longest run performed by a Sunderland engine was still to Bishop Auckland!

	1923	1933	1939	1954
A8 4-6-2T	-	-	2	6
F8 2-4-2T	3	-	-	-
G5 0-4-4T	19	19	21	12
G6 0-4-4T	2	-	-	-
398 0-6-0	4	-	-	-
J21 0-6-0	8	6	4	-
J24 0-6-0	4	4	1	-
J25 0-6-0	12	9	9	-
J27 0-6-0	10	8	10	18
J39 0-6-0	-	-	1	2
44 0-6-0T	2	-	-	-
J71 0-6-0T	1	2	-	-
J72 0-6-0T	4	6	4	5
J77 0-6-0T	1	1	1	-
J94 0-6-0T	-	-	-	6
N8 0-6-2T	5	4	-	2
N9 0-6-2T	-	2	4	-
N10 0-6-2T	2	2	2	1
Y3 0-4-0T	-	1	1	-
4MT 2-6-0	-	-	-	1
	77	64	60	53

With the introduction of diesel railcars the passenger tank engines were no longer required and in 1958 alone Sunderland lost G5 67246/53/4/9/61/5/70/97,67329 for scrapping. The A8 4-6-2T managed to survive a little longer but in 1960 Sunderland said farewell for the last time to 69850/3/4/5/7/8/9/70/3/4/5/8/

83/9, until eventually the shed housed only freight and mineral engines. For instance in 1965 (June) the allocation comprised 2 K1 2-6-0s; 9 Q6 0-8-0s; and 11 J27 0-6-0s.

Until well into the 1960s it was possible to see the shed's fleet of J27 0-6-0s grouped round the turntable of the roundhouse on a Sunday, all facing the same way, with their fat smokeboxes leering at intruders who came to look at them and take their numbers. The fact that these engines alone could be seen inside the shed was due to the turntable being only 42ft in diameter and thus the Q6 0-8-0s and WD 2-8-0s could not be housed under cover. However, it was the practice to disconnect engine and tender when the larger engines were required in the shed for repairs.

Finally the day came for the complete abandonment of steam in the north east, by which time Sunderland was down to twelve engines:

J27 0-6-0   65811/55/79/82/94
Q6 0-8-0   63395
WD 2-8-0   90009, 90135, 90348/78/82, 90417

Q6 63395 and J27 65894 were specially cleaned by local enthusiasts for their last days at work and both engines have, in fact, been purchased by the North Eastern Locomotive Preservation Group and, at the time of writing, are intended for use on the North Yorkshire Moors Railway Preservation Society's line, formerly part of the old Pickering & Whitby line opened in 1836.

DURHAM

The first railway to reach Durham (in name at least) was the Durham & Sunderland, which actually terminated at Shincliffe, to the south of the city. This was originally a rope worked line and although it did eventually change over to locomotive haulage no trace of any engine shed has been found in NER records.

It is probable also that a shed was built at Gilesgate for the opening of the line from Belmont Junction in 1844, for on 18 June 1885 it was reported that the 'old disused engine stable at Gilesgate is in a very dilapidated condition and no longer required and is to be taken down'. Although the shed disappeared many years ago the former Gilesgate passenger station continued in use for goods traffic until very recently.

It must be remembered that originally the main Durham station was not on the east coast main line but on a branch from Leamside to Bishop Auckland. It was not until the links were put in from Gateshead (via the Team Valley) to Newton Hall Junction (north of Durham), and from Relly Mill Junction (south of Durham) to Ferryhill, that through running via Durham became possible. However, on 24 October 1862, before the above links were built, it was decided to build a shed for four engines at Durham New Station: a tender of £1,253 2s 6d was accepted and when the building was completed in 1864 there was an additional £55 17s 5d to pay. No further mention of a shed has been found and it seems probable that this is the building which remained in use until 8 December 1958 and was demolished three years later.

In 1923 the complement of the shed was 2 J21 0-6-0s; 1 J22 0-6-0; 1 398 0-6-0; and 3 1440 2-4-0. The 2-4-0s were used on the three passenger workings which the shed had at that time. Each turn was operated by a single set of men, although two of the engines were used for additional periods each day by a set of relief men. The No 1 turn involved leaving Durham at 5.15am and working to Leamside, thence Middleton in Teesdale - Sunderland - and back to Durham to finish at 12.19pm. No 2 engine worked four afternoon return trips Durham to Waterhouses, thence to Newcastle, Ferryhill and back to Durham. No 3 worked the 2.38pm to Middleton in Teesdale and the 5.35pm return, ending its day with a trip to Waterhouses and the relief men worked the same engine to Ushaw Moor and Waterhouses on late evening trips on certain days of the week.

As the Class 1440s were withdrawn Durham shed received five 'Tennant' 2-4-0s to replace them but as these in turn were withdrawn they were replaced by G5 0-4-4Ts. These particularly useful little engines then remained Durham's motive power for more than thirty years as 67320 was not withdrawn from Durham until 20 November 1958. From September 1957 Durham shed had housed three of the much larger A8 4-6-2Ts - 69873,69883 and 69893. The latter was withdrawn in November 1958 but the other two managed to remain until the shed was closed, when they were transferred to the parent shed at Sunderland.

Tyne Dock

An engine shed and a repair shop for mineral wagons at Tyne Dock were recommended by Mr T.E.Harrison in a report dated 26 February 1858 and these buildings, to cost approximately £15,000, were sanctioned by the NER Board. Work on the engine shed was actually commenced in 1861 and it was probably completed in the following year. In December 1869 Mr Fletcher reported that large numbers of engines had to stand exposed to the weather at various stations, amongst these being Tyne Dock, and a new shed was authorised. In March 1870 plans were submitted for buildings costing £3,100 but two months later a tender of £8,469 2s 6d was accepted 'for additions to the shed'. Accommodation for a further twenty engines was provided in 1877 following the acceptance in the previous year of a tender amounting to £9,942 7s 9d.

Unfortunately, once again, it has proved impossible to tie in the various extensions quoted above with the known buildings, although by 1880 there were two roundhouses and a straight shed and it seems probable that these were the buildings sanctioned in 1870 and 1877. However, the most northerly building, latterly a straight shed accommodating Class 9F 2-10-0 engines, appears to have been converted from a roundhouse. A further roundhouse, known as No 1 shed but with a larger turntable(50 ft) was added on the west side but the date of this has not yet been located.

Tyne Dock was responsible for four passenger turns in 1923, one of which was manned by one set of men, one by two sets, and two by three sets. These were all employed working trains between Newcastle, South Shields and Sunderland using F8 2-4-2Ts: in fact the last of these engines finished their days on these workings in 1938, when the Newcastle to South Shields line was electrified.

Duties in 1939 were down to three using locomotives, although there were three Sentinel railcar duties requiring five sets of men. No 1 locomotive turn required two sets of men to work between Newcastle-Sunderland and Durham. No 2 was a complicated two set roster, taking the engine and men as far as Middleton-in-Teesdale. The turn was booked for a tank engine, presumably a G5 0-4-4T as Tyne Dock had nothing larger. No 3 turn covered trains between South Shields and Sunderland, with the last trip extended from Sunderland to West Hartlepool via Wellfield. This involved the notorious Seaton Bank and on Fridays a J39 0-6-0 was specified for this turn to handle pigeon traffic on the 8.57pm Sunderland-West Hartlepool.

Tyne Dock's main responsibility as far as freight and mineral working was concerned was the one-time Stanhope & Tyne main line between South Shields, Washington, Consett, Waskerley and Stanhope. Much of this had originally been rope worked inclines but in the 1890s it became possible to work with locomotives throughout. The western end of the line served a large number of collieries which needed to get their coal to the coast, and fortunately traffic was available in the opposite direction in the form of iron ore for the large ironworks at Consett.

On these services the North Eastern 0-8-0 engines put in some good and hard work, developing from the earliest Wilson Worsdell T and T1 engines (LNER Q5), through the Raven T2 (LNER Q6) locomotives, to the Raven three-cylinder T3 (LNER Q7) design. Finally, of course, the BR 9F 2-10-0s took over in the 1950s and a fleet of Westinghouse pump fitted engines was stationed at Tyne Dock shed solely for these duties. A day's work for a crew was one trip to Consett with a full load, returning with the empties, banking assistance being usually provided by engine of the same class up the bank from South Pelaw Junction.

For local goods and mineral working Tyne Dock had a stud of about twenty 0-6-0 tender engines, with a number of 0-6-0T engines for local and dock shunting. Also provided for work on the docks were nine 0-4-0Ts of Class Y7 but these became redundant when Tyne Dock itself was taken over by the Tyne Improvement Commission in 1938. At the other end of the scale were the large 4-8-0Ts used for marshalling the mineral trains at Tyne Dock in readiness for the coal being teemed into the ships berthed at the staiths.

Eventually the ore trains were taken over by diesel-electric locomotives and the direct line to Consett via Washington was broken, leaving the shed to come to an end on 9 September 1967 when K1 2-6-0 62007/11/45/50 were transferred away. No 62005 of the same class was transferred to Holbeck shed (Leeds) on the following day and is still in existence, two and a half years later awaiting preservation and restoration. It seems probable that it will find a new home on the North Yorkshire Moors Railway between Grosmont and Pickering.

	1923	1939	1947	1954
F8 2-4-2T	7	-	-	-
G5 0-4-4T	-	5	-	-
J21 0-6-0	2	-	-	-
J22 0-6-0	1	-	-	-
J24 0-6-0	5	-	1	-
J25 0-6-0	8	9	4	6
J26 0-6-0	2	7	-	-
J27 0-6-0	5	-	-	-
J39 0-6-0	-	2	-	-
J71 0-6-0T	8	5	2	2
J72 0-6-0T	4	2	3	5
J73 0-6-0T	2	-	-	-
J77 0-6-0T	2	-	-	-
N8 0-6-2T	-	-	2	1
N9 0-6-2T	-	2	2	3
N10 0-6-2T	-	-	-	1
O4 2-8-0	-	-	19	5
Q5 0-8-0	1	2	11	4
Q6 0-8-0	32	9	1	2
Q7 0-8-0	1	4	15	15
T1 4-8-0T	5	2	-	2
Y1 0-4-0T	-	-	1	-
Y3 0-4-0T	-	2	2	-
Y7 0-4-0T	9	5	3	-
8F 2-8-0	-	-	3	-
WD 2-8-0	-	-	-	4
	94	56	69	50

ANNFIELD PLAIN

Here again no reference to the shed has been located except for a Minute dated 4 May 1893 authorising the relaying of the shed floor with hard scoriae bricks at an estimated cost of £108. However, it is thought that the shed was erected in 1885/6 when a diversion was opened to allow locomotives to work between Stanley Bank Head and Consett. Until then the line at Annfield Plain had been merely a short almost level section between two rope-worked inclines, together with the branch to Tanfield Moor.

The shed, which was closed on 9 September 1940, was situated immediately west of the level crossing over road A6067 but the buildings have been demolished and more recently the level crossing has been taken out, with the line terminating adjacent to the

Stanhope & Tyne Railway Inn. The shed, built of stone, was approximately 100ft long, with two roads, and photographs taken in the 1930s show a very dilapidated building, although it remained standing until the early 1950s.

In 1933 the shed allocation comprised J25 0-6-0 536 and 1993, N9 0-6-2T 1648 and 1652, Q5 0-8-0 643, 785, 1110, 2116 and 2124, and Q7 0-8-0 629. In 1937 the five Q5 engines were exchanged with a similar number of Q6 engines from Tyne Dock, 1264, 1285, 1291, 1294 and 2232 as 'a stronger type of engine required at Annfield Plain'. With the closure of pits in north-west Durham the number of engines stationed at Annfield Plain decreased until, when the decision was made to close the depot, it had only four Q6 0-8-0s on its strength. These four – 1264, 1291, 2215 and 2232 – were transferred to Consett on 9 September 1940, together with the three remaining engines at Waskerley, closed on the same day.

PELTON LEVEL

Nothing is known of the original shed here. The second building was authorised in October 1893 to replace 'the dilapidated shed'. For many years it housed one or two North Eastern tank engines for working this level section between two inclines on the old Stanhope & Tyne Railway; until 1934 these were two J73 0-6-0Ts, but 552 was transferred to Consett on 22 May 1934, leaving only 549 of the same class at Pelton. This was transferred to Alexandra Dock shed at Hull on 26 October 1937 and replaced by 1652, an N9 0-6-2T from Gateshead. In December 1948 1652, which by this time had been renumbered 9424, was transferred to Sunderland, displacing N8 9400 to Tyne Dock: henceforward Tyne Dock supplied an engine of Class N8, N9 or N10 to Pelton Level, which ceased to have an allocation of its own.

CHAPTER V

Waskerley, Shildon, Ferryhill

Waskerley

The first shed was authorised in October 1845 at an estimated cost of £370, to accommodate four engines and tenders as a result of the decision to build a new railway community high on the moors between Consett and Stanhope, at the end of the section from Stanhope and at the top of Nanny Mayor's Incline. A sizeable village sprang up at Waskerley, with its own church and school, the latter provided with a schoolmaster at the expense of the Stockton & Darlington Railway to educate the children of the company's employees.

In January 1854 it was decided to provide a new shed, or alternatively, to lengthen the existing building, but as no records have been discovered of any subsequent alterations or additions it seems probable that a new building was actually erected, as there were two sheds when the depot closed on 9 September 1940. One of these was a two-road through shed and the other a two-road dead-end building, which finally housed J24 0-6-0 1846 (transferred to Darlington) and N10 0-6-2T 1148 and 1683 (both transferred to Consett).

The engines at the shed were mainly employed on local goods and mineral workings in the area, and in fact, until not long before it closed Waskerley was a more important shed than Consett, having usually eight or nine engines on its allocation compared with Consett's three or four.

The allocation over the years was:

	1923	1930	1935	1939
D2 4-4-0	-	-	1	-
D22 4-4-0	1	1	-	-
J21 0-6-0	-	1	1	-
J22 0-6-0	1	-	-	-
J26 0-6-0	-	-	1	2
J27 0-6-0	-	-	1	-
N8 0-6-2T	7	6	4	3
	9	8	8	5

It will be noted that Waskerley for many years had a passenger 4-4-0 on its strength — this was for working two trips a day from Blackhill to Darlington and back — the men changed at Burnhill on the first return trip from Darlington. Between 1926 and 1930 the service was worked by D23 23 and, after that engine was withdrawn in August 1929, by 678 of the same class. Class D23 engines were getting scarce for the Stainmore line services because of withdrawals in 1930 and so 678 was transferred to Kirkby Stephen on 11 July 1930 and replaced by D22 777 from Hull. 'Three sevens' — perhaps the most accident prone engine on the NER — was withdrawn on 22 May 1935 and replaced by former GN 4-4-0 4386 from York. Waskerley persisted with this engine for two months and then managed to get it transferred back to York. Henceforward they relied on their J21 to work the passenger turns. No 807 had actually been transferred from York to Waskerley in February 1927 to replace J22 0-6-0 498 (withdrawn December 1926). However, on 28 February 1936 807 was sent to Gateshead as 'not required at Waskerley' — presumably by this time Waskerley had lost its passenger turn.

Two large 0-6-0s were transferred to Waskerley on 7 January 1935 because of extra work; these were J26 1366 and J27 0-6-0 1013 but in June 1937 the J27 was sent to Sunderland in exchange for J26 1676 'to avoid having one engine of a type at a depot'.

The shed buildings have now been demolished but the site, together with the remaining houses, are worthy of a visit. Until recently the office building still carried its Stockton & Darlington house number plaque but this has now vanished.

CONSETT

On 12 January 1875 Mr Fletcher reported that 'the engine running the last passenger train from Crook to Benfieldside has to run back to Waskerley and to go from Waskerley to its work in the morning. It is recommended that an engine shed be provided at Benfieldside'. Consequently in May 1875 it was agreed to provide accommodation for two engines, and a tender of £961 3s 7d was accepted two weeks later. The shed was later known as Blackhill and finally as Consett. Strangely enough in the *1923 Passenger Engine Working* book the Blackhill to Crook and Darlington turns are worked from Waskerley shed, leaving Consett with only two N8 0-6-2Ts for local shunting duties. However, one Consett engine was used on Sundays to work a morning passenger train to Newcastle and return via Annfield Plain and Birtley, and an afternoon train to Newcastle and back via Lintz Green and Scotswood.

By 1929 Consett had also acquired two J39 0-6-0s (1465 and 1473) and as the outbreak of World War II brought extra work to the area four J26s — 412, 434, 1366 and 1676 were transferred to Consett between September 1939 and July 1940. With the closure of Annfield Plain and Waskerley sheds on 9 September 1940 a re-arrangement of the workings in the area took place and Consett received four Q6 0-8-0s from Annfield Plain, losing the four J26s to Darlington. At the same time N10 0-6-2T 1148 and 1683 were transferred from Waskerley to Consett and N8 0-6-2T 861 from York to Consett.

Further development of industry in the area led to an increased demand for motive power and by 1947 Consett shed was the home of twelve Q6 0-8-0s as well as one N8 and two N9 0-6-2Ts, and A8 4-6-2 69861. The A8 commenced its working day on the 6.17am Consett to Newcastle (via Scotswood) and ended it on the 10.5pm Newcastle to Blackhill (via Birtley). Altogether five return trips to Newcastle were made during the day, requiring the engine to be manned by three sets of men, the engine being coaled at Blaydon shed between 10.8 and 10.50am daily. Although booked to work this duty until 4 May 1947 the A8 was exchanged with N8 0-6-2T 9384 of Sunderland in February 1947.

To accommodate its sixteen engines Consett could provide only a single road dead-end shed 105ft long — just enough to house two

J26 0-6-0s under cover. However, at a date unknown but probably in the 1950s, a new single road shed was built alongside, to the west of the original building and about twice as long: even so at week-ends most of Consett's steam locomotives had to stand outside.

As traffic in the area decreased, and with the advent of diesel locomotives, the shed was gradually run down until on 24 May 1965 it closed to steam locomotives, although remaining in use as a signing-on point for exactly a year longer.

Shildon

This was, of course, the headquarters of the Stockton & Darlington Railway locomotive department and it appears that for many years the locomotives in normal running use were housed and maintained with the locomotives undergoing heavy repairs and overhaul. It was not until January 1848 that a separate running shed was proposed 'for 6 or 8 engines, with proper coke depots, furnace and sand drying place, with water laid on'. This was approved and a plan of c 1849 shows a nine-road straight shed (accommodating one engine per road) situated immediately west of Mason's Arms level crossing. Next, in 1852, came a building 'in which to wash the locomotive engines', and in the following year a new shed costing an estimated £2,345 7s 2d was authorised. This was opened in April 1854, and may have been the first roundhouse. The building or area was known as Sebastopol and although the Crimean War started in 1854 the fall of Sebastopol was not until the following year, or a year after the shed was opened. A further shed, to hold twenty-four engines was authorised in June 1856 and was, presumably, the second roundhouse while a tender for another circular shed was accepted in December 1864 at a cost of £3,916 4s 5d.

In January 1873 Mr Bouch reported that additional accommodation was necessary 'partly to meet the increased number of engines, but mainly because of the recent arrangement for giving access to Bolckow Vaughan & Co Furnace Pit, having deprived the company of accommodation for twelve engines at the square shed'. A new shed was authorised as a result of Mr Bouch's representations but it is not clear from the Minutes which shed is referred to — a shed additional to the three roundhouses is not known.

However, it is known that there were three circular sheds in the 1870s and in 1886 a start was made on extensive rebuilding. A new turntable was ordered from Cowans Sheldon for No 1 shed in 1886 (£388) and following this a start was made on rebuilding No 2 Shed. No 3 Shed followed in 1891/2 but in this case the turntable was not renewed until 1906, when it was reported that 'the turntable in No 3 Shed is not worth repairing' and a replacement was ordered from Cowans Sheldon, this time at £870 for a 50ft table.

In 1915 No 3 Shed was adapted to house the ten electric locomotives built for working the line to Newport (Middlesbrough) and although an NER electric sectioning diagram shows eleven stalls as being fitted with overhead wiring, an LNER diagram of January 1929 states that all stalls in No 3 Shed were equipped to house the electric locomotives. Each stall carried a number between 3 and 12 on a large board above the track, presumably to indicate in which stall each locomotive should be stabled as their numbers ran from 3 to 12. However, photographs taken in May 1932 with eight engines grouped round the turntable show only half of them in their correct stalls.

The electric locomotives ceased to work in 1935 and on 8 July the shed was closed and the steam locomotives dispersed. The allocation at the time was:

J21 0-6-0: 16, 93, 582, 944, 1323, 1507/50/3
J25 0-6-0: 1973,·2054   J71 0-6-0T: 40, 241, 802, 977
J27 0-6-0: 1015/29, 1221   Y3 0-4-0T: 148

The electric locomotives were sent to Darlington Works and stored for many years in the Paint Shop before moving to South Gosforth.

	1923	1933
A7 4-6-2T	5	-
G5 0-4-4T	1	2
398 0-6-0	4	-
J21 0-6-0	8	10
J22 0-6-0	1	-
J23 0-6-0	-	1

J24 0-6-0	-	1
J25 0-6-0	8	11
J26 0-6-0	-	1
J27 0-6-0	13	3
44 0-6-0T	1	-
J71 0-6-0T	5	5
J72 0-6-0T	1	1
J77 0-6-0T	1	-
N12 0-6-2T	-	1
Q5 0-8-0	15	14
ELECTRIC 0-4-4-0	10	10
	73	60

Once again a shed with almost entirely freight and mineral duties, Shildon in 1923 was responsible only for some very minor passenger turns. No 1 was actually worked by a relief set of men, who ran light engine to Darlington to work the 8.0pm to Crook, which was extended to Tow Law on Wednesdays and Saturdays. They returned light from Crook to Shildon each night except Saturday, although on Wednesdays they had to work the empty set back from Tow Law to Crook in readiness for the next day's working before they finished. On Saturdays they worked in addition the 9.42pm from Tow Law to Bishop Auckland and the 10.30pm Bishop Auckland to Crook before running home light.

The only other passenger turn ran on Saturdays and involved working the 1.5pm to Sunderland and the 6.28pm return as far as Bishop Auckland: then to Cockfield Fell and back and Ferryhill and back, returning empty to Shildon at 11.40pm.

After closure the shed buildings remained out of use for some time before being taken over by the adjacent wagon works, and although they are still standing they are difficult to identify as once belonging to the important Shildon shed.

Photographs of the original buildings are almost non-existent but the well-known Locomotive Publishing Co view of the double-ended locomotive 'Wilberforce' shows in the background what is probably the original circular shed.

Shildon engines and men were responsible for working over the notorious Stainmore line of the South Durham & Lancashire

Union Railway, working coke westwards as far as Cockermouth on the Cockermouth, Keswick & Penrith line. Due to heavy loads and the long and heavy gradients accidents on this line were numerous and the Shildon footplate crews had some hair-raising experiences. The one I like best occurred on 18 April 1882 on the Cockermouth, Keswick & Penrith Railway. This involved a double-load mineral train from Shildon to Cockermouth, which were regularly worked throughout by Shildon engines. With a double-load two engines and two brake vans were used and the train conveyed twice the load allowed for one engine. Each van carried a guard, who was supposed to remain in his own van, but on this particular day the rear van became uncoupled between Braithwaite and Bassenthwaite Lake stations with both guards in it. On reaching Embleton the driver of the leading engine (George Sanderson) noticed that they had lost a brake van, so leaving the train-engine driver to work forward to Cockermouth with the train, he returned to Bassenthwaite Lake, still in possession of the staff for the section.

After waiting at Bassenthwaite Lake for a few minutes one of the guards came hurrying along from the stranded van, and because he stated that the other guard had gone back to Braithwaite to stop following trains they set off for the van on the engine. On the outward journey the train had used a ticket from Braithwaite to Bassenthwaite Lake, leaving the staff to be carried by the following mineral train. Although the signalman at Bassenthwaite Lake had noticed that the first train had passed him without a tail lamp he accepted a second mineral train from Braithwaite and this was stopped by hand-signals by the guard who had gone back towards Braithwaite. On learning that the engine was carrying the staff the guard assumed that it was being left to him to remove the stranded van, although before they parted the guards had agreed that the one who went forward should be responsible for removing it.

After buffering up to the van the second mineral train commenced to propel it towards Bassenthwaite Lake, at the same time hauling its own train, but they had not gone very far when they saw steam from the light engine returning for the van from the Bassenthwaite Lake end. Although both drivers made attempts to stop, the light engine collided with the van and derailed it.

Before the light engine hit the van the driver had reversed the engine and all on the footplate abandoned ship by jumping off seconds before the collision. However, before any of them could recover their senses the engine had set off back towards Bassenthwaite Lake with no-one on the footplate. Although the driver said that the regulator was closed before he jumped off the engine was reported to have gone through Bassenthwaite Lake station at 50mph! In fact so fast that the signalman did not notice that there was no-one aboard.

A few minutes later the driver came dashing up and gasped out that the engine was running away with no-one on the footplate, and would they telegraph Cockermouth immediately. Fortunately a telegraph message got through to Cockermouth immediately and by some quick action the station staff managed to detrain some twelve passengers from a Maryport & Carlisle Railway train standing at the platform. This was accomplished with only seconds to spare before the runaway engine crashed into the rear of the stationary train. However, this was not the end of their troubles. The crew on the footplate of the engine standing on the other end of the train had taken shelter when they saw a collision was imminent, leaving their own engine unattended. The shock of the collision uncoupled their engine and away it went down the gradient west of Cockermouth station, again with no-one on the footplate. Fortunately a porter was able to run after it, climb aboard, and apply the brake after it had travelled only about twenty yards. So ended a mishap which caused collisions some six miles apart and which might have had much more serious consequences.

Driver Sanderson of the runaway engine was born in 1847 and commenced work with the Stockton & Darlington Railway in 1866 as a shunter. He was appointed fireman in 1867 and driver in 1871. He retired in 1913. For the part he played in the Bassenthwaite Lake collision his pay was reduced 6d (2½p) per day for one year. In 1912 he was cautioned for his actions whilst working the 7.5am goods from York to Shildon with Class T 0-8-0 engine 2118 on 22 December 1911. As his engine was low in water at Northallerton he wished to pick up water at Wiske Moor troughs, but realising that he was not travelling fast enough he brought his train to a stand just north of Northallerton. He then uncoupled the engine from the train and ran forward as fast as he could over the troughs, picking up water. He then returned for his train, coupled up and set off for Shildon.

The Shildon district sheds merged with the Darlington district from 20 June 1932.

WEST AUCKLAND

This depot, also known as Fieldon Bridge or Fylands Bridge, was opened in 1887, having been authorised in December 1885 at an estimated cost of £17,650 but this included thirty-two cottages and a house for the Locomotive Foreman. It consisted of a single roundhouse of typical NER pattern with eighteen stalls and two entrance roads.

It was first closed on 13 April 1931 as an economy measure, when N9 0-6-2T 1646 and 1651 were transferred to Wear Valley Junction and Darlington respectively, and J21 0-6-0 1323 and thirteen J25 0-6-0s (1727, 1971/2/5/80/8/95, 2038/44/5/74/9, 2130) to Shildon.

Four years later it was decided to close Shildon and Wear Valley Junction sheds and to reopen West Auckland: initially West Auckland received eight J21 0-6-0s (16, 93, 582, 944, 1323, 1507/12/53), J25 1973, J27 1029, J71 0-6-0Ts 50, 241, 802, 977, and Y3 0-4-0T 148. Of the fifteen engines only 1323 had been allocated to West Auckland when it closed in 1931.

In 1922/3 the shed worked only one daily passenger turn which required two sets of men and took them to Ferryhill, Barnard Castle and Stockton. There was also a Saturday turn requiring one set of men to work to Crook and Durham.

In 1939 there were three regular passenger turns:

No 1 To Wearhead, Durham and Darlington	2 sets of men
No 2 To Ferryhill, Durham and South Shields	2 sets of men
No 3 Darlington	1 set of men

On these duties J21 0-6-0s were used.

The allocations were as follows:

	1923	1939	1947	1954
A8 4-6-2T	-	-	6	6
F8 2-4-2T	1	-	-	-

G6 0-4-4T	2	-	-	-
J21 0-6-0	1	7	2	5
J22 0-6-0	1	-	-	-
J25 0-6-0	17	-	12	3
J27 0-6-0	-	1	-	-
J39 0-6-0	-	-	-	3
J71 0-6-0T	-	4	4	2
J72 0-6-0T	-	-	2	5
J77 0-6-0T	-	-	-	1
N9 0-6-2T	2	-	1	-
Q5 0-8-0	-	-	2	-
Q6 0-8-0	-	-	-	2
V1 2-6-2T	-	-	3	-
Y1 0-4-0T	-	-	2	2
Y3 0-4-0T	-	1	1	-
2MT 2-6-0 (LM)	-	-	-	4
2MT 2-6-0 (BR)	-	-	-	6
3MT 2-6-0	-	-	-	7
	24	**13**	**35**	**46**

By 1949, when the shed had six A8 4-6-2T on its strength, the number of passenger turns had been increased to five, all requiring two sets of men. The locomotives rostered for these were two G5 0-4-4Ts and three A8s (two G5s had arrived at the shed in 1947 subsequent to the date of the allocation quoted in the accompanying table). An engine also had to be provided to work the 5.0pm workers' train from Heighington to Crook.

Shildon shed had been responsible for the mineral train workings over Stainmore Summit from the 1860s and thus when that shed was closed West Auckland took over some of the duties and these increased with World War II. After the war, with the lifting of some of the restrictions on engines allowed over the viaducts, it became possible to use larger engines and West Auckland used 4MT 2-6-0s of both LMS and BR designs. These were also used on the through Newcastle-Blackpool passenger trains on Saturdays, which West Auckland worked as far as Tebay.

The final closure took place on 2 February 1964 when the allocation was dispersed as follows:

Q6 0-8-0   63344/61/98,63443/6 to Thornaby

	63343, 63407 to Darlington
LM 4MT 2-6-0	43133 to Goole
	43138/41 to Hull Dairycoates
BR 3MT 2-6-0	77003/10 to Stourton

The shed was demolished in 1965.

WEAR VALLEY JUNCTION

On 21 January 1848 John Dixon and John Graham reported that an engine shed 'ought to be built here against another winter' but nothing appears to have transpired until 12 January 1875, when it was suggested that 'a shed to accommodate not less than eight engines should be built at Wear Valley Junction, and about 16 houses. Shildon accommodates 72 engines but 112 stand there and about 8 Shildon engines have to go to their work at Wear Valley Junction, losing time and obstructing the line'. The following month plans were submitted for a circular shed to hold 9 engines, so that it could be extended to hold 20 engines if ultimately found necessary. The estimated cost was £2,955 plus £780 for a turntable and in May 1875 a tender for £3,378 10s 0d was accepted, plus £1,080 for a turntable, and a ninety-nine years lease was taken on the necessary land. Before work commenced it was decided to provide additional accommodation for 'two more locomotives and four tank engines' and expenditure of a further £1,220 was authorised. The building was completed in December 1876 and additional expenditure of £408 14s 6d was necessary.

The actual size of the shed raises some queries. Certainly the original plans show a nine-road segment, but where were the 'two more locomotives and four tank engines' accommodated when the LNER diagram and contemporary photographs of the shed show it as having only six stalls?

The shed was situated at the junction of the Wearhead branch with the Bishop Auckland to Crook line and although referred to by the NER Board as Wear Valley Junction it was actually known as Witton Junction originally.

In 1932 the shed housed five engines:

G5 0-4-4T 408	Transferred to Wear Valley Junction on the closure of Stanhope shed on 1 May 1930. Remained until closure.
J21 0-6-0 1553	No record of transfer from Wear Valley

	Junction to Shildon but transferred Shildon to West Auckland when Shildon closed 8 July 1935.
J25 0-6-0 25	Transferred to Cudworth 29 June 1934.
N9 0-6-2T 1646	Transferred to Wear Valley Junction 11 April 1931 on the closure of West Auckland shed, and transferred to Sunderland 2 June 1932.
Y3 0-4-0T 148	Transferred to Wear Valley Junction from Hull Dairycoates 15 June 1931 and transferred to Shildon (to work at Bishop Auckland) on 7 March 1932.

On 8 July 1935 there was a reorganisation of locomotive distribution in this corner of south west Durham: West Auckland shed was reopened: at the same time Shildon and Were Valley Junction sheds were closed. By this time only G5 408 remained at Wear Valley Junction and this engine was transferred to Darlington.

Until the closure of Stanhope shed and the transfer of 408 to Wear Valley Junction the shed handled only freight and mineral trains.

STANHOPE

As the line pushed up Weardale an engine shed was established first at Frosterley, then Stanhope, and finally at the head of the valley at Wearhead. Stanhope was reached in October 1862 and three years later it was decided to move the shed from Frosterley to Stanhope. As Stanhope shed was latterly a solidly built stone structure it is not clear if this was done or if a new building was erected. Perhaps for the sake of economy the stone structure at Frosterley was dismantled and re-erected at Stanhope? However, whatever happened, in 1876 it was agreed that the accommodation at Stanhope should be increased to take six instead of four engines and a tender for £745 was accepted for this work.

In June 1905 it was decided to reorganise the workings on the branch and Stanhope was left with one engine for working the passenger trains. This method of working continued until the shed closed from 1 May 1930 when the engine, G5 0-4-4T 408, was transferred to Wear Valley Junction shed.

After the 1876 additions the shed consisted of three roads, each holding two engines, but at some period during LNER ownership it was reduced to a single road shed. To this remote spot went 'Locomotion' No 1 and 'Derwent' for safe keeping during World War II.

WEARHEAD

This small single-road shed at the terminus of the branch from Wear Valley Junction was erected when the final extension up the valley took place in 1895.

From 1923 (or even earlier) a G5 0-4-4T was shedded at Wearhead but from 8 July 1935 J21 0-6-0 1566 from Ferryhill replaced G5 1881. In October 1935 J21 314 from West Hartlepool replaced 1566 and the former then remained at Wearhead for almost eighteen years as it was still stationed there when the passenger services were withdrawn and the shed closed from 29 June 1953. Unfortunately 314 — by now renumbered 65064 — was not used on the last trains up and down the valley on the evening of 27 June and 65078 took its place. Wearhead at the time of closure was a sub-shed of West Auckland and by some oversight 65064 was not transferred to West Auckland on paper until 16 May 1954.

The two sets of men stationed at Wearhead were, in 1923, responsible only for working as far as Wear Valley Junction but in 1939 they worked through to Darlington twice each day and on Saturdays ran as far as Richmond. By this time (1939) the engine worked a trip to Bishop Auckland and back on summer Sundays.

After the shed was closed the building was used by a road haulage company as a workshop and the engine pit used to reach the undersides of motor vehicles instead of G5 and J21 engines.

Ferryhill

This three-road single-ended straight shed was first mooted in 1879 and towards the end of the year a building to hold nine engines was authorised at an estimated cost of £2,780. A tender for £1,995 4s 8d for the building alone was accepted on 15 January 1880 and the shed was opened in 1881. Although primarily a goods engine shed it did have one passenger turn at

Grouping and this occupied the engine (a G5 0-4-4T) from 6.35am to 8.59pm (10.40pm on Saturdays) taking it to Battersby and Newcastle: the two 0-4-4Ts were 427 and 1882.

By 1938 the passenger workings had shrunk to two on Saturdays only, No 1 being manned by two sets of men who changed at Ferryhill at 2.36pm. The first set left Ferryhill at 6.37am and worked first a return trip to Stockton, Middlesbrough and Battersby, followed by a trip to Newcastle and back via Leamside. The second set worked to Battersby, returned as far as Stockton and then worked to Guisborough: they then worked a train from Guisborough to Middlesbrough, ran light engine to Stockton, and ended their day on the 9.5pm Stockton-Ferryhill. The other engine worked three return trips to West Hartlepool, commencing with the 1.20pm from Ferryhill and ending with the 9.20pm from West Hartlepool. On Sundays in the summer one engine worked to Redcar and back, and the other worked to Seaton Carew and back if required.

Ferryhill No 11 Goods Engine turn picked up the empty workmens' coach at Bowes at 4.32pm and worked it to Hulands platform, returning with the 4.32pm Hulands to Barnard Castle, carrying the LNER workmen employed at Hulands Quarry. The engine then ran light to Ferryhill.

These turns could be worked by the G5 0-4-4T (1882) that remained at Ferryhill until the shed closed on 7 November 1938, or by three engines normally employed on freight duties — J21 0-6-0 800, J39 0-6-0 1490, or N9 0-6-2T 1651, all of which were fitted with automatic vacuum brakes. The allocation of Ferryhill shed at various dates was:

	1923	1933	1938 (at closure)
G5 0-4-4T	2	1	1 (1882)
398 0-6-0	5	-	-
J21 0-6-0	-	3	1(800)
J22 0-6-0	4	-	-
J24 0-6-0	1	1	-
J25 0-6-0	1	2	8 (1962/72/85/8/ 95, 2059, 2130/9)
J26 0-6-0	1	2	-
J27 0-6-0	9	11	5 (888, 1064/6, 1222/9)
J39 0-6-0	-	-	1 (1490)

J72 0-6-0T	-	2	2 (581, 2326)
J73 0-6-0T	5	2	2 (544/5)
J76 0-6-0T	1	-	-
N9 0-6-2T	-	1	1 (1651)
Q5 0-8-0	-	5	9 (83, 430/43/74, 648, 773, 1186, 1685/96)
	29	30	30

In World War II some of the locomotives and rolling stock from the Railway Museum at York were evacuated to Ferryhill and the shed housed Fletcher 2-4-0 910, Stockton & Darlington 0-6-0 1275, Stirling 4-2-2 No 1, Stockton & Darlington coach 59, and the Bodmin & Wadebridge vehicle, from 1941 until they returned to York in 1947.

In 1951 the building was used for storing surplus G5 0-4-4T engines and 67242/72/94, 67318/31 were noted there. The building has since been demolished.

BYERS GREEN

In 1869 Mr Fletcher, the locomotive superintendent, reported that 'a large number of engines have to stand exposed to the weather at various stations for want of engine shed accommodation' and amongst the places where additional accommodation was recommended was Spennymoor. In 1874 it was suggested that an engine shed be erected at Todhills 'for engines at present standing at Spennymoor' and on 22 October 1874 preparation of the plans and estimates for a shed at Byers Green was authorised. The exact date of opening has not been located but the year 1878 has been quoted.

The shed was built on what was originally the West Durham Railway, at the top of the Todhills Incline, about one mile west of Burnhouse Junction, near where the West Durham Railway and Clarence Railway made an end-on junction. Byers Green station was some distance away and was actually on the later line from Burnhouse Junction to Bishop Auckland, via Coundon.

The three road brick built building accommodated some eight mineral engines of Class 398 and 163, 488, 941, 990, 1372, 1374, 1386 and 1455 are known to have been there in 1920-2. Three of these were withdrawn in 1920 (1372, 1374 and 1455) and 941 went for scrap in 1921. To the four remaining engines were added another Class 398 engine (1405) and a P2 (406) and these six engines were there when the shed closed on 17 July 1922. After many years disuse the shed was eventually sold for use as a brickworks and as such it is still in use and in quite good condition.

PART TWO
Southern Division

SOUTHERN DIVISION SHEDS IN 1914

MAIN SHED *Sub-shed(s)*	ENG-INES	MEN	CIRCULAR SHEDS		STRAIGHT SHEDS	
			Adjacent	Separate	No	Roads
YORK	116	722	4	2	2	3/4
Normanton	8	33	-	1	-	-
LEEDS (NEVILLE HILL)	97	476	4	-	-	-
Starbeck	51	209	-	-	1	2
Thirsk	11	51	-	-	1	2
Ilkley	1	5	-	-	1	2
Bradford	1	5	-	-	-	-
Pateley Bridge	1	5	-	-	1	1
Masham	1	5	-	-	1	1
HULL (DAIRYCOATES)	139	677	6	-	2	2/3
Botanic Gardens	45	193	2	-	-	-
Doncaster	3	18	-	-	-	-
Bridlington	4	39	-	-	1	3
SELBY	65	299	2	-	1	1
MIDDLESBROUGH	85	369	-	3	-	-
Newport	100	403	2	-	-	-
Saltburn	15	37	-	-	1	2
Carlin How	6	19	-	-	1	3
Rosedale	3	12	-	-	1	2
Guisborough	1	5	-	-	1	1
SCARBOROUGH	22	70	-	1	1	8
DARLINGTON	97	484	-	1	3	3/3/3
Northallerton	10	33	-	-	2	1/1
Barnard Castle	6	30	-	-	1	2
Richmond	1	5	-	-	1	2
Hawes Junction	1	5	-	-	1	1
Middleton in Teesdale	1	5	-	-	1	1
WHITBY	16	57	-	-	1	2
Pickering	5	12	-	-	1	1
MALTON	15	50	-	-	1	2
KIRKBY STEPHEN	13	63	-	-	1	4
Penrith	1	5	-	-	1	2
STOCKTON	52	217	-	-	1	8
Haverton Hill	12	66	-	-	1	4
TOTAL	1005	4685				

CHAPTER VI

York

York

When travelling along the East Coast main line from London to Scotland in steam days railway enthusiasts invariably gave extra attention as the various large locomotive depots were passed. Peterborough (New England), alas was usually obscured by rows of mineral wagons; Grantham was too far away and partially screened by station buildings; whilst Doncaster was also difficult to see because of intervening wagons, although the engines fresh from overhaul at the Plant were usually visible at the north end of the shed yard. In the North Eastern Area, Selby usually hid its complement of locomotives behind the shed buildings; Darlington was usually clear but as the engines 'on shed' were in rows parallel to the main line it was possible to see only the nearest line of engines. Only the tip of Gateshead shed was visible as main line trains crossed the River Tyne on the King Edward Bridge, although trains via Gateshead East did pass the shed yard. There was not much to see at Heaton - perhaps a glimpse of one of the Quayside electric shunting locomotives at the south end and some V1 2-6-2Ts at the north end. Tweedmouth accommodated a number of North Eastern Atlantics and some K3 2-6-0s, then over the Royal Border Bridge and into Berwick with the Scottish Border only a few miles further on. In Scotland, however, there was nothing of note until Edinburgh was reached and then St Margarets shed was passed so quickly that it was impossible to see many of the engines standing there.

York, without a doubt, was the most fascinating and productive main line shed. As most trains stopped there (and those that did not stop were reduced to a crawl) the shed was passed slowly and thus it was possible to see much of interest. Entering the station from the south there were sheds on both sides of the line (until 1932), that on the up side housing the 'foreign' visitors to York, whilst York's own stud of smaller engines occupied the three (latterly two) roundhouses on the down side.

North of the station there was the panorama of locomotives standing in the yard at the North shed. This stretched for some distance along the side of the main line and it was possible to see many types of locomotives being coaled, watered and turned in readiness for their next trip.

The first railway to serve York was the York & North Midland - George Hudson's inaugural line - of which the initial section to Gascoigne Wood was opened on 29 May 1839. Workshops to maintain the locomotives were built at York, on the south side of the line, adjacent to the temporary terminus just outside the City walls. These buildings are still in existence, occupied by the Railway Museum. In addition, about the same time, a two road locomotive shed for six engines was built on the north side of the line, roughly on a site now occupied by platform 11, but this shed was demolished in 1875 or 1876 to make way for the present station. However, an 1860 plan of York station shows a three road shed on this same site and perhaps the two road shed was replaced by a larger building at some date not yet located.

On 4 January 1841 the first permanent station at York was opened by the York & North Midland. It was reached through an arch cut in the City walls, and from 30 March 1841 the station was also used by the Great North of England Railway, which opened its line from Darlington on that date. The lines of these two companies diverged immediately outside the walls, with the Y & NM passing via Chaloner Whin, Milford Junction and Altofts to Normanton, whilst the GNE followed a northerly course to reach the first station out of York at Shipton (later Beningbrough). A curve from the GNE to join the Y&NM at Hob Moor gave a route to the south without the need for reversing in the station, which was a terminus.

It was in this triangle of lines that eventually five further locomotive sheds were built - three roundhouses and two straight sheds. The first circular shed was built about 1850 (it was certainly in use by 1851) and in October 1850 a similar shed was authorised at an estimated cost of £1,600. This second shed appears to have been opened late in 1851 or early in 1852. The two sheds were only a few feet apart at one point and each had sixteen stalls served by a 42ft turntable. It is not known when the first built ceased to be used for locomotive purposes, but by 1921 it was being used for repairing wagon sheets. However, one of the NER petrol-engined inspection saloons was kept in the shed but the saloon and the building were both destroyed by fire on 21 October 1921. The second roundhouse remained in use until May 1961 when the practice of stabling pilot engines at the South shed ceased, although surplus locomotives were stored there for some time longer. The building was eventually demolished at the end of 1963.

The third roundhouse on the site was larger than the other two as it had a 45ft turntable serving eighteen roads. It was also of a different type of construction, with each stall having its own ridged roof — the gable-ends of this shed can be seen in many old photographs taken at the South shed. The central roof was circular and the whole was surmounted by a large weathervane with a 2-2-2 locomotive (probably a 'Jenny Lind') in place of the usual 'cock'. This building was authorised on 5 June 1863 at an estimated cost of £5,271.6s.0d but excess expenditure of £555.15s.11d was authorised on 2 December 1864, shortly after the shed had been completed. This roundhouse had a life of almost a century as it too was demolished at the end of 1963.

In conjunction with the new layout at York, which involved building a new through station in place of the old terminal building, a shed to hold sixty engines was authorised on 5 November 1875 at an estimated cost of £36,700 and this building was erected at Clifton, on the west side of the line at the north end of the new station. The new shed consisted of three adjoining roundhouses in the shape of an L, each with twenty roads and a 45ft turntable.

On 19 May 1879 the Swinton & Knottingley Joint line was opened for passenger traffic, bringing an influx of Midland Railway locomotives to York. In the following month the Midland requested shed accommodation for their engines which remained at York overnight and after some discussion the North Eastern decided to provide accommodation 'by appropriating for Midland Railway use one of the circular sheds in the new engine stable'. However, this recommendation does not seem to have been put into effect, or if it was, then only for a short time, because the third roundhouse at the south end of the station — the shed opened in 1864 — became the Midland shed. In January 1883 an agreement was drawn up between the North Eastern and the Midland, whereby the latter was to pay the North Eastern £25 per annum for each engine stabled at York, plus gas and water at cost, the agreement being back dated to 17 May 1879, or two days prior to the opening of the S&K Joint line. The Midland engines used this roundhouse at the south end of the station until the Grouping of 1923, when they moved across to join the former Lancashire & Yorkshire engines at Queen Street shed.

The four-road straight shed at Queen Street was opened in 1909 when alterations and extensions were carried out at the south end of the station (including the provision of a new Locomotive Yard signal box with 295 levers). It had previously been the boiler shop of the York Locomotive Works, which had been developed from the Y & NM works mentioned earlier. In addition to the L & Y, Great Central and Great Eastern engines also used Queen Street shed until the Grouping, when the two LNER constituents moved across to the roundhouses in exchange for the Midland engines.

The LMS engines remained at Queen Street until 1932 when they moved across the main line to the South shed, whilst Queen Street became redundant for locomotive stabling purposes. For a short period in BR days part of the building was used for the maintenance of diesel shunters, but latterly its main use has been to accommodate the various inspection saloons provided for the use of Regional and District officers.

For a time the shed yard at Queen Street was used by LNER engines from other sheds which merely required turning and watering before taking up their return workings, and the turntable adjacent to the entrance of the Railway Museum was in frequent use until the advent of the diesels. The yard was also used by the emergency engine provided as a replacement for any main line trains which suffered an engine failure.

Now to consider the two straight sheds at York South, as the

depot came to be called, and although little documentary evidence
has been found regarding either of them it is the writer's considered opinion that one was the shed built for the Great North of
England Railway in 1841. The building referred to is the three-
road shed which was only demolished at the end of 1963. Prior to
nationalisation and transfer of the former LMS locomotives to the
North shed this building was used by the LMS, but before 1923 it
was the Great Northern shed. An agreement to stable four GN
locomotives at York was signed on 5 November 1850, shortly
after the route from Doncaster was opened via Knottingley and
Burton Salmon, but it is not known exactly when the Great
Northern took over the building. However, it must have been in
the 1850s as in 1859 the North Eastern agreed 'to carry out
alterations to the roof of the GN shed'.

The reason for thinking that this was originally the GNE shed is
because the style of building was identical with the GNE shed at
Darlington, although the latter had only two roads whereas York
had three. Both buildings were notable for the large clerestory on
the roof, but although the Darlington shed still stands and retains
this feature the shed at York had the whole roof replaced at some
date not yet located, probably in the 1930s. The new curved roof
was built on the old walls and it completely changed the appearance of the building, making it look more like a farmer's Dutch
barn than an engine shed!

Apart from its designation as an engine shed on old plans of
York station nothing is known of the origins of the other straight
shed at the south end of the station. This building also had three
roads and latterly it was used as the Signal Fitting shop, until it
was demolished in 1936/7 to make way for platforms 15 and 16.
It stood at an angle of about 45 degrees to the lines through the
present station, but in this position it was almost parallel to the
GNE line to the north from the original station. In the 1909
alterations the building had one corner removed to give more
space beyond No 14 platform.

That covers all the known sheds at the south end of the station
and we must now return to Clifton (or York North) shed, where
the three integral roundhouses were opened early in 1878,
together with a new coal stage. In 1891 the original 45ft turntable
in No 2 shed was replaced by a 50ft 'table, and in 1911 two new

electric 60ft turntables were ordered from Messrs Cowans, Sheldon of Carlisle at £2,170 the pair. One of these replaced the 45ft turntable in No 3 shed whilst the other was used in the new No 4 shed, authorised on 9 February 1911 at a total estimated cost of £28,700. In addition to the turntables this amount included a new coal stage (the old one had to be demolished to make way for the new shed) and a hot water washing out plant. Two 25 ton wheel drops and a 6 ton hoist were also authorised at an additional cost of £860. These works were completed in 1915 and cost £1,809 more than the original estimate. The new shed was built on to the north end of the existing building.

The next major alterations at the North shed were the provision of a 70ft Mundt non-balancing electric turntable (which could be operated by hand-winch in an emergency) and a mechanical coaling plant with four coal chutes and a bunker capacity of 500 tons, both in 1932. The turntable was supplied by Messrs Ransomes & Rapier Ltd and the coaling plant by Mitchell Conveyor & Transporter Co Ltd.

Ten years later, on 29 October 1942, the shed suffered severe damage when German planes bombed the city. One bomb dropped between A4 Pacific No 4469 'Sir Ralph Wedgwood' and B16 4-6-0 No 925, both of which were considered to be beyond repair. The A4 had been receiving attention on the wheel-drops and the centre driving wheels were not blown from under the engine by the bomb as photographs might lead one to believe. Other engines involved in the bombing were not damaged enough to warrant withdrawal and after repairs they all continued in traffic, whilst the shed itself was rebuilt and it is still in use today.

In the meantime a 70ft turntable had been provided in No 4 shed to allow Pacific engines to be accommodated under cover, although York did not receive its first Pacific until A2 No 2401 'City of Kingston Upon Hull' was transferred there on 9 February 1934 to work the 8.12pm express from York to Newcastle. The first Gresley Pacifics to be stationed at York — 2570 'Tranquil' and 2576 'The White Knight' — followed in November 1936 to take the place of the Raven Pacifics withdrawn from service.

The final alterations at York took place in 1957/8 when Nos 1 and 2 roundhouses were demolished and replaced by a straight shed: at the same time Nos 3 and 4 sheds were remodelled and re-roofed but remained as roundhouses, and it is these buildings which are earmarked for the National Transport Museum to replace Clapham Museum.

In addition to the running sheds mentioned above there was also a small corrugated iron building erected to house Sentinel locomotive No 45. This engine was provided in 1930 to shunt the Engineer's Yard situated on the down side of the main line north of the station. The Sentinel was replaced by Departmental No 84, a Ruston Hornsby diesel-mechanical locomotive, in 1959.

Little is known about the engines stationed at York in the very early days although, of course, they would be York & North Midland engines and later, no doubt, joined by Great North of England locomotives. In true North Eastern Railway days, from 1854, Fletcher engines would predominate until the influence of Locomotive Superintendents began to be felt — McDonnell in 1882, T.W.Worsdell in 1885, Wilson Worsdell in 1890, and Vincent Raven in 1910. Fortunately there are photographs in existence covering the last decade of the nineteenth century and up to 1914: postwar York was a mecca for many of the famous railway photographers and the period between 1923 and 1939 is well covered photographically.

E.L.Ahrons capably describes the great variety of engines to be seen at York at the end of the nineteenth century in his *Railway Magazine* series (and the subsequent reprint in book form) of *Locomotive and Train Working in the Nineteenth Century.*

The Midland and Great Northern visitors have already been mentioned. London & North Western engines commenced working regularly into York from Leeds on 1 July 1893 but ceased at the end of 1904. However, they continued to work to York on excursions and specials (as distinct from running powers trains) bound mainly for Scarborough. The Great Eastern commenced working their own trains into York on 1 November 1892; the Great Central from 15 March 1899; and the Lancashire & Yorkshire from 1 May 1894, working over the North Eastern from the frontier points at Shaftholme Junction, Ferrybridge Junction, and Altofts Junction respectively.

Now to the engines themselves. Latterly the Midland engines at York were Class 2P, 3P and 4P 4-4-0s with Class 4F 0-6-0s as frequent visitors on excursions. The engines transferred from

Queen Street to the South shed when the former closed in 1932 were 4-4-0 Nos 400,401,402,563,727,728,729 and 1091, together with 0-6-0 No 3715. Stanier Class 5 4-6-0s started to work into York shortly after their introduction and about 1939 the LMS Garratts began to appear on iron ore trains from Northampton-shire. In BR days a number of Stanier and Fairburn 2-6-4Ts made their appearance but perhaps the strangest sight was the use of 3F 0-6-0Ts on station pilot duties in place of the faithful J71 and J72 of North Eastern origin.

Great Northern engines used included 2-2-2s, 2-4-0s and the famous Stirling 8ft 'singles'. Subsequently the various types of 4-4-0 and 4-4-2 appeared and, in fact, there were ten GN 4-4-0s and two 4-4-2s stationed at York in 1923. The two Atlantics were soon joined by two more and for years York used C1 4424 and 4447, and C2 3984 and 3986 indiscriminately and did not restrict their workings to the Great Northern section. In fact the two small Atlantics remained at York until scrapped in 1937, and the two larger Atlantics until transferred away in 1943. Some of the 4-4-0 engines, such as 4180,4386,4387 and 4398 remained at York until 1937-9.

It is not clear if the LNWR engines were stationed at York or if they worked in from the Leeds end, but the three most common were 2-2-2 No 1 'Saracen' and 1434 'Eunomia', and 2-4-0 No 1220 'Belted Will'.

The Great Eastern types known to have used the South shed were the 2-2-2, 4-2-2 and 2-4-0, built in 1893, 1898 and 1891-1902 respectively, followed by the various classes of 4-4-0. Class B12 were never common at York but they were noted on the shed on various occasions in their original form and as rebuilt to Class B12/3. The various types of Great Eastern 0-6-0 also appeared at times.

Allocations were as follows:

	1923	1933	1954
A1 4-6-2	-	-	5
A2 4-6-2	-	-	1
A2/2 4-6-2	-	-	3
A2/3 4-6-2	-	-	4
A7 4-6-0T	2	3	-
B1 4-6-0	-	-	15
B13 4-6-0	-	1	-

B15 3-6-0	6	7	-
B16 4-6-0	27	19	36
C1 4-4-2	2	2	-
C2 4-4-2	-	2	-
C6 4-4-2	4	5	-
C7 4-4-2	15	19	-
D2 4-4-0	10	5	-
D20 4-4-0	15	11	2
D21 4-4-0	7	-	-
D49 4-4-0	-	9	7
1440 2-4-0	1	-	-
901 2-4-0	1	-	-
G5 0-4-4T	-	2	-
G6 0-4-4T	3	-	-
398 0-6-0	3	-	-
J21 0-6-0	8	6	-
J23 0-6-0	-	3	-
J24 0-6-0	1	9	-
J25 0-6-0	-	1	6
J26 0-6-0	11	5	-
J27 0-6-0	5	5	10
J39 0-6-0	-	2	-
J71 0-6-0T	11	16	10
J72 0-6-0T	9	11	10
J77 0-6-0T	5	8	1
J78 0-6-0T	-	1	-
J94 0-6-0T	-	-	9
K3 2-6-0	-	13	-
N12 0-6-2T	-	1	-
Q6 0-8-0	-	1	-
V2 2-6-2	-	-	30
X3 2-2-4T	1	1	-
WD 2-8-0	-	-	10
	147	168	159

At Grouping, York shed had thirteen top link main line workings to Newcastle and back, almost all on express passenger trains,
although one or two turns did work parcels trains or braked goods
in one direction. At the same time there were ten Local link
workings;

No	SETS OF MEN	WORKED
1	3	Scarborough, Leeds & Sheffield
2	3	Pickering (twice) and Normanton
3	2	Leeds and Harrogate
4	2	Pocklington, Doncaster, Scarborough and Leeds
5	2	Hull and Doncaster
6	2	Harrogate, Leeds, Selby and Hull
7	1	Selby and Leeds
8	3	Normanton and twice to Leeds
9	2	Normanton, Scarborough and Doncaster
10	1	Lincoln

For the winter 1949-50 period the Main Line workings were:

CLASS OF ENGINE	SETS OF MEN	TO WORK
A2	-	To be available as emergency engine (north) throughout the 24 hours
A2	2	Emergency engine (south) 9.10am-3.30pm; 5.40pm-6.30pm and 11.30pm-3.30am
A1	1	Engine to Kings Cross but York men only to Doncaster
A2	2	Engine to Kings Cross but York men to Peterborough only
A1	3	Harrogate, Leeds, Newcastle, Wakefield
A1	2	Newcastle –Leeds–Newcastle
A1	2	Twice to Newcastle
A2	1	York engine worked by York and Heaton men to Newcastle and back
A1	1	Newcastle
V2	1	Newcastle
B1	2	Twice to Sheffield
B16	1	Darlington
B16	1	Doncaster and Heaton
V2	2	Darlington and Newcastle
B16	1	West Hartlepool
B16	1	Doncaster and Heaton
V2	1	Darlington
—	1	York men on Eastern Region engine to Grantham
—	1	York men on Heaton engine to Peterborough
—	1	York men on Heaton engine to Grantham

—	1	York men on Heaton engine to Grantham
—	1	York men on Eastern Region engine to Grantham
—	1	York men on Gateshead engine to Newcastle
—	1	York men on Eastern Region engine to Newcastle
—	1	York men on Heaton engine to Newcastle

The local workings for the same period (winter 1949-50) were:

CLASS OF ENGINE	SETS OF MEN	TO WORK
B1	3	Leeds (twice) and Harrogate
B1	2	Twice to Sheffield
B1	2	Lincoln and Leeds
B1	2	Leeds and Doncaster
B1	2	Scarborough and Leeds
D49	2	Normanton and Doncaster
D49	2	Twice to Hull
D49	2	Twice to Scarborough
D49	2	Twice to Pickering
D49	2	Selby, Hull and Leeds

In addition there were five J71 pilot engines: South end, up side; South end, down side; Scarborough side; North end, down side; and Clifton carriage sidings. Four of the engines worked from 6.0am Mondays to 6.0am Sundays, and the fifth worked continuously. However, the engines spent one or two spells of 60 to 90 minutes on shed each day for locomotive duties — coaling, cleaning the fire etc.

NORMANTON

Throughout the existence of the NER the main line of the company was always regarded as commencing at Normanton and not Shaftholme Junction. Actually the York & North Midland Railway connected with the North Midland Railway at Altofts Junction, a mile north of Normanton Joint Station, and the station was the physical point of exchange for passenger traffic.

In January 1850 the Joint Committee responsible for the

working of the station decided to provide a shed, sidings and a turntable for the use of the various companies using the station 'to be repaired and upheld at the separate expense of the companies which may require them'. The NER obtained accommodation for four of their engines in 1860 and in 1864 complaint was made regarding the amount of space taken up by the North Eastern Railway. This led to the provision of a new shed, for which a tender of £8,800 was accepted in February 1866. In 1881 the Lancashire & Yorkshire Railway expressed a wish to stable twenty engines at Normanton to save light running to and from Wakefield and this was approved in 1882, when a shed costing £10,553.8s.9d was authorised, plus £2,000 for the coal stage and £194.2s.3d for gas lighting. This building was opened on 27 July 1884.

The building authorised in 1866 is believed to have been the roundhouse (now demolished) which was shared by North Eastern and Midland engines, whilst the Lancashire & Yorkshire shed was the straight shed, which remained in use until the depot closed. In 1889 a further shed was suggested but the North Eastern complained that this was only necessary because the Midland used the shed for local purposes and the scheme was shelved.

The *Railway Magazine* stated in 1906 that the Midland stabled fifty-eight engines at Normanton and the North Eastern stabled twelve — although the roundhouse had only twenty four roads, of which three were entrance/exit lines.

On the formation of the LMS the Midland and Lancashire & Yorkshire engines continued under separate control until 7 November 1927, when the L&Y engines were brought under Midland Division supervision: thenceforward the North Eastern Area engines used the straight shed as well as the roundhouse, although a diagram issued by the LNER in 1930 shows that any eight stalls in the roundhouse were for the use of the North Eastern Area engines.

From 1 October 1938 the LMS assumed full control of the shed and from that date the LNER paid a rental for their engines actually stationed at Normanton.

The engines stationed at Normanton usually comprised a number of tank engines for shunting in the Castleford/Whitwood area and one or two mixed traffic locomotives for working to York or Hull. For instance in 1922 there were four shunting tanks, together with an ageing Fletcher 0-6-0 and a B16. The B16 was used on freight during the week but on Sundays had to be used on Normanton's only passenger working. This was a long drawn out duty involving two sets of Normanton men and one set of Hull men, with the engine commencing work on the 7.58am to Hull. The Normanton men returned home as passengers and their engine was used by Hull men on the 3.20pm Hull-Selby and the 6.55pm Selby-Church Fenton, before they too returned home as passengers on the 7.47pm ex Church Fenton. The second set of Normanton men travelled as passengers to Church Fenton and then worked home using their own engine. The journey took exactly 30min and for the half hour running, plus stabling, they received pay for 5hr 20min. In fact the whole duty, involving simply a working from Normanton to Hull and back (with a short diversion to Church Fenton) necessitated the payment of wages for a time totalling 19hr 5min to the drivers and firemen!

By 1938 the number of passenger duties had increased. One involved working the 8.15pm Class B goods from Normanton to York on Saturdays only, returning with the Sunday 2.5am express passenger from York to Normanton. On Sundays there was a return working to Hull by the early turn men, and a return trip to Selby by the late shift men. Presumably they used their sole J21 0-6-0 1809 on these turns

The allocation in 1923, 1939 and 1950 was:

	1923	1939	1950
B16 4-6-0	1	-	-
398 0-6-0	1	-	-
J21 0-6-0	-	1	-
J71 0-6-0	1	3	3
J72 0-6-0T	1	-	-
J77 0-6-0T	2	-	-
Q5 0-8-0	-	-	1
	6	4	4

The Q5 left Normanton early in 1951 and in January 1952 the three J71 0-6-0Ts 68238/92/4 were transferred to the control of the London Midland Region, although remaining at Normanton. On 1 January 1957 Normanton (together with a number of other sheds in the West Riding of Yorkshire) was transferred from the London Midland Region to the North Eastern Region and recoded 20D to 55E. By this time the J71 engines had been scrapped and they had been replaced by two J72 0-6-0Ts, 68681 and 68701, to be joined by 68726 in February 1958. J71 68275 was also at Normanton between September 1959 and February 1961, when it was withdrawn from service. The J72 engines were also withdrawn about this time — 68701 in October 1960; 68681 in November 1960; and 68726 in June 1961. However, this did not end the North Eastern's long association with Normanton for on 12 June 1966 the four Q6 0-8-0s remaining at Neville Hill were transferred to Normanton, where they remained until 2 October 1966 before being transferred to Tyne Dock.

The shed closed completely on 1 January 1968.

CHAPTER VII

Leeds

In October 1898 it was proposed that as the accommodation at Holbeck was inadequate a move should be made to Neville Hill, on the eastern outskirts of Leeds, where eleven acres of land were available. In November 1899 overall plans were approved for sidings, engine shed, repair shops, coal stage, carriage and wagon sidings, and a washing shed at an estimated cost of £132,971, and the whole scheme was approved. Plans for a locomotive shed to hold 96 engines were submitted in December 1901 and in the same month tenders for the building were received.

The shed, comprising four adjoining roundhouses under one roof, was opened in October 1904 and the engines and men transferred from the cramped premises at Holbeck to a spacious shed and yard. The exact number of locomotives stationed at Neville Hill at that date is unknown but by 1923 there were eighty-two engines there of twenty-four different classes. Not all engines working into Leeds from other sheds went to Neville Hill for locomotive duties and those from Hull, Scarborough and York were often turned and watered at the shed at the west end of New Station.

Although Raven and Gresley Pacifics did work to Leeds in the 1920s and 1930s they could not be turned and it was the practice for those that worked in via York to return via Harrogate and vice versa. This included the engines off the Pullman trains into Leeds Central station, which ran tender first to Geldard Junction and then to Leeds New station to work home via York. The Newcastle Pacifics arriving at Leeds New station worked forward to Geldard

Junction, and then reversed up to Central station for their return working via Harrogate.

	1923	1939	1954
A3 4-6-2	-	-	5
A6 4-6-2T	1	-	-
A7 4-6-2T	-	3	-
A8 4-6-2T	-	3	2
B1 4-6-0	-	-	13
B13 4-6-0	6	-	-
B15 4-6-0	1	2	-
B16 4-6-0	3	9	20
C6 4-4-2	-	2	-
C7 4-4-2	3	2	-
D17/2 4-4-0	5	-	-
D18 4-4-0	2	-	-
D20 4-4-0	7	3	1
D21 4-4-0	2	6	-
D49 4-4-0	-	15	4
F8 2-4-2T	5	-	-
G5 0-4-4T	3	5	5
G6 0-4-4T	1	-	-
H1 4-4-4T	5	-	-
398 0-6-0	2	-	-
J21 0-6-0	9	5	-
J25 0-6-0	5	2	-
J26 0-6-0	1	-	-
J27 0-6-0	2	1	-
J39 0-6-0	-	3	11
J71 0-6-0T	2	-	-
J72 0-6-0T	-	2	2
J76 0-6-0T	3	-	-
J77 0-6-0T	4	2	1
N8 0-6-2T	1	2	-
N10 0-6-2T	4	2	-
N13 0-6-2T	-	-	5
Q6 0-8-0	5	6	2
Y3 0-4-0T	-	1	-
	82	76	71

In 1939 one of the four 55ft turntables at Neville Hill was replaced by a 70ft 'table and on 2 December the first Gresley Pacifics were transferred to Leeds — 2573 'Harvester' from Gateshead, and 2580 'Shotover' and 2597 'Gainsborough', from

Heaton — for working trains to Newcastle. However, their stay at Leeds was very short and on 28 February 1940 they were transferred to York in exchange for three D49 4-4-0s: 292 'The Southwold', 297 'The Cottesmore', and 366 'The Oakley'. For many years during World War II the 9.0am Liverpool (Lime Street) to Newcastle was worked by a pair of D49 engines between Leeds and Newcastle — a turn for which the Pacifics had been scheduled. The official reason given for the transfer of the Pacifics from Neville Hill was 'Re-allocation due to extra coal trains and war traffic, and curtailment of passenger services'.

On 29 September 1945 Pacifics 2507 'Singapore', 2570 'Tranquil', and 2577 'Night Hawk' were transferred from Leeds in readiness for new engine diagrams which came into force on 1 October, but as these ceased from 6 May 1946 the engines were transferred away again a few days later. Early in 1948 522 'Straight Deal', 524 'Herringbone' and 60526 'Sugar Palm' were transferred to Neville Hill but departed again after a few months.

Early in 1949 Leeds again received Pacific engines for its top link jobs: initially 60036 'Colombo', 60073 'Harvester', 60081 'Shotover', and 60086 'Gainsborough', followed a few months later by 60084 'Trigo'. Was it by coincidence that of the four original engines of 1949 three were the same as the A3 engines of 1939?

Their duties were:

No 1   5.35am Leeds-Darlington (via Ripon and Thirsk)
        Light engine Darlington-Northallerton
        9.40am Northallerton-Leeds (via Thirsk and Ripon)
        4.40pm Leeds-Newcastle (via Ripon:2.15pm ex
        Liverpool Lime Street)
        8.15pm Newcastle-Leeds (via York:4.0pm ex
        Glasgow)
No 2   8.40am Leeds-Newcastle (via York)
        2.5pm Newcastle-Leeds (Central) (via Ripon: up
        Queen of Scots)
        8.20pm Leeds-Stockton No 1 Express goods
        12.30am Stockton-Leeds No 1 Express goods
No 3   11.27am Leeds-Newcastle (via Ripon and Darlington:
        9.0am ex Liverpool Lime Street)
        4.15pm Newcastle-Leeds (via West Hartlepool and

Harrogate)
10.0pm Leeds-Darlington Express goods
3.5am Darlington-Leeds Express goods

The fourth A3 engine worked a relief to the 11.27am to Newcastle at 11.7am *if required* and returned *as required* meaning that it had no booked return working and could therefore be returned working any suitable train.

The working of No 1 turn was later modified so that after working to Darlington and back the engine was taken over by the Heaton men who had worked the 10.0am Newcastle-Leeds (via York) and they returned to Tyneside working the 3.20pm Leeds (Central) to Newcastle (down Queen of Scots). After servicing, the Heaton engine was used by Leeds men on the 4.40pm Leeds-Newcastle. They were relieved by Heaton men at Newcastle (Central). The Leeds engine which the Heaton crew had worked on the down Queen of Scots was then brought from Heaton shed by yet another set of men and the Leeds crew took over the engine and then coupled on to the 4.0pm Glasgow-Leeds for the journey home.

No 3 turn was also altered, so that the engine ran light from Leeds to Starbeck and worked the Darlington Express goods from there.

The 11.27 Leeds-Newcastle was booked to be assisted by a Starbeck engine between Leeds and Harrogate, and the 4.15pm Newcastle-Leeds to be assisted by a Starbeck engine between Ripon and Leeds.

Some of the trains worked by the Leeds Pacifics were old established trains. For instance the 8.50am to Newcastle (and Glasgow) appears to have first run in the summer of 1901 as the 8.47am to Edinburgh and was eventually extended to Glasgow. In British Railways' days it carried the name The North Briton.

In 1922 Leeds had only two main line turns – the 8.55am to Newcastle and the 1.6pm return, and the 11.15am to Newcastle (ex Liverpool) and the 4.11pm return – and for these had three Class Z Atlantics, 2201, 2207 and 2210. Due to increased work they were joined by 718 and 2203 in 1924, and by 729,2202 and 2206 in November 1926. The following year delivery of new D49 'Shire' class engines started and Neville Hill received seven, displacing a similar number of Atlantics, 2201,2202,2203 and 2206 to Gateshead and 718,729 and 2207 to Tweedmouth in February, March and April 1928; 2210 remained at Leeds until June 1929 when it was transferred to Heaton.

The new 'Shires' were soon hard at work on the following five duties:

No 1	Leeds	-	2.0am
	York	2.34	2.53
	Newcastle	4.35	6.15
	Sunderland	6.39	7.4
	York	9.20	10.5
	Leeds	10.40	-
No 2	Leeds	-	2.50am
	York	3.26	3.50
	Newcastle	6.0	7.35
	York	9.32	10.32
	Leeds	11.35	-
No 3	Leeds	-	8.55am
	York	9.30	9.38
	Newcastle	11.10	12.5
	York	2.38	3.30
	Leeds	4.8	-
No 4	Leeds	-	11.15am
	Newcastle	2.21pm	4.19
	Leeds	7.25	-
No 5	Leeds	-	8.3pm
	York	9.6	9.38
	Newcastle	11.41	1.50am
	York	3.31	4.15
	Leeds	4.55	-

Another duty on which they were to be seen was the 5.5pm Leeds-Hull and the 8.40pm 'mail' return working and it was on this turn that the first D49s were seen in Hull.

Except for the brief spells in 1939/40 and 1945 when generally Pacifics were available for the top jobs Leeds had to rely on D49 4-4-0s until the new Thompson B1 4-6-0s came along. To help the D49s on mixed traffic duties Neville Hill built up a fleet of K3 2-6-0s but in 1947 these, together with some of the D49s were displaced when the new B1 engines arrived. The first B1 to be seen in Leeds was actually the prototype engine, 8301 'Springbok', which worked there on the Darlington running-in turn during the first week the engine was in traffic in December 1942, but the first B1 to be stationed permanently at Neville Hill did not reach there until August 1946 when 1060 arrived, closely followed by 1062, 1065, 1068 and 1069, and further engines followed over the next two years. Thus, except for a short spell in January and February 1948, until the Pacifics returned in 1949 the B1 4-6-0s were the main engines and worked the turns previously listed for the Pacifics. After the arrival of the Pacifics for the Newcastle turns the B1 engines took over the medium distance expresses, such as those to Hull, Scarborough, Stockton and Darlington: on these turns the engines were usually manned by two sets of men, although one duty (involving two return trips to Hull and a Leeds-Harrogate-York-Leeds round trip) was manned by three sets.

For many years Leeds used former North Eastern 4-4-0s on its main jobs and even after the allocation of three Atlantics to Leeds the D20 engines played a large part in the semi-fast workings to Hull and Scarborough, assisted to some extent by the large D21 4-4-0s. Until they were withdrawn in 1930 the two D18 4-4-0s with 7ft 7¼in coupled wheels, 1869 and 1870, were at Leeds, as were some of the D17/2 engines also with clerestory cabs but with 6in smaller wheels. At one time the Smith three-cylinder compound 4-4-0 1619 was stationed at Neville Hill and there is in existence a commercial postcard of it standing in Leeds New station at the head of the morning Newcastle train.

As the diesel locomotives and railcars took over, the steam loco-motives at Neville Hill were gradually transferred away or withdrawn from service, until on 12 June 1966 the time came for closure to steam, when only seven steam engines remained: 4MTT 42184, 42196, 42699 and Q6 0-8-0 63344, 63387, 63420 and 63426. The four eight coupled engines were transferred to Normanton − a shed which had not previously housed North Eastern Q6 engines − but after a few months in the West Riding they were transferred to Tyne Dock, to be on their home ground and with others of the same class.

In 1960 two roundhouse sections of the shed were demolished and the remainder re-roofed, while at the same time a new diesel railcar depot was built and the old steam repair shop converted for use with diesel locomotives. In 1969 a new carriage washing plant was erected adjacent to the depot and the old carriage sheds on the opposite side of the main line were abandoned.

In 1931 a mechanical coaling plant was authorised to be built at Neville Hill to replace the old North Eastern pattern coal stage. The coaling plant was built by the Mitchell Conveyor & Transporter Co Ltd for £7,897 12s 10d (£7,897.64).

In the 1930s Neville Hill had on its strength one of the three 250hp Armstrong-Whitworth diesel-electric railcars which were purchased by the LNER for use in the North Eastern area. Unfortunately this car — 'Northumbrian' — gave a fair amount of trouble and its duties (covered by Carriage Roster 496) frequently had to be covered by normal steam hauled trains. When it was in working order it was due to leave the shed at 7.48am for the station to work Leeds-York-Harrogate-Wetherby-Leeds-York-Church Fenton-York-Leeds-Horsforth-Leeds-York-Harrogate-Leeds-York-Leeds, arriving back at Neville Hill at 8.29pm.

At the same time — the mid-1930s — Neville Hill also had a duty for one six-cylinder Sentinel steam railcar. This left the shed at 6.0am to run light to Micklefield and subsequently worked Micklefield-Leeds-Horsforth-Leeds-Ilkley-Leeds-South Milford-Harrogate-Leeds-Ilkley-Leeds-Horsforth-Leeds-Cross Gates, thence to Harrogate-Leeds-Ilkley-Horsforth-Leeds-Cross Gates, thence to shed from 9.0pm to 9.35pm before ending its day on the 9.55pm Leeds-Wetherby and the empty return working at 10.40pm, due on shed at 11.5pm. The coach was manned by three sets of men during the day.

During World War II Leeds was the home of two Southern Railway ex London, Brighton & South Coast 4-4-0 engines, 2051 and 2068. These arrived at Neville Hill on 14 November 1940 and they were used on some of their lighter 4-4-0 turns until they moved on to York on 11 July 1942.

Also during World War II a large number of American 2-8-0 engines were in use in this country until they were required for the invasion of Europe. Darlington Works put quite a number of them in working order before they were released to traffic and a number of them were 'run in' from Darlington shed. The allocation of these engines to the North Eastern comprised fifty engines, divided equally between Neville Hill and Heaton.

The first to arrive at Leeds was 2146 on 3 June 1943 and the last 2121 on 10 August 1943. The engines actually allocated to Leeds were 2104-7/15/7/20/1/3-8/46 and 2250-3/86/7/95/6/8/9: after a year's service they were recalled by the United States Authorities and all twenty-five departed from Leeds between 28 August and 19 September 1944, leaving an urgent need for engines, filled by the transfer of fifteen Q6 0-8-0s from various sheds.

On 7 January 1935 the 'hush-hush' engine was transferred to Neville Hill. This was of course, the 4-6-4 engine 10000 with the Yarrow water-tube boiler, built at Darlington in 1929. The engine had done a lot of trial running from Darlington Works and Gateshead shed and as a last resort it was decided to carry out some extensive trials between Leeds and Hull, using the dynamometer car and the counter-pressure locomotive. During this period 10000 was fitted with a double blast pipe and chimney, and also some experimental cowls to lift the smoke clear of the cab. Unfortunately in July 1935 it was decided to abandon the whole project and 10000 was put on one side at Darlington for over a year before it was sent to Doncaster for rebuilding in October 1936.

The Leeds district sheds were merged with the York district sheds from 11 October 1937, under a new district locomotive superintendent at York.

STARBECK

In 1854 it was reported that an engine shed was required at Low Harrogate; a report also 'pointed out the danger of lighting up the engines in close proximity to the Goods Warehouse in which flax is stored'. Although a shed was not provided until 1857 there is no report of the flax catching fire! However, the location of this shed is unknown although it is presumed it was at Starbeck, even though Starbeck is not Low Harrogate. In 1864 it was recommended that the shed should be lengthened to accommodate two further engines in consequence of the closure of Brunswick station in Harrogate, but it is not clear if there actually was a shed at Brunswick. In June 1877 it was decided to extend the shed again, this time 'in connection with the running of trains through from Harrogate to Bradford: estimated cost of £625' but it was decided to build eight cottages as well, which brought the price up to £1,432.

On 1 March 1888 it was decided to lengthen the shed yet again, this time at a cost of £1,840, and this extension can only have just been completed when the Midland Railway asked that accommodation be provided for two of their engines. It was recommended that the shed should be lengthened once again, to the extent of 150ft and, with a re-arrangement of the line, the cost would be £2,254. As the Midland were only to pay £25 a year per engine it was not a very profitable deal!

Further unspecified alterations took place in 1900/1 and the final modification took place when a new roof was installed after World War II. In 1930 a new shed was proposed between Starbeck North Junction and Dragon Junction but this was not proceeded with.

Allocations in 1923, 1933 and 1954 were:

	1923	1933	1954
A7 4-6-2T	4	6	-
A8 4-6-2T	-	1	-
B16 4-6-0	-	-	1
D3 4-4-0	-	1	-
D17/2 4-4-0	1	1	-
D20 4-4-0	-	1	-
D21 4-4-0	1	2	-
D22 4-4-0	2	1	-
D23 4-4-0	3	1	-
D49 4-4-0	-	-	16
G5 0-4-4T	10	11	-
G6 0-4-4T	2	-	-
H1 4-4-4T	5	3	-
398 0-6-0	1	-	-
J21 0-6-0	6	4	-
J22 0-6-0	1	-	-
J25 0-6-0	-	3	-
J26 0-6-0	2	1	-
J27 0-6-0	2	2	-
J39 0-6-0	-	-	12
J71 0-6-0T	2	2	-
J72 0-6-0T	-	2	-
J77 0-6-0T	2	2	3
N8 0-6-2T	4	4	-
Q5 0-8-0	2	1	-
Q6 0-8-0	-	3	-
Y3 0-4-0T	-	1	-
	50	53	32

Starbeck turned out thirteen engines daily for passenger trains in 1922/3, and this required twenty-two sets of men, as nine of the engines were manned by two sets, and four engines by one set. The services worked radiated in all directions from Harrogate — to York, Leeds, Bardford, Pilmoor, Selby, Pontefract and West Hartlepool. It will be seen from the allocation totals that at that time the majority of the work was performed by the useful G5 0-4-4T, with the longer turns in the hands of the various 4-4-0 engines. The D3 4-4-0 - a reminder of when Great Northern engines were stationed at Starbeck for working through trains to and from Kings Cross - was at this time largely used for piloting duties between Ripon and Leeds and I remember seeing it arrive at Leeds Central station assisting the Uniflow Atlantic 2212 on the up Queen of Scots Pullman train.

In addition to the goods work on the branches Starbeck was responsible for working goods trains north and south: between Starbeck and Leeds the A7 4-6-2T were used and could make two trips to Armley and back in an eight hour shift. How they must have roared through Bramhope Tunnel, with their three cylinders and small wheels.

Although not brought out in the allocation totals Starbeck became the home for many D20 4-4-0s and in 1939 had thirteen on its strength - 712,1026,1042,1206,1217,1236,1258,1672,2020, 2101, 2104, 2105, 2107, and these, together with the eleven G5 0-4-4Ts and four D21 4-4-0s, were responsible for the following turns:

No	ENGINE	WORKING TO	SETS OF MEN
1	G5	Leeds,Selby,Bradford,York	2
2	G5	Knaresborough and Leeds	2
3	-	Leeds and West Hartlepool	
5	-	York(return with goods)	1
7	-	Leeds	2
8	-	Bradford,Northallerton,Leeds	2
9	-	Leeds and York	2
10	D20	Leeds and Selby	2
11	G5	York,Leeds,Knaresborough	2
12	G5	Bradford,York,Selby	2
13	-	Leeds,Pilmoor,Bradford	2

14	B15	West Hartlepool (return with goods)	1
16	-	Doncaster(Pullman) and Leeds	1
17	-	Leeds and Ripon	2
18	G5	Leeds and Castleford,Pateley Bridge	1
19	-	Ripon,Northallerton and West Hartlepool	2
20	-	Leeds and Doncaster	2
21	-	York and Leeds	2
22	-	Leeds(part duty on Starbeck Sentinel Railcar)	1
23	-	Ripon(part duty on Starbeck Sentinel Railcar)	1
24	G5	Pilmoor,Bradford,Knaresborough (Push-and-Pull unit)	2

34

In addition there was a Sentinel steam railcar working solely between Harrogate and Knaresborough for fourteen hours each day, manned by two sets of men. The other Sentinel car was worked partly by Starbeck No 23 men (above) and Leeds men.

In 1922/3 the only Sunday duty worked by Starbeck shed during the winter months was the 8.20am empty to Pateley Bridge, returning on the 9.10am milk train. Although not a fair comparison the 1939 summer working comprised one G5 trip to Leeds and back, and three Sentinel cars employed solely between Harrogate and Knaresborough, with five trips extended to and from York.

The Harrogate-Knaresborough section was one of three in the North Eastern Area where Sentinel cars were allowed to run coupled whilst carrying passengers (the others were Sunderland-Durham and Whitby Town-West Cliff). Only coaches of the same type were allowed to run coupled and both cars had to face the same direction so that a boiler compartment was next to a driving compartment. Both coaches, of course, had to carry a driver and fireman.

The shed was closed on 13 September 1959 when the following twenty-three engines were dispersed:
D49 4-4-0 62727/38/53/9/63

    J25 0-6-0 65726
    J39 0-6-0 64706,64821/45/55/7/9/61/6,64942/4
    WD 2-8-0 90044/54, 90457,90518
    3FT 0-6-0T 47438/62, 47581

The roof was removed and the walls left standing until partly demolished during the great gale of 1962, and the remaining portions have since been demolished and the site cleared.

THIRSK

The first known reference is dated 24 April 1857 and concerns the provision of 'an engine pit, sand drying house, and cabin for engine men at Thirsk Junction'. A shed for two engines did not follow until 1887, having been authorised in November 1886. In April 1896 extensions were authorised to increase the accommodation to five engines, at an estimated cost of £800, followed in September 1897 by a supplementary estimate of £60 for an office and store.

The engines at Thirsk were mainly employed on local goods workings and even the single passenger turn was combined with goods train workings. This was the 7.26 am Thirsk to Melmerby, thence empty to Ripon, followed by the 8.54am Thirsk, Northallerton and West Hartlepool. Return from West Hartlepool was on a goods leaving at 12.20, due Thirsk 2.26pm. After changing men the engine continued on the 2.55pm goods to Ripon, and after shunting there it returned on the 7.30pm Ripon-Thirsk goods. At this period (1923)the allocation comprised

A7 4-6-2T	2	J21 0-6-0	1	
G5 0-4-4T	1	J25 0-6-0	7	
398 0-6-0	1	J77 0-6-0T	2	Total 14

Within a matter of a few months the allocation was drastically reduced to six engines:

| A7 4-6-2T | 1 | J25 0-6-0 | 3 |
| J77 0-6-0T | 2 | | |

In 1927 another A7 was transferred to Thirsk but on 12 December both these engines - 1176 and 1179 - were transferred away, the former to Leeds and the latter to Starbeck. In their place Thirsk received Q5 0-8-0 715, followed a little later by 443 of the same class. The two 0-8-0s departed in 1929, leaving two J25 0-6-0s and one

J77 0-6-0T. One J25, 1723, was transferred to Starbeck on 8 October 1930 when the Thirsk-Helmsley goods was withdrawn, leaving J25 2142 to go to Starbeck, and J77 604 to go to Northallerton, when the shed closed on 10 November 1930. The shed remained standing until 1965 but on 14 June of that year demolition commenced and the site was cleared.

ILKLEY

A shed for the joint use of the North Eastern Railway and Midland Railway was reported ready for use on 1 July 1866: this shed was close to the station and in July 1888, in connection with the opening of the line between Ilkley and Skipton, and because of complaints regarding smoke nuisance at the shed, it was decided to look for a new site. In January 1889 a site some 25 chains east of the station was recommended as it was 'about ten chains from the nearest dwelling house and public road'. Six engines were to be stationed at the shed – three North Eastern and three Midland – and with a 50ft turntable the cost would be £3,800. It was reported that the Ilkley Local Board would contribute to the cost of removal, but nine months later, when they were asked for £1,830, they refused to pay up.

However, the Otley & Ilkley Joint Committee decided to proceed with the alterations, but in July 1891 the site of the shed was changed from the south to the north side of the running lines, with accommodation for eight engines. A tender of £3,795 15s 8d was accepted on 11 April 1892 and completion must have been effected before the end of the year as on 30 December it was decided to remove the old shed, turntable, and water column, to make way for additional carriage sidings. E. L. Ahrons states that Nos 10, 62, 65, 276, 957 and 1461 were the BTP engines stationed at Ilkley at various times.

The BTP engines were replaced by the LNER G5 engines with similar wheel arrangement, although the earliest known allocation list of December 1923 states that no LNER engines were stationed at Ilkley at that date. However, 1096 spent some years at Ilkley before being transferred to Starbeck on 5 November 1928. This was part of a three point move to enable a G5 fitted with Raven fog signalling apparatus to be transferred to Darlington, this being 439 from Starbeck. In exchange for 1096 Ilkley received 468 from

Darlington. Driver Douglas of Ilkley was very attached to 1096 and he immediately put in a request to have 'his engine' returned to him, particularly as it was not the actual engine required for Darlington but had only gone as a substitute to Starbeck. His appeal was successful and on 3 December 1928 1096 returned to Ilkley and 468 went to Starbeck. However, on 16 July 1930 1096 was moved to Neville Hill in exchange for 1884 and this remained at Ilkley until the panic move of 9 September 1939 when it was transferred back to Neville Hill. When the Emergency Timetable was instituted from 2 October 1939 1884 returned to Ilkley,

The next move was on 23 May 1942 when 1096 was joined by 1695 of the same class - an engine recently fitted with push-and-pull gear - and a fortnight later 1884 was transferred to Botanic Gardens. 67337(formerly 1695) was transferred to Starbeck in March 1951 and a new method of working from Ilkley commenced: henceforward a G5 engine was supplied to Ilkley by Neville Hill but this was operated by former LMS men. From 3 April 1954 a revised scheme came into operation and all workings from Ilkley were worked by former LMS engines from Holbeck, Manningham, or Ilkley, including the trips to Leeds via Arthington. At this time, as a sub-shed to Manningham, the shed usually stabled two Class 3 2-6-2Ts, one Class 2 2-6-2T, and three L&Y 2-4-2Ts. The shed closed on 5 January 1959.

In spite of the LNER Allocation List statement that no engine was stationed at Ilkley in December 1923 there was certainly a North Eastern locomotive working in force from 2 October 1922. This involved an early start for the Ilkley men as the first turn set booked on duty at 3.50am and worked light engine to Arthington at 4.35am to return with the 5.5am Arthington-Ilkley. The engine continued to work between Ilkley, Arthington and Leeds for the rest of the day, finishing with the 9.0pm Leeds to Ilkley, Wednesdays and Saturdays excepted, and on the 11.9pm Arthington to Ilkley on Wednesdays and Saturdays only.

On the outbreak of World War II the working was very similar except that the last train worked was the 9.22pm Leeds-Ilkley on each day of the week. Because of the long day involved the Ilkley engine was worked by Neville Hill men between 12.40pm and and 3.40pm.

BRADFORD (MIDLAND RAILWAY)

North Eastern engines were stationed at the Midland shed at Manningham for working to Harrogate and E.L. Ahrons records that at the end of the nineteenth century there were three engines there - a BTP 0-4-4T; a Class 447 2-2-2; and a Class 901 2-4-0. Later Class 1440 2-4-0 486 was known to be there, and there is also a photograph in existence of Class D23 4-4-0 1120 in Manningham shed in 1924, although still in NER livery. No 328 of the same class was there in 1931 and was replaced on 30 October by the larger D22 4-4-0 115 from Starbeck. When 115 was withdrawn in December 1933 it was replaced by 1120, noted earlier, and when this in turn was withdrawn in May 1935 it was replaced by D17/2 4-4-0 1903. On 12 August 1935 1903 was transferred to Starbeck and replaced by 1908 of the same class from Neville Hill. Finally, on 4 February 1938 1925, also Class D17/2, replaced 1908 and this engine remained at Manningham until the LNER ceased to station an engine there from 31 October 1938; 1925 was then offically withdrawn from service.

In LNER days the sole engine at Manningham required only one set of men as the engine performed only one trip per day, working the 7.12am from Bradford to Harrogate; forward at 8.33am to York, returning to Bradford at 10.25am from York.

At this period the driver was Albert Hoole (no relation to the writer) and he achieved fame on two occasions: whilst working to Harrogate one morning in March 1924, he noticed that a quantity of rock had fallen from the cutting side near Esholt Junction and he managed to stop the 7.25am Guiseley-Bradford train before it hit the obstruction. In January 1931 on the same turn, and with engine 328, Driver Hoole's train hit a motor lorry which had crashed through the level crossing gates at Hopperton, on the Great North Road. The collision set fire to the lorry and its load of celluloid film and before the train could be brought to a stand it was festooned with blazing film. The regular passengers on the train, grateful for their escape, sent the driver and fireman a letter of appreciation accompanied by a sum of money.

PATELEY BRIDGE

This shed was at the extremity of one of the typical North Eastern branch lines that meandered up the Yorkshire valleys

Page 121 Interior of York North (or Clifton) shed 1948

Page 122 Two of the roundhouses at York South shed. That on the left was at one time the Midland shed

Page 123 New shed at Darlington Bank Top 2 October 1940. The clock tower of Bank Top Station is in the distance

Page 124   (above) The remaining portion of Stanhope shed 18 August 1959;
            (below) Boroughbridge, closed 1886 and subsequently used as a
            goods warehouse. B16/2 61438 on pick-up goods alongside 16
            August 1962.

Page 125   *(above)* One of the two roundhouses at Leeds Holbeck, closed circa 1904 and subsequently used by Thomas Marshall and Son Ltd, with a portion on the far side used as a garage and filling station 3 March 1961; *(below)* Hexham as rebuilt post-1945 21 August 1964. Derelict turntable in foreground.

Page 126   (above) Coaling by hand at York circa 1908; (below)Coaling by crane at Ferryhill circa 1908

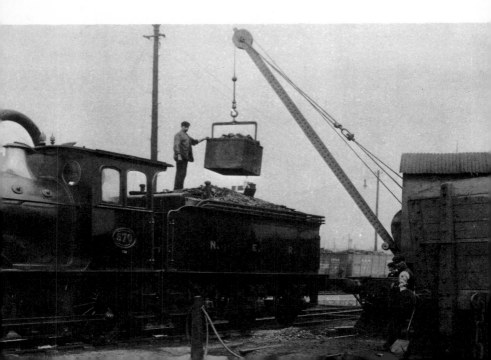

Page 127   *(above)* Coaling stage and mechanical coaling plant at Selby 29 August 1963. The lean-to shed at the rear of the coal stage was built to accommodate the petrol-electric railcars used on the Cawood branch; *(below)* Coaling plant at Thornaby under construction 1958.

Page 128 (above) Whitby shed and yard 31 July 1955; (below) Bridlington 12 July 1959. Closed the previous year. Engines awaiting return excursion trains

Page 129　　(above) Middlesbrough 22 April 1956. Originally a roundhouse;
　　　　　　(below) North Blyth shed interior 10 April 1965.

Page 130   The light and airy interior of the new straight shed at Thornaby 1958

Page 131   Gateshead shed with new roof 1957. Soon afterwards the tracks and turntables were removed and the building was converted into a straight shed for diesel locomotives

Page 132 The new order at Gateshead. D9008 at the east end of the rebuilt shed 1964

— in this case the valley of the River Nidd. Pateley Bridge was
the hub of Nidderdale and although for many years the station was
at the end of the line a Light Railway was eventually built for a
further six miles up the valley to Lofthouse. Beyond this the line
served only the Bradford Corporation reservoirs. Although
through trains did not run from the North Eastern, over the Light
Railway, to Lofthouse through coaches conveying special parties
could be worked between the two systems, utilising the connection
between the two stations at Pateley Bridge.

No details are known of the original stone built engine shed
which, judging by its architecture, involving the use of stepped
gables, was built at the same time as the branch and station,
namely 1862. At some date as yet unknown it was replaced by a
wooden structure but the reason for this is not known. Mr
J.D. Petty suggests that it was due to subsidence caused by the
weight of the building on the bank of the river. It is also probable
that the river bank was affected by the change in water level
brought about by the extensive Bradford Corporation reservoirs
higher up the valley.

Most readers will recall E.L. Ahrons' account of workings on the
branch and he quotes 2-4-0 62 and 65 as regular performers between
1876 and 1880. Another 2-4-0 was 372, built by Hawthorn in
1849 and fortunately a photograph exists of this engine at
Pateley Bridge c 1886. Eventually a BTP 0-4-4T was shedded at
Pateley and finally a G5 0-4-4T. For many years this was 1839,
which worked all day between Pateley and Harrogate, with a
morning trip to Wetherby and back. By 1939 the working had
changed little, although two trips to Knaresborough and one
through to Pilmoor were introduced to fill in the engines' stop-
over time in Harrogate.

When push-and-pull working was reintroduced in the north east
in 1938 it was decided to utilise this method of working on the
Pateley branch and thus on 20 March 1939 G5 380 was transferred
from Starbeck in exchange for 1839, whose long association with
the branch was broken. No 1839 was transferred from Starbeck to
West Hartlepool on 13 June 1939 but this must have been a paper
transaction, as at that time 1839 was in Darlington Works being
fitted with push-and-pull equipment. When this was completed
1839 was transferred back to Pateley and the interloper, 380, was

133

packed off to Kirkby Stephen to start a push-and-pull service there. No 1839 continued to work at Pateley — latterly as 67253 — until the passenger service was withdrawn on 1 April 1951, when the shed was closed. It has since been demolished (or removed).

MASHAM

In July 1874 Mr Fletcher reported that a shed for two engines would be necessary on the opening of the branch to Masham, and that coaling and watering facilities, together with four cottages, would be required. The cottages were completed by March 1875 and the shed was nearly ready: the branch was actually opened in June 1875.

The engine shedded at Masham for many years before its closure on 1 January 1931 was G5 0-4-4T 1911. On this date the branch was closed to passenger traffic but it remained open to freight traffic until 11 November 1963.

The engine commenced duty on the 7.0am Masham to Harrogate and the 8.53am return, then worked the 10.10am to Ripon, ran back empty to Melmerby and worked the 12.20pm Melmerby-Masham, giving a connection out of the 10.52am from Leeds and the 9.15am from Hartlepool. The engine then worked the 1.0pm to Ripon with the late turn men and at 1.45pm on Mondays, Wednesdays and Fridays worked a goods to Newby Wiske and back: on Tuesdays, Thursdays and Saturdays, at the same time from Ripon, the goods went to Masham and back. Finally the 5.5pm passenger Ripon-Masham, another Masham-Ripon return trip at 5.50pm from Masham and 7.25pm from Ripon and the engine was finished for the day.

The shed, which was unusual for the North Eastern in that it could only be reached via the turntable, was demolished about 1941.

CHAPTER VIII

Hull

Hull (Dairycoates)

Hull Dairycoates, the largest shed on the North Eastern Railway, consisted of six roundhouses (a type of building much favoured by the NER) and two straight sheds. From 1915, when the extensions were completed, five of the circular sheds were contiguous and it was a wonderful sight on a Sunday to stand at one end of the shed and to look down the length of the building, across the five turntables, with more than a hundred steam locomotives standing in their stalls on either side.

The first mention of a shed at Dairycoates comes in November 1857, when Mr Fletcher, the locomotive superintendent of the North Eastern, reported 'a great want of engine shed room at Hull' and that the engines, in consequence, suffered from exposure to the weather. Mr Fletcher, together with Mr Harrison (the engineer) and Mr Cabry (the divisional engineer) were instructed to investigate the area and they decided on an area adjacent to the line from Selby, some two miles from Paragon station and out in the country, near Dairycoates Farm.

By February 1858 an estimate had been prepared for the proposed shed which, exclusive of permanent way, was to cost £13,000. However, the go-ahead was not given until March 1861, when a tender of £13,965 was accepted, for a new shed, fitting shop, and an unspecified number of cottages. In June 1861 a 42ft turntable at £420 was ordered, and this building, completed in 1863, eventually became known as No 1 shed.

The next two roundhouses (Nos 2 and 3 sheds) were authorised in June 1873 at a cost of £21,753, although the lowest tender was actually for £15,482. These two sheds were to accommodate forty engines, and two turntables were obtained from Cowans Sheldon at £517 each. The size of the original turntables is not known but at that time the wheelbase of the largest engines was about 37ft and it seems probable that both turntables were 42ft diameter. However, they were listed as 50ft diameter early in this century and they were, in fact, replaced by two new 50ft 'tables in 1914 at a cost of £987 10s 0d each. Nos 2 and 3 sheds cost £995 2s 8d over the tendered price and they were opened in 1876. At the same time as they were being built modifications were made to the earlier shed at a cost of £193 6s 3d.

A photograph of Dairycoates shed on a Sunday in 1913 shows how short was the accommodation but at that time extensions had already been commenced. These had been authorised in August 1911 at an estimated cost of £70,000 which included £37,950 for the three sheds themselves, £2,940 for the three 60ft turntables from Cowans Sheldon, and £5,433 for a mechanical coaling plant. There was also a twin-track elevated wheel-drop building, with hydraulic lifts to allow the wheels to be lowered and to be run into the fitting shop at ground level; a hot water boiler washing out plant; a breakdown train shed; and extensive stores; offices; mess rooms etc.

The coaling plant at Dairycoates, although not the first in the country, was the most advanced. It was designed by the chief mechanical engineer's department of the NER and erected by Spencer & Co Ltd of Melksham. Two tenders were received for the plant — Spencer's at £5,433, and from Cowans Sheldon of Carlisle at £5,863. The tender was accepted in October 1913 and the plant was brought into use on 27 March 1916.

The installation was operated electrically, using current supplied by a dynamo coupled to the engine operating the machinery in the repair shop of the shed. Coal was tipped from wagons into an underground hopper, and it was then transferred into the upper bunkers via a chain of light steel buckets. Small coal went direct into the upper bunkers but large coal was crushed before being transferred. The underground hopper could be fed direct from bottom-door wagons, or from end-door wagons. The latter required an electric hoist to lift the end of the wagon opposite to the doors, and thus a wagon turntable was required to get the wagon the right way round.

Two upper bunkers were provided, for different grades of coal, one holding 100 tons and the other 200 tons, and there were two chutes from each bunker so that four locomotives could be coaled at the same time, taking about two minutes per engine. Some 135 engines a day were coaled when the plant was first opened but this had risen to 166 per day ten years later. Each locomotive required about 2 tons of coal and thus the plant only required to be in full operation during the day: during the night there was enough coal in the bunkers to last until the following morning. The coal required for each engine was obtained by the fireman and this was delivered to the tender in amounts of 10cwt at a time.

For many years the daytime plant attendant was George William Lidguard, who took charge when the installation opened. He actually transferred to the NER from the old Hull Dock Company in 1898 and between 1904 and December 1915 he was the driver of one of the petrol-electric autocars which first worked at Scarborough, and later between Selby and Cawood. The coaling plant was demolished in 1967.

At Hessle, the first station out of Hull on the Leeds and Doncaster lines, a large water softening plant was installed in 1902. The chalk Yorkshire Wolds gave the water a high lime content and all water in the Hull area passed through the plant, which was doubled in size in 1908 to enable it to handle a million gallons of water a day, making it probably the largest single water softening installation in the country.

At the time of the Grouping in 1923 there were 150 engines stationed at Dairycoates shed, almost all of which were for freight, mineral, or shunting work: the passenger engines for the area were stationed at Botanic Gardens shed. However, the freight working was not entirely divorced from the passenger working and a few turns involved working a passenger train out from Paragon station (to Doncaster) and a freight or mineral back, and vice versa. By 1932 there were 175 engines at Dairycoates, the increase being largely accounted for by the increase of 4-6-0 engines from 22 to 34; 0-6-2Ts from 29 to 35; and large tanks (4-6-2T and 4-8-0T) from 4 to 10. Other types remained remarkably constant –

for instance the 0-8-0s at 37 and the 0-6-0Ts at 22.

By 1954 the allocation was down to 129 engines – the 37 0-8-0s had been replaced by 27 WD 2-8-0s and the 34 4-6-0s by 23 K3 2-6-0s. The once numerous 0-6-0s of Class J21 had given way to 15 4MT 2-6-0s, of LMS design, and one of BR origin. By this time the diesel electric shunters had gained a foothold and the number of steam engines gradually decreased as more shunters appeared; followed by main line diesel locomotives, until in June 1967 Dairycoates lost its last steam engine.

On 24 June B1 4-6-0 61002, 61255 and 61289, and WD 2-8-0 90262, 90265 and 90450 were condemned and withdrawn from stock, and on the following day B1 61306 and WD 2-8-0 90009 90378, 90478, 90627, 90677 and 90695 were transferred away However, Dairycoates continued to handle 'dead' steam locomotives for a couple of years longer. These were from various Eastern Region and London Midland Region sheds on their way to a nearby scrapyard for cutting up.

On 5 October 1969 Dairycoates lost all its main line diesel locomotives (6730-41, 6781/2/3/4/8/9/90, 6835/6, 8310-15) and was left with only shunters. Almost a year later, on 21 September 1970, the remaining engines (2100/68/71/2/4, 3070/4/5/7/9/80/1, 3232/3/4/6, 3313/8/23, 3675/6, 3944/5 and 12121 were transferred to Botanic Gardens shed and Dairycoates closed as a locomotive depot.

The duties at Dairycoates fell into four main categories:
1. Long distance freight and mineral trains worked by 4-6-0s and 0-8-0s
2. Short distance freight and mineral trains worked by 0-6-0s
3. Trip working between the various docks and marshalling yards worked by 0-6-2Ts
4. Shunting – light by 0-4-0Ts and 0-6-0Ts; heavy – by 4-6-2Ts and 4-8-0Ts

In the 1920s and 1930s the short distance freight working engines of Class J21, with continuous brakes, were used at times of pressure on passenger trains to Hornsea, Withernsea and Bridlington, and they also put in a lot of work on race specials to Beverley.

The 4-6-0s worked simultaneously to Scarborough, Leeds and Doncaster. The same pattern was followed in British Railways

days, with the 4MT 2-6-0 engines on short distance freights and
also on transfer trips, with passenger working at holiday times:
the K3 2-6-0s were on the longer freights to Doncaster, Leeds,
York etc during the week and heavy passenger trains to and from
Bridlington, Filey Holiday Camp, and Scarborough on Saturdays
and Sundays.

Prior to 1914 the longest regular working from Hull was the
goods lodging turn to Newcastle, worked usually by a Class S
(LNER B13) 4-6-0 engine, although records exist of Class C
(LNER J21) engines on this job when a 4-6-0 was not available.
The duty involved the men booking on at 7.35pm to work the
8.35pm from Sculcoates to Newcastle Forth, where they were
due at 6.0am the following morning. By the time the engine got
to Gateshead shed and the men were relieved their time on duty
could reach 12½hr. After lodging at the Company's hostel (where
accommodation was free plus a lodging allowance of 1s 9d) they
returned on the 11.1pm from Park Lane (Gateshead). This could
lead to an even longer day! For instance, on 19 September 1907
Driver Howcroft, with 4-6-0 768, arrived at Hessle Junction at
7.5am but was unable to dispose of his train and get to Dairycoates
shed until 10.30am. He booked off at 10.45am after a 13½hr day.
Even these long spells of duty were nothing when crews were
booked to work with ballast trains — Driver Howcroft logged 15½hr
with P1 0-6-0 2058, and 15hr 40min with Class 59 0-6-0 1106
on 25 September and 25 October 1907 respectively. Unfortunately
he died in November 1907 after receiving injuries from the
reversing lever of his usual engine 768.

In LNER days turns were introduced to Colwick and Manchester
and although in the 1950s Kings Cross men and engine worked
through to Hull there was no similar working from the Hull end.
However, Hull men did work through to London on Wembley
Exhibition specials in 1924 and 1925.

With the establishment of a large new marshalling yard at
Gascoigne Wood in 1908 mineral traffic from the surrounding
collieries was concentrated at this yard and forwarded to Hull
in block loads. If they fulfilled certain conditions the crew of each
train received a bonus of up to 4s 0d (20p) per day, divided so
that the driver received 2s 0d (20p), and the fireman and guard
1s 0d (5p) each. This involved working two return trips over the

35 miles between Hull and Gascoigne Wood. At Class B speed they were allowed 82min from passing Hessle Junction to arriving at Gascoigne Wood, and 83min in the opposite direction, and at Class C speed these timings were 103 and 104min respectively. The two scales in the following table take note of the speed when reckoning the hours:

Double Trip Working Between Hull and Gascoigne Wood

Whenever Train Men working these double trip turns, running at Class B speeds, obtain 800 wagon miles per traffic train engine hour with a P2 or P3 engine, or 900 wagon miles with a Class T engine, in any one day's work, a bonus will be paid on the following scale:

P2 or P3 Engine Wagon Miles	T Engine Wagon Miles	Total Bonus	Driver	Fireman	Guard
800-874	900-974	2s6d(12½p)	1s3d(6p)	7½d(3p)	7½d(3p)
875-924	975-1024	3s0d(15p)	1s6d(7½p)	9d(4p)	9d(4p)
925-974	1025-1075	3s6d(17½p)	1s9d(9p)	10½d(4½p)	10½d(4½
975 and over	1075 and over	4s0d(20p)	2s0d(10p)	1s0d(5p)	1s0d(5p

but when both outward trips with empty trains from Hull to Gascoigne Wood run at Class C speed, the following scale will apply:

750-824	850-924	2s6d(12½p)	1s3d(6p)	7½d(3p)	7½d(3p
825-874	925-974	3s0d(15p)	1s6d(7½p)	9d(4p)	9d(4p)
875-924	975-1024	3s6d(17½p)	1s9d(9p)	10½d(4½p)	10½d(4½
925 and over	1075 and over	4s0d(20p)	2s0d(10p)	1s0d(5p)	1s0d(5p

104 minutes for 35 miles (20mph) may not seem very fast but when it is remembered that in those days traffic was heavy and the mineral trains had to take second place to the Hull to Leeds and Doncaster passenger trains, not forgetting the task of getting through Selby, then it was a creditable performance

Anyone who has not experienced the traffic conditions in the north east will probably be unaware that the mineral trains did not run to a timetable. Certainly paths were provided in some cases but normally the trains ran to order only when required. This was because the coal traffic had to be shipped and thus loading was dependent on the weather and tides, and the availability of a suitable berth - and the wagons had to be unloaded before they could become returned empties.

The jump in emigration of people from Europe to America in the early days of this century created a large amount of traffic for the North Eastern. Most of the emigrants travelled from German ports to Hull, then across England by train to embark again at Liverpool for their journey to the New World. From Hull paths were provided for the emigrant trains via four routes:

1. Selby,Leeds,Huddersfield,Stalybridge,Stockport,Liverpool
2. Selby,Normanton,Wakefield,Sowerby Bridge,Rochdale,Wigan, Liverpool
3. Selby,Pontefract,Sheffield(Midland),Chinley,Padgate Junction, Liverpool
4. Goole,Doncaster,Penistone,Stockport,Padgate Junction, Liverpool

Ten paths were provided via each route, five for heavy trains and five for light trains.

Dairycoates men worked through to Liverpool and returned with the same engine and stock after resting. For instance on 23 September 1907 Class S 4-6-0 2006 worked the 8.15am from Hull with thirteen coaches (182 tons). Hull was left 26 minutes late and, after travelling via Doncaster and Penistone, Liverpool was reached at 1.9pm, 50 min later. The crew then took 2006 to Brunswick shed and after stabling the engine they booked off at 3.0pm. After ten hours rest they prepared their engine and then ran light to Halewood, picked up their train, and returned to Hull, arriving back at 1.10pm and booking off at 1.40pm.

On 27 October 1907 the same driver worked via Leeds and the LNWR route with 4-4-0 1633 of Class M, and a couple of weeks later over the same route with 1626 of the same class, stabling engines at Edge Hill LNWR shed.

Dairycoates also provided accommodation for engines of other companies and Ahrons refers to Midland Railway 2-4-0 53,54 and 55 at Hull in 1883 for working the Sheffield (via Milford Junction) service which commenced in 1881. However, it is not certain that these engines were at Dairycoates - they *may* have been stationed at the old Paragon shed - the forerunner of the Botanic Gardens passenger shed. The same applies to the Manchester, Sheffield & Lincolnshire 4-4-0 also mentioned by Ahrons, which worked a Liverpool-Hull service from 1874.

Certainly the London & North Western engines were shedded

at Dairycoates between 1893 and 1915. They paid £25 per year
for the privilege and were supplied with coal at 13s 6d (67½p)
per ton, water at 6d (2½p) per tank, lighting up cost 1s 0d (5p)
a time, and washing out was 9d (3½p) a time.

The Lancashire & Yorkshire started working goods trains to
Hull in 1886 but it is not clear if they stationed any engines at
the Hull end. They certainly did when they commenced through
Hull - Liverpool passenger trains on 1 May 1900 and the engine
was one of the famous Atlantics. In LMS days 2P 4-4-0 586 was
stationed at Dairycoates for working one trip to Wakefield and
back each day, with a load which often consisted of no more
than two coaches.

The Great Central also stationed an Atlantic at Hull prior to
1914 for working to Sheffield Victoria but the dates of this
working have not been located.

	1923	1932	1954
A7 4-6-2T	2	5	10
B1 4-6-0	-	-	3
B13 4-6-0	15	6	-
B15 4-6-0	2	5	-
B16 4-6-0	-	23	-
D17/1 4-4-0	1	-	-
E5 2-4-0	1	-	
J21 0-6-0	25	22	-
J22 0-6-0	2	-	
J25 0-6-0	3	-	-
J26 0-6-0	-	2	-
J27 0-6-0	2	-	-
J28 0-6-0	-	4	-
J39 0-6-0	-	-	8
398 0-6-0	2	-	-
J71 0-6-0T	4	7	7
J72 0-6-0T	7	9	5
J76 0-6-0T	4	-	-
J77 0-6-0T	7	6	-
K3 2-6-0	-	-	24
N8 0-6-2T	21	18	3

N9 0-6-2T	1	5	-
N10 0-6-2T	7	9	10
N11 0-6-2T	-	3	-
Q5 0-8-0	17	7	-
Q6 0-8-0	16	30	-
Q7 0-8-0	4	-	-
T1 4-8-0T	2	5	-
Y1 & Y3 Sentinel 0-4-0T	-	4	4
Y8 0-4-0T	5	5	-
WD 2-8-0	-	-	27
4MT 2-6-0 LMS	-	-	15
4MT 2-6-0 BR	-	-	1
350hp d/e shunters	-	-	12
	150	175	129

HULL (BOTANIC GARDENS)

Botanic Gardens shed was completed in 1901, superseding the shed adjacent to Paragon station. Named after nearby pleasure gardens (now a cemetery) Botanic Gardens shed housed the majority of the passenger engines operating in the Hull area and working to Doncaster,Leeds,York,Scarborough,Hornsea and Withernsea. In North Eastern days most of the longer runs were worked by 4-4-0 tender engines, which had replaced 2-4-0 engines about the turn of the century, and the local services by 2-4-2T and 0-4-4T. In LNER days many of the local services were worked by Sentinel steam railcars and also by an influx of ex Great Northern 4-4-2T engines.

When displaced from main line duties at the end of 1924 the five Class S1 4-6-0 engines spent a few weeks at Botanic Gardens before going on to Dairycoates and, except for trials with K3 2-6-0 1108 and 1119 and B16 4-6-0 848 and 849 on the heavy Sheffield trains in 1931/2, Botanic Gardens had to rely on 4-4-0 locomotives until the arrival of B1 4-6-0 1010/71/4/80/4 in 1946. Thus for some fifty years Hull's main passenger services were worked by 4-4-0 engines.

The origin of the shed is tied up with the decision to extend Paragon station, taken in November 1897, when the General Manager reported that the site of the shed at Paragon station would be needed for the proposed extensions and a new shed would be required. This was authorised to be built on the new site at an estimated cost of £30,428 to provide accommodation for 44 engines. Two 50ft turntables were ordered from Messrs Cowans Sheldon at £638 each, with each 'table being suitable for 24 roads or stalls. Thus, with an allocation of some fifty engines Botanic Gardens was one shed where few locomotives had to stand outside. A tender of £21,355 was accepted for the building in August 1898 and the shed was completed early in 1901.

Coaling was originally from the standard pattern of NER coal stage, where the coal was shovelled into small hand trucks, then wheeled across the stage to be tipped into a chute leading to the tender or bunker of the engine. In 1932 a new coaling plant built by Messrs Babcock & Wilcox Ltd was brought into use at a cost of £6,239. On this coaling plant only one bunker was provided and it was filled by hoisting up the loaded coal wagon and tipping the contents direct into the bunker. The time taken to lift the loaded wagon was two minutes five seconds, and to lower it after the load had been tipped one minute twenty seconds.

In 1956/7 extensive alterations took place and a new building was erected over the existing turntables and stalls. However, the steam locomotive was on its way out and within a couple of years the turntables had been removed, the pits filled in, and the building was converted to a straight shed to house diesel railcars: the official date of re-opening as a diesel car shed was 13 June 1959.

This was not, of course, Hull's first experience of railcars. Between 1927 and 1946 Botanic Gardens maintained a fleet of Sentinel steam railcars, mostly of the two-cylinder variety, but an odd six-cylinder car was allocated for the more arduous turns. In 1935, for instance, Botanic Gardens had eleven two-cylinder cars (Valliant,Brilliant,Tally Ho,Rockingham,Highflyer,Eclipse, Yorkshire Huzzar, Perseverance, Teazle, North Star and Neptune) and one six-cylinder car (Cornwallis) for six railcar duties

Mondays to Fridays, seven on Saturdays, and three on Sundays. The need for twelve cars to cover a maximum of seven duties illustrates the unreliability of the vehicles! The names carried by the Sentinel cars were formerly used on horse-drawn stage coaches.

At the same time the Armstrong Whitworth diesel-electric car Lady Hamilton was stationed at Botanic Gardens and worked trips to York and Pontefract. When this car was out of action it was replaced by a two-coach train worked by a Class D17 4-4-0 of 1896 vintage or, on rare occasions, by the 2-2-4T 957 allocated to Hull for working the District Engineer's saloon.

For many years Hull's main passenger engines were the LNER D20 4-4-0 perhaps better known as the North Eastern Class R, which survived at Hull until British Railways' days. In 1923 for the lighter duties the Class M(LNER D17/1), Class F(LNER D22), and Class G(LNER D23) 4-4 0s were used, of which there were 6,11 and 11 respectively, plus the Smith three-cylinder compound 4-4-0 1619. There were also seven D22s sub-shedded at Bridlington. In the mid 1920s the D23 engines were gradually transferred away and the D17s increased in number to 12: three of the D22s were also transferred away but in 1925 8 D17 engines were sent to Bridlington in exchange for a similar number of D22 engines, bringing the total of such engines at Botanic Gardens up to 16. By this time three D21 4-4-0s had arrived at Botanic Gardens to work the 8.55am and 2.50pm Sheffield trains — Hull's heaviest passenger turns. Thus at 31 December 1925 Botanic Gardens shed accommodated 35 ex NER 4-4-0s, together with the five ex Hull & Barnsley 4-4-0s transferred from Springhead on the closure of Cannon Street station, with eight 4-4-0s sub-shedded at Bridlington.

As the older 4-4-0s were gradually withdrawn Botanic Gardens received D20 engines in replacement until in 1931 there were eleven stationed at Hull: these had in turn been displaced from other sheds by the new D49 engines built in 1927-9. Botanic Gardens eventually did get some modern 4-4-0 engines, but even these were engines which had been displaced from other sheds by new engines. They were in fact, five of the D49/3 Shire engines with Lentz oscillating Cam poppet valves: 318 Cambridgeshire, 320 Warwickshire and 322 Huntingdonshire from Leeds and 327 Nottinghamshire, and 335 Bedfordshire from York, together with a single piston valve Shire , 253 Oxfordshire, also from York.

Five of the engines were used daily on the following turns, with one spare engine:

1. 5.58am and 2.50pm Hull-Sheffield, and return
2. 8.55am to Sheffield and 5.5pm to Doncaster, and return
3. 9.10am Doncaster and 5.0pm to York, and return
4. 8.25am to York, returning via Leeds, and 4.30pm to Sheffield and return
5. 9.0am and 8.40pm to Leeds, and return

Botanic Gardens did finally get some new engines when in 1934 D49/2 205 'The Albrighton' and 214 'The Atherstone' arrived from Darlington Works, followed by 377 'The Tynedale' in 1935. As the North Eastern 4-4-0s gradually disappeared on their last journey to the scrap yard at Darlington further D49 engines were transferred to Hull, until at the end of the LNER in 1947 there were 17 D49s at Botanic Gardens.

Prior to the introduction of the Sentinel railcars on the local services they were worked by 0-4-4Ts of class BTP(3) and O(4) together with 2-4-2Ts of class A(3). The last BTP disappeared in 1929 and the last Class A in 1932. In 1930 the number of Class O(LNER G5) increased to a maximum of nine but that year also saw the introduction of the wheezy ex Great Northern C12 4-4-2T and as the number of C12s increased some of the G5 engines were transferred away. December 1935 saw the loan of A8 4-6-2T 1520 to Botanic Gardens (from Scarborough) for trials on the 6.50am Hull to Goole train, and after proving successful the engine was transferred to Hull six months later, to be joined later in 1936 by 1517,2159 and 2160.

Post war years saw further large passenger tank classes working in the Hull area, such as A5 4-6-2T,L1 2-6-4T, and V1 and V3 2-6-2T. The most surprising (and most unsuccessful) transfer was that of eight ex LMS 3MT 2-6-2Ts in 1954.

The first British Railways diesel multiple unit railcar arrived at Hull on 9 August 1956 and after extensive trials commenced regular work in January 1957. For a time the cars were stabled at the former Hull & Barnsley shed at Springhead but they moved to their proper home at Botanic Gardens when the shed was converted to a diesel depot in 1959. Over the years the steam locomotive stock at Botanic Gardens had gradually been reduced until on 14 June 1959 the last engines were transferred away in one sweep. At that time they were:

      B1 4-6-0 61010/68/80, 61215/89, 61304/5/6

      D49 4-4-0 62701/7/10/7/20/2/3/60

      V1 & V3 2-6-2T 67635/8/40/63/77/82/4/6

      J73 0-6-0T 68363

      3MT 2-6-0 77001

Allocations in 1923, 1932 and 1954 were:

	1923	1932	1954
D22 4-4-0	11	2	-
D23 4-4-0	11	-	-
D17/1 4-4-0	6	3	-
D20 4-4-0	5	11	-
D19 4-4-0	1	-	-
X2 2-2-4T	1	1	-
G6 0-4-4T	3	-	-
G5 0-4-4T	4	6	11
F8 2-4-2T	3	-	-
J71 0-6-0T	2	-	-
C12 4-4-2T	-	10	8
Y1 0-4-0T	-	2	-
D24 4-4-0	-	5	-
D49 4-4-0	-	6	11
J77 0-6-0T	-	1	-
D17/2 4-4-0	-	1	-
J73 0-6-0T	-	-	1
A5 4-6-2T	-	-	5
3MT 2-6-2T	-	-	8
B1 4-6-0	-	-	6
L1 2-6-4T	-	-	7
	47	48	57

DONCASTER (GREAT NORTHERN RAILWAY)

In 1922 there were two North Eastern passenger duties worked from Doncaster. The first involved two sets of men, each of which worked a return trip to Hull, leaving Doncaster at 8.55am and 4.48pm, and Hull at 11.32am and 9.24pm. The other turn commenced with the 7.18am to York and then the 10.5am forward to Hull, returning from Hull to Doncaster on the 12.30pm fish train.

The 10.5 York-Hull train remained a Doncaster turn long after the North Eastern had ceased to exist, at first worked by the North Eastern men who had been integrated into the former Great Northern staff at Doncaster, and later by any Doncaster driver who had signed for the road. In early LNER days this brought ex Great Eastern B12 4-6-0s on to the train, and later the three B17 engines at Doncaster, 2832 'Belvoir Castle', 2833 'Kimbolton Castle', and 2835 'Milton'.

BRIDLINGTON

The date of the original shed at Bridlington has not been discovered but it probably opened with the line from Hull on 6 October 1846. A new shed was authorised to be built at 'the end of the present shed' in 1875 and a tender of £522 was accepted for this work. In June 1892 a tender of £3,439 was accepted for a three-road shed to hold nine engines, and a new turntable was ordered from Messrs Cowans Sheldon at £385 delivered. This building remained in use until 1958 - and it is still standing at the time of writing, although now in a very bad state of repair. The shed sidings and turntable were abandoned in October 1968 but the approach road was left in place to provide a shunting neck for the up sidings.

The duties worked by the shed were almost wholly passenger trains to Hull, Scarborough and Leeds and on these turns before World War I Class 901 and Class 1265 2-4-0s were used. From 1914 Class G 4-4-0s took over and these were later replaced by seven (later 8) of the larger Class F(LNER D22) until 1925 when they were in turn replaced by a similar number of Class M(LNER D17/1) 4-4-0s. The following year the Smith three-cylinder compound 1619 also went to Bridlington and it worked from there until withdrawn in October 1930, still in its LNER green livery.

The D17/1 engines spent some nine years at Bridlington before two new D49 'Hunt' class arrived and in that time they put in some really good work and were popular with their crews, handling trains of four to six coaches in the winter months and up to ten on summer Saturdays. They also put in some speedy running, perhaps not to be wondered at after their exploits in the

1895 Races to Aberdeen when only a couple of years old. One turn involved running the 8.5am Bridlington to Hull train over the 31 miles in 37min. Speeds of 70mph were regularly obtained between Beverley and Driffield and the journey was often accomplished in 34 or 35 min provided a clear run into Paragon station at Hull was obtained. Another interesting turn was that involving two trips to Leeds and back, commencing with the 7.52am from Bridlington and ending with the 4.52pm from Leeds. The intermediate trips at 10.40am Leeds to Bridlington and 2.12pm Bridlington to Leeds ran during the summer months only. At one time Bridlington men worked a service to Sheffield with Class J 'singles' but this ceased with World War I.

Bridlington shed used about ten sets of men daily, most engines being double-shifted, with one engine on wash-out and one spare each day. In 1932 the ten duties were reduced to nine and split into links of three and six turns: the three sets of men worked both on locomotives and the Sentinel steam railcar 'Criterion,' whilst the other six sets were employed solely on locomotives. By this time there were also two Sentinel steam locomotives at Bridlington, 174 for shunting the local goods yard, and 100 for shunting at Driffield each day. As two men were required on the footplate when 100 was running to Driffield a shunter was trained to ride with the driver and they also shunted the yards at the intermediate stations of Carnaby, Burton Agnes, Lowthorpe, and Nafferton.

In August 1934 Bridlington received two new D49/2 'Hunt' class engines from Darlington Works, 230 'The Brocklesby' and 238 'The Burton', the only engines known to have gone new to Bridlington! However, Hull soon got its covetous eyes on these new engines and in 1935 they were exchanged for older D49/3 engines, 318 'Cambridgeshire' and 335 'Bedfordshire'. The former was renowned in the area for its extremely bad riding.

In 1939 a great redistribution of motive power in the North Eastern Area meant the transfer of six C6 4-4-2s to Bridlington, five in June (700,742,784,1776, and 1792), and one (1794) on the last day of July. What a comedown for these Atlantics, once the pride of the East Coast main line between York and Edinburgh. Bridlington men certainly did not like them and did not want them: they were too big and clumsy after the engines they had been used to, and the fire took much more throwing out at the end of the day, with no drop grate and only limited facilities at the small depot. In addition Class R (LNER D20) 4-4-0 1234 and 2016 joined the Atlantics.

After eighteen months at Bridlington the increased traffic due to the war meant that the C6 engines could be better employed on the main line again rather than on light branch line trains and all six left for Heaton (4) and Gateshead (2) in November and December 1940. At this time the services worked by Bridlington shed were severely curtailed and in place of the six Atlantics only two D20 4-4-0s (2024 and 2101) were sent to join 1234 and 2016. 1234 was withdrawn in May 1943 and 1078 eventually arrived from Gateshead as a replacement: 1947 saw the same four D20s still at Bridlington, by now renumbered 2345/53/60/83. Between 1947 and 1951 there were frequent exchanges of D20 engines between Bridlington and other sheds and 62355/62/5/75/87/97 all spent a period there.

In 1949 D49 engines returned in the shape of 62701 and 62707 from Botanic Gardens, followed in 1950 by 62703 and 62750 from Hull and 62766 from Gateshead, and this class worked the passenger trains until displaced by diesel railcars in September 1957.

The run-down of the Sentinel shunters in the 1950s led to two new classes being allocated to Bridlington for when 68148 was transferred away in December 1953, after almost 25 years at Bridlington, it was replaced by N8 0-6-2T 69378. Later two G5 0-4-4-Ts appeared (67280 and 67341) and these were the last steam locomotives stationed at Bridlington. They were actually transferred away on 8 June 1958 but the shed was not closed until 1 December 1958. For a few more years the shed provided turning, watering and stabling facilities for engines working summer trains to the coast but none of these were stabled overnight.

In 1914 the locomotive foreman in charge of the shed was James Dunn, who received £143pa. His son also joined the North Eastern and was eventually passed a fireman at the shed. In the 1930s a shed chargeman by the name of Ned Ford was responsible for the running of the shed and when he retired a foreman fitter was appointed. At this time the shed was under the direct control of the Hull district locomotive superintendent - for years a well-known ex North Eastern man, O.P. Hutchinson, formerly of Tyne Dock and finally district locomotive superin- tendent at Darlington. In an effort to obtain efficiency and economy the LNER created the post of stationmaster & loco - motive shedmaster and Bridlington was one of the first depots to come under this new arrangement. There was still a man in charge at the shed but he was responsible to the stationmaster for the clerical and operating side of the work, and to the district loco- motive superintendent for the technical and stores side. This meant that if an engine was late off the shed the stationmaster could take up the matter with the man in charge. Previously he would have had to write to his superior, the district operating superintendent, who would then have to write to the district locomotive superintendent, who would then have to write to the man in charge of the shed. The reply would have had to go back the same way.

No 1

Bridlington		7-17
Selby	8-51	11-57
Burton Salmon	12-14	12-27
Bridlington	3-7	

No 2

Bridlington		6-57
Hull	8-11	8-55
Scarborough	10-33	4-20
Hull	5-58	7-10
Bridlington	8-22	

No 3

Bridlington		8-0
Hull	8-41	10-43
Bridlington	11-26	

No 4

Bridlington		7-52
Leeds	9-24	10-40
Bridlington	12-21	2-12
Leeds	3-56	4-52
Bridlington	6-22	8-34 ThO
Hull	9-45	10-50 ThO
Bridlington	11-40	

No 5

Bridlington		8-10
Hull	8-59	2-15
Bridlington	3-0	3-30
Selby	5-0	6-2
Bridlington	7-34	

No 6   *SX*

Bridlington		2-20
Hull	3-18	5-30
Bridlington	6-13	

No 7

Bridlington		12-28
Selby	1-28	5-52 SX
Bridlington	7-9	
Selby		2-54 SO
Bridlington	3-55	

No 8   *SO*

Bridlington		8-50
Selby	9-55	2-15
Burton Salmon	2-38	3-20
Selby	3-36	3-38
Bridlington	4-41	

No 9   *SO*

Bridlington		2-25
Selby	3-29	5-52
Bridlington	7-9	

No 10   *SO*

Bridlington		3-38
Scarborough	4-25	9-45
Bridlington	10-54	

No 11   *SO*

Bridlington		11-33
Scarborough	12-20	2-10
Bridlington	3-1	

No 12   *SO*

Bridlington		3-7
Hull	4-13	10-50
Bridlington	11-40	

No 13   *SO*

Bridlington		2-4
Scarborough (Excn Stn.)	2-50	4-3
Bridlington	4-44	

CHAPTER IX

Middlesbrough, Stockton

Middlesbrough

This shed was undoubtedly the most decrepit building to be taken over by British Railways from the North Eastern Area of the LNER. Years of neglect had left the buildings in a sorry state, no doubt hastened by the polluted atmosphere of Tees-side, and bomb damage had led to one roundhouse being demolished, leaving the engines to stand round the turntable in the open air. What a difference the staff must have found when they were transferred to the new depot at Thornaby when it opened in 1958.

The earliest reference to a shed at Middlesbrough is dated November 1845 and this deals with the proposed extension to an existing building. In January 1849 a further shed was authorised 'to be erected nearly opposite to the sail-cloth factory'. Early in 1854 the accommodation was still only sufficient for four engines although six locomotives were stationed there, and a new shed for sixteen engines was commenced in the same year. Before it was actually completed it was fitted with gas lighting and benches. to allow work to proceed on the engines. The same shed is referred to in 1859 and again in 1865, by which time twenty-seven engines were stationed at Middlesbrough. The same 1865 item records 'some engine shed accommodation will be obtained by the transfer of the Cleveland Railway, but not much more than will be required for the engines working on that line'.

Events then moved quickly and on 22 November 1865 a tender of £4,566 was accepted for a circular shed, followed in a matter of days, by a request for still further accommodation. Evidently decisions were taken quickly in those days because on 27 December

1865 a tender for a second circular shed was accepted. This was submitted by Messrs Shaftoe & Barry, the contractors for the first shed, and was for £4,500. The two circular sheds appear to have been completed in August 1866 and February 1867 respectively, for there are the usual statements of excess expenditure amounting to £1,478 2s 2d for the first shed and £688 14s 8d for the second. A third roundhouse was authorised in 1870 at an estimated cost of £5,500 and this was completed early in 1872, when an excess expenditure of £982 1s 1d was allowed.

An unspecified shed was demolished to make way for the new Middlesbrough station opened in 1877 and this was undoubtedly the shed for sixteen engines mentioned above, although it is not known if it was a straight shed or a roundhouse. The three circular sheds of 1866-1872 remained in use until the depot was closed on 31 May 1958 and they were demolished in 1959/60.

Middlesbrough shed's main function was to supply engines for working the sidings at the numerous iron and steel works on the south bank of the River Tees, together with shunting engines for the docks. The loads from the ironworks had to be worked to the marshalling yards at Newport, west of Middlesbrough, and the usual engines for such turns were 0-6-0 tender engines: note the allocation of twenty-eight small 0-6-0s in 1923. The passenger turns were mainly local in character although in 1923 there were five return trips to Newcastle worked by Middlesbrough G5 0-4-4T engines. The Middlesbrough-Newcastle trains gradually got heavier and heavier until the G5 engines were unable to cope but the final blow came in September 1938 when a start was made in using LNER corridor stock in place of the old North Eastern vehicles. Various classes of engine were then tried on the Newcastle expresses, including A5 and A8 4-6-2Ts, D20 4-4-0s, and J39 0-6-0s, but it was not until five V1 2-6-2Ts were received from Blaydon (in exchange for a similar number of A8s) that the services were mastered. These five V1s – 419, 423, 465, 479 and 484 – arrived at Middlesbrough in January 1939.

Until 1933 the services along the Yorkshire coast to Whitby and Scarborough were worked by Saltburn shed but with a change of route Middlesbrough shed became increasingly responsible for such workings. The A6 engines, specifically designed for the route in 1907, proved ineffective and the most suitable engine found for working the heavy summer traffic was the J39 0-6-0. Unfortunately a nasty derailment at Whitby put a stop to the use of these engines and Class A8 4-6-2Ts were drafted to the route as quickly as they could be rebuilt at Darlington Works. Thus when Middlesbrough lost five A8 engines to Blaydon in exchange for the V1 2-6 2Ts some A8s were retained for the Whitby and Scarborough services. It was not until ten years later that V1 and V3 engines appeared on the Scarborough workings, after the lifting of restrictions on their use south of Loftus.

In 1923 the local tank engine workings were to West Hartlepool, Eston, Battersby, Eaglescliffe, Ferryhill, Port Clarance, Leamside, Saltburn and Darlington, although Middlesbrough men played an insignificant part in the Darlington to Saltburn workings.

In winter months, however, the Scarborough service was worked by Sentinel steam railcar 2281 'Old John Bull' or Armstrong-Whitworth diesel-electric car 'Tyneside Venturer'. The Sentinel car was actually rostered for No 1 Steam Coach duty, leaving Middlesbrough for Saltburn at 6.30am and working Saltburn-Middlesbrough-Guisborough-Middlesbrough-Guisborough-Middlesbrough-Guisborough-Middlesbrough-Scarborough-Middlesbrough to end its day at 9.25pm. The diesel-electric car was booked to work the 6.25am to Scarborough and back then two trips to Guisborough and back and one return trip to Stockton, returning to shed at 10.30pm. However, these two duties appear to have been interchangeable and the steam or diesel car could turn up on either duty.

In 1947 Middlesbrough had six turns, all of which except one, were manned by two sets of men while the sixth utilized three sets of men. The four main duties involved working Newcastle expresses and each called for a V3 engine and the engines worked filling in turns to Battersby, Haverton Hill, Low Fell and Saltburn. The treble manned duty involved the engine leaving the shed at 3.30am and not returning until 11.0pm and the three sets of men covered all but 85min of the 24hr on the one engine. Two A8 turns were rostered: one covered local workings, the furthest afield it reached being West Hartlepool, Saltburn and Darlington,

whilst the other worked a return trip to Scarborough and then
another trip to Scarborough, returning the following day and
alternating with a Scarborough A8 engine. There was another
A8 duty but this involved only the pilot and stand-by duty
from 5.0am to 7.35pm, with particular reference that it must
be used for the 4.20pm to Scarborough if required.

Allocations were as follows:

	1923	1939	1954
A5 4-6-2T	-	5	-
A6 4-6-2T	-	3	-
A8 4-6-2T	-	9	7
D20 4-4-0	-	2	-
F8 2-4-2T	5	-	-
G5 0-4-4T	5	4	-
G6 0-4-4T	4	-	-
E5 2-4-0	2	-	-
J21 0-6-0	13	3	-
J24 0-6-0	10	5	-
J25 0-6-0	5	11	-
J26 0-6-0	1	5	4
J27 0-6-0	2	-	1
J39 0-6-0	-	7	2
J71 0-6-0T	5	-	4
J72 0-6-0T	5	6	10
J77 0-6-0T	5	5	3
J79 0-6-0T	2	-	-
Q5 0-8-0	-	15	-
Q6 0-8-0	-	-	19
V1/V3 2-6-2T	-	-	7
4MT 2-6-0	-	-	7
	64	80	64

When the time came for closure of Middlesbrough the following
engines were transferred to Thornaby from 1 June 1958:

A5 4-6-2T	69830/1/4/42
A8 4-6-2T	69860/6/9/82/91
J25 0-6-0	65720
J26 0-6-0	65737/75/6/9
J27 0-6-0	65870
J50 0-6-0T	68908/42/8
J71 0-6-0T	68245/60/92, 68312
J72 0-6-0T	68684/8/9/90,68712/21/40,69006/19
L1 2-6-4T	67754/9/64/5/6
Q6 0-8-0	63340/9/55/64/8/9/73/5/80/93/6,
	63401/5/9/11/7/20/4/35/42/52
4MT 2-6-0	43054/7/71/2/3,43102 TOTAL 63

This shed, situated in the centre of the extensive marshalling yards between Middlesbrough and Thornaby, was essentially a freight engine shed, although at summer holiday times its J39 engines were used on passenger trains to the coast. From February 1943 it had an actual allocation of six passenger engines - D17/1 4-4-0 1629 and D20 4-4-0 1026,1184,1209, 1232, and 1672 - but these were there solely for assisting heavy freight trains up the three mile long bank at 1 in 170 between Yarm and Picton, en route to Northallerton and the south. It will be seen from the allocation table that in 1923, 1939, 1954 and 1958 there was nothing but six and eight coupled engines at Newport.

Between November 1943 and October 1944 Newport received a large number of War Department 2-8-0 engines - 47 in all - and these were returned to the W D between December 1944 and February 1945. With the end of the war this class started returning to Newport in November 1945 and by the end of the year twenty-four had arrived back on Tees-side.

With the opening of the new shed at Thornaby all the Newport engines were transferred from 1 June 1958 and the buildings at Newport were demolished in 1959 to make way for the new Tees Marshalling Yard.

The first suggestion for a shed at Newport had come in November 1876 but the original site under discussion was 'in the fork between the main line and the goods lines near Bowesfield Lane', where a two-road straight shed 120ft long was proposed. At a meeting in December it was reported that the land mentioned was being used by the contractor constructing the Bowesfield Lane subway and it was decided to consider the alternative site at Newport. However, nothing further was done until 1880, when Mr Fletcher suggested a shed for twenty engines: an estimate submitted in June of that year quoted £8,580 for a shed with extra deep foundations, plus £1,813 for the coal stage, and these were authorised on 15 July. In spite of the extra deep foundations the shed became unsafe due to subsidence and on 31 May 1888 it was recommended that the shed be rebuilt on a new site, together with an additional shed to hold a further twenty engines. The cost of rebuilding the old shed and constructing the new was estimated at £13,250 and work was completed in November 1890, when an excess expenditure of £394 5s 11d was authorised.

The 1890 building consisted of two turntables and their associated stalls under one roof but in November 1901 extra sidings were required at an estimated cost of £350 'owing to the re-arrangement of traffic working in the Middlesbrough area and the transfer of a number of engines from Middlesbrough to Newport'. During World War II a lightly constructed straight shed was built adjacent to the east wall of the building, to provide much needed facilities for carrying out repairs to the engines. In the 1930s the main building was allowed to get into a bad state of repair, largely due to neglect and economy, and this culminated in the collapse of part of the roof in January 1939, killing the foreman cleaner.

Allocations to Newport in 1923, 1939, 1954 and 1958 were:

	1923	1939	1954	1958 (To Thornaby)
A7 4-6-2T	-	1	-	-
398 0-6-0	9	-	-	-
J22 0-6-0	4	-	-	-
J24 0-6-0	10	2	-	-
J25 0-6-0	3	-	-	-
J26 0-6-0	6	5	41	38
J27 0-6-0	18	22	1	-
J39 0-6-0	-	24	-	-
J73 0-6-0T	-	2	-	-
J77 0-6-0T	5	5	-	-
J94 0-6-0T	-	-	7	5
Q5 0-8-0	27	30	-	-
Q6 0-8-0	5	18	14	11
T1 4-8-0T	2	3	8	-
WD 2-8-0	-	-	32	30
	89	112	103	84

The Stockton & Darlington Railway was extended from Redcar to Saltburn on 19 August 1861, and two years later it was decided to move the locomotive shed from Redcar to Saltburn 'in consequence of the early and late trains going to and from Saltburn'. Approval for the expenditure of £350 was given in November 1863 and on December a tender for £411 13s 6d was accepted for a building to hold two engines. In February 1864 it was decided to have a building to hold four engines instead of two at the cost of a further £250 and the shed was extended again in 1877 to hold six engines.

On 17 April 1907 the roof was completely destroyed be fire and Class 901 853 was damaged. A new roof was erected on the old walls later the same year and the two-road shed continued in use until 27 January 1958, when it was closed, largely due to the Darlington services being taken over by diesel railcars.

The shed was mainly responsible for passenger train working on the lines to Darlington and Scarborough and at Grouping operated six turns, four of which worked solely between Saltburn and Darlington, one also ran to Whitby as well as Darlington, and the sixth worked to Scarborough. Three of the turns were manned by two sets of men, one by three sets, and two by only one set. In addition there was an autocar duty worked by three sets of men and during the day it ran between Saltburn and Guisborough, Eston, Nunthorpe, and Loftus. On Saturdays the autocar worked as far as Whitby West Cliff.

At this time the Darlington services were worked by the Class D 4-4-4Ts, LNER H1s, and the Scarborough services by the Class W, LNER A6, 4-6-2Ts, with two BTP 0-4-4Ts for the autocar service. In May 1928 seven of Saltburn's H1s were exchanged for a similar number of A5 4—6—2Ts from Blaydon and Gateshead because of the 'unsatisfactory working of the Class D engines on the Saltburn-Darlington line'. Nos 2144/6/8 went to Gateshead in exchange for 1766/7/84, and 2149-52 went to Blaydon in exchange for 1738/56/60/90. In June 1930 the remaining two 4-4-4Ts at Saltburn (1327 and 2155) were transferred to Heaton, supposedly in exchange for two more A5s, 1712 and 1719. However, three A5s were required at Heaton for boat train workings to Tyne Commission Quay and the transfer of 1712 was cancelled.

In March and April 1939, in connection with the provision of V1 2—6—2Ts for the Middlesbrough—Newcastle services, another reshuffle of tank engines took place and Saltburn had its A5 engines replaced by seven A8 4-6-2Ts - rebuilds of the H1 class 4-4-4T Saltburn had last accommodated eleven years earlier: these were 1503/18/9/22/4/8/9. Eventually Saltburn housed nine A8 engines but by the time of closure the shed allocation was a mixture of four A5s (69830/1/4/42) and two A8s (69866/9): these were all transferred to Middlesbrough on 26 January 1958 and the shed was closed, although the yard did accommodate engines requiring to stand awaiting return excursions.

In 1939, with A8 engines, Saltburn was responsible for six duties all of which involved working Darlington trains: one of the turns also had a working to West Hartlepool but the other five remained solely in use between Saltburn and Darlington. Of these, five turns were manned by two sets of men and the sixth by one set. In addition there was a Sentinel steam railcar mainly employed between Saltburn and Brotton, utilising two sets of men between 6.48am and 9.39pm SX (10.35pm SO).

The allocation totals between 1923 and 1954 were:

	1923	1933	1939	1947	1954
A5 4-6-2T	-	8	8	-	-
A6 4-6-2T	2	2	-	-	-
A8 4-6-2T	-	-	-	9	9
E5 2-4-0	1	-	-	-	-
G6 0-4-4T	2	-	-	-	-
H1 4-4-4T	9	-	-	-	-
J24 0-6-0	1	3	1	-	-
J26 0-6-0	-	-	1	1	-
Y3 0-4-0T	-	1	-	-	-
4MT 2-6-0	-	-	-	-	1
	15	14	10	10	10

The three J24s in 1933 were the three former Rosedale engines, 1860, 1893 and 1950, retaining their tender cabs.

The shed building was demolished in 1960.

CARLIN HOW

In his well-known series on *Locomotive & Train Working in the Latter Part of the Nineteenth Century* E.L. Ahrons ends his section on the North Eastern Railway by describing a shed full of old engines 'somewhere on the north east coast'. This has puzzled many of his readers and I have been asked numerous times if I know where this shed could be. Although I have no proof I am sure, from circumstantial evidence, that this shed was at Carlin How, adjacent to Skinningrove Ironworks.

Ahrons states that the time he visited the shed was 'about twelve years ago' and his NER series appeared in 1916 and 1917, Thus putting the date about 1904 or 1905. At this time Carlin How shed had been closed because of a depression in the iron ore traffic and stored in the shed were seven engines withdrawn from traffic and awaiting sale or scrap. Certainly this does not tally with Ahrons' estimate of 'some thirty engines' but the only other shed known to house stored engines at this time was Battersby—and this was far from 'the sound of surf beating upon the rocks'; other engines similarly stored were in the open near Port Clarence —and there are no rocks or cliffs there. Support for Carlin How comes from his reference to 'an iron-bound coast'—the district is honeycombed with ironstone mines and Skinningrove Ironworks are just across the tracks. And it could have been to the Ironworks that his friend had gone on business. As Ahrons and his friend no doubt travelled by train to their destination they would see the spray from the sea as they traversed Huntcliff, on the very edge of the headland and high above the sea. Everything fits into place except for the number of engines – but could Ahrons have embroidered the story to give it more effect?

The position regarding the origins of the shed is rather confused because of references to sheds at Skinningrove, Kilton, and Carlin How itself: however, they are all believed to have resulted in one and the same shed. The earliest mention is dated 8 March 1865, when it was resolved that tenders be requested 'for an engine shed on the Cleveland Extension Railway', and on 17 January 1866 a tender of £1,261 13s 0d was accepted.

Only seven years later, in January 1873, it was suggested that Kilton engine shed be converted to a goods depot and the engines transferred to Middlesbrough. If this suggestion was carried out it must have been only temporary for in November 1875 it was decided to extend the shed at Carlin How to accommodate four additional engines 'using the wooden shed now passing out of use at Shildon, at an estimated cost of £200'.

In June 1876 it was decided to build a shed at Kilton Bank Top, located at either Pennington Ings or near Carlin How signal cabin. It seems possible that the original shed had been damaged by mining subsidence because later in the year it was suggested that the shed and houses should be built of wood as they would then be less liable to damage from subsidence. On 10 May 1877 expenditure of £9,500 was authorised on shed and cottages but the plans were not approved until four months later. The next brief reference comes in 1893 when, on 9 February, alterations and additions costing £1,000 were authorised.

Fortunately quite extensive records have survived of the mineral traffic handled at Carlin How and in 1885 there were ten former Stockton & Darlington long-boilered 0-6-0 engines stationed at the shed for working the ironstone traffic to the blast furnaces on Tees-side, Nos 1004,1013,1028,1049,1109,1126,1128,1148, 1167 and 1220. In addition there were three Class 1037 0-6-0T engines for shunting (1037,1292 and 1294) and one BTP 0-4-4T for working between Loftus and Middlesbrough. This BTP, No 1115, had replaced on the same duties the former Stockton & Darlington 2-4-0 with the same number. By 1892 some of the 0-6-0 engines had changed; one of the 0-6-0Ts had departed, and the solitary BTP remained. The 0-6-0s were now:

1004	Driver Lancaster	1148	Driver G. Glover
1028	Driver Warrior	1201	Driver M. Glover
1047	Driver Moore	1220	Driver Morris
1049	Driver R. Glover		

The 0-6-0Ts were designed specifically for work on the zig-zag line leading down from Carlin How to the valley floor at Skinningrove. No 1294 came to grief on the zig-zag about 1905 when it got out of control descending the second leg and finished up hitting the buffers with wagons piled up around it.

A more serious accident happened on 12 July 1880 when 0-6-0 1220 also got out of control and crashed into the buffers. On this occasion there were six people on the footplate; the driver and fireman, a boy who had brought the driver's tea, a locomotive inspector and his son, and a youth hitching a lift from his work in one of the mines to his home at Skinningrove. The engine was overpowered by the load and after hitting the buffers at the bottom of the second leg of the zig-zag the engine ran about 8ft up the bank and the tender was tilted up, trapping the inspector's son, who was scalded to death by steam escaping from a broken gauge glass. The accident was attributed to the driver not having had sufficient wagon brakes pinned down before descending the incline, which was 1,290yd long with gradients varying between 1 in 41 and 1 in 27.

On 31 July 1902 a heavy blow struck this small railway community when the general manager of the NER recommended that 'owing to the closing of Liverton Mines and the consequent reduction in work it is recommended that the shed be closed and the engines and men removed as follows' :

> 1 engine and 2 sets of men to Saltburn
> 2 engines and 2 sets of men to Haverton Hill
> 6 engines and 6 sets of men to Middlesbrough

The shed was duly closed on 1 October 1902. However, it reopened in March 1907, only to close again in 1921. The building remained standing until 1954 but the site can still be located by the shed floor and the filled-in inspection pits.

ROSEDALE

With the upsurge in interest in the historical aspect of railways the Rosedale branch has come into a larger than usual share of research. Over the last fifteen years or so I have had more enquiries about the Rosedale line than any other North Eastern project. Perhaps it is its remoteness on the wild upland moors of North Yorkshire that makes it a favourite with many people, or is it the gigantic incline, almost a mile long, which had to be climbed to gain the plateau above Battersby, where the line left the former North Yorkshire & Cleveland Railway line heading along the Esk Valley towards Whitby?

Fortunately the line was an attraction even when railway enthusiasts were few and far between and thus it is possible to find quite a number of photographs of the line covering its history and development (and its downfall) between about the turn of the century and the present day.

It is not known what type of engine worked the line when it was first opened in 1861 but early records do mention 422, 423, 564 and 571. These were all 0-6-0s, the first two built by Robert Stephenson & Co in 1860 and the other two by R.&.W Hawthorn & Co in 1866. Another source, referring to a collision which took place on the line on 13 December 1890, quotes the engines involved as 568 and 569, also built by Hawthorn & Co in 1866. By 1903 ex Stockton & Darlington long boiler 0-6-0s were in use and these engines worked the line until about 1920. When an engine needed to go from Rosedale to the Works for overhaul it was the practice to leave the replacement engine at Rosedale shed and not to send back the newly overhauled engine, thus saving unecessary trips up and down the incline. The same practice was followed with regard to the Q5 0-8-0 engines at Kirkby Stephen but there, of course, it was the dismantling for the passage over Belah Viaduct that was obviated.

Consequently a number of different 1001 class engines spent some time at Rosedale and those known include 1108,1126, 1128, 1129, 1192, 1193, 1195, 1255, 1282 and 1286. Class 1196 0-6-0 1766 is also believed to have been at Rosedale prior to its being withdrawn in August 1908. Another odd engine at Rosedale was McDonnell Class 59 0-6-0 1489, which was there from about 1915 to 1919. Finally, in 1919 and 1920, three North Eastern P 0-6-0 engines were sent up the Incline and they worked the line until it closed on 29 September 1928. Thre three engines concerned were 1860, 1893 and 1950 and they were all fitted with cabs on their tenders for the better protection of the enginemen, perpetuating the tender cabs fitted to the 1001 class engines that worked the line. No 1950 was transferred from Rosedale to Saltburn on 22 August 1927, when only two engines were required at Rosedale, and the other two followed on 24 January 1929, after assisting with the dismantling of the line.

The duty of the engines was to haul wagons of ironstone from the mines at East and West Rosedale to the Incline Top, where the wagons were lowered down the Incline and taken forward by another engine. At the top the engine worked empty wagons back to the mines. A little general freight traffic was carried but it was insignificant when compared with the ironstone traffic.

The shed was situated at West Rosedale and the first building was authorised in April 1860, to accommodate three engines.

Mr Cail, the contractor building the line, was approached to submit a tender and this amounted to £760, with the stipulation that the roof should be boarded instead of plastered. Extensions were asked for by Mr Fletcher in September 1862 and in the following month a tender of £330 15s 0d was accepted. However, the contractor went bankrupt five months later and the work was awarded to the next lowest at £334. The task was completed by the end of the year and for once the actual cost was less than the amount authorised, although by only £18 10s 3d. No alterations appear to have taken place after that date and the shed continued to provide shelter for the engines until closure.

The shed was demolished in the 1930s and the stones were used to build the village hall at Hutton-le-Hole, a village some four miles away. However, the floor of the shed and the filled-in inspection pits can still be seen at West Rosedale.

GUISBOROUGH

In 1923 the Guisborough engine commenced work on the 5.12am to Middlesbrough: a train run for the steel workers in Middlesbrough. The footplate crew booked on at 4.10am to prepare the engine for this early start. At this time the train was actually an autocar - a BTP 0-4-4T engine with a coach at each end, with the driver using the leading coach in which ever direction the train was travelling. After working from Middlesbrough to Loftus, Saltburn, Guisborough and back to Middlesbrough the Guisborough crew returned to Guisborough as passengers and the engine was worked to Guisborough later, where the second set of men took over at 2.0pm to work until 9.55pm, visiting Saltburn and Brotton. On Saturdays the autocar set was replaced by normal locomotive worked coaches from 9.2am until finishing at Guisborough at 11.32pm.

In the early days of the LNER the BTP engines were being withdrawn steadily and as Guisborough lost one, another was transferred there to take its place. Thus between 1923 and 1929 the shed housed 226, 358, 416, 595 and 1436: 1436 was actually the last example of this well known class to remain in service. Thus, when no further replacements were available a new engine suitable for Guisborough had to be found and F8 2-4-2T 685 was transferred from Middlesbrough on 29 July 1929. In November of the following year Guisborough lost its

locomotive and acquired the 12 cylinder Sentinel steam railcar
'Old Blue'.

The railcar still made an early start and worked the 5.14am
to Middlesbrough, returning empty to its home station to work
the 6.43am to Middlesbrough. During the course of the day the
car also visited Stockton, Battersby and Loftus, arriving back at
Guisborough in the hands of the second set of men at 9 32pm:
between 12.3 and 3.7pm the car was worked by Middlesbrough
men. The last turn on a Friday evening - the 8.3pm Middlesbrough
-Loftus and the 9.11pm empty Loftus to Guisborough - was worked
by a steam train to provide additional accommodation between
Guisborough and Middlesbrough on Saturdays, and to allow the
railcar boiler to be washed out at Middlesbrough shed. The
Guisborough men retrieved their Sentinel for the 11.10pm
Middlesbrough - Guisborough Saturdays Only working in readiness
for the normal working on the Monday .

The railcar was withdrawn for scrapping in 1941 and on 15
September G5 0-4-4T 1883 replaced it at Guisborough. This
engine was one of the first of the class to be fitted with the LNER
pattern of push-and-pull apparatus and it remained at Guisborough
(latterly as 67281) until the shed closed on 20 September 1954.

Nothing is known about the original shed at Guisborough which
was probably constructed for the opening of the Middlesbrough
& Guisborough Railway in 1853 However, it is known that the
building was destroyed by fire on 27 February 1903 and replaced
some five years later by a corrugated iron structure, which has
now been demolished.

Stockton

It might be thought that this shed was descended from the
Stockton & Darlington Railway but this was not so: the
Stockton & Darlington and Leeds Northern stations were some
distance apart and the modern shed (closed in 1959) was
descended from the Leeds Northern, Stockton & Hartlepool,
and Clarence Railway developments on the north side of Stockton.
In fact until 1893 the main station at Stockton was known as
North Stockton.

The exact origins of the Leeds Northern station are unknown
166

but it dated from the time the company reached Stockton in 1852. An engine shed must have been completed with the line because by 1862 increased accommodation was required and the shed was doubled in size at a cost of £1,093 10s 6d: a plan of the area prepared c 1873 shows a six-road shed, with each road only long enough to hold one or two engines, immediately west of the station.

In consequence of the forthcoming enlargement of the station (completed in 1893) a search was made in 1889 for a new site for the shed and when plans were submitted on 3 October 1889 the estimated cost was quoted as £16,500, with accommodation for twenty-four engines. A tender for £12,099 7s 7d was accepted on 14 November but this was amended to £12,520 2s 9d in the following month. The shed was completed in 1891 after excess expenditure of £445 10s 0d had been authorised.

The resulting single-ended eight-road straight shed, very similar in design to the building at Scarborough of the same period, was closed on 13 June 1959 and the engines dispersed. After standing empty for a time the building was taken over by a private firm.

Stockton shed was responsible for passenger and goods workings but the former were very local and in 1923 only one turn took an engine as far afield as Harrogate. No 1 turn (2 sets of men) worked to Yarm, West Hartlepool and Wellfield; No 2 (two sets of men) ran to Eaglescliffe, Hartlepool, Ferryhill and Yarm; No 3 (one set of men) worked to Battersby and Guisborough; No 4 (two sets of men) to Battersby and Wellfield; and No 5 (with two sets), after a morning trip to Wellfield, worked the 8.47am Stockton—Harrogate and the 11.41am return.

In 1939 there were four locomotive turns, plus three Sentinel railcar duties:

		Sets of Men
No 1 G5	Port Clarence, West Hartlepool and Battersby	2
No 2 A8	West Hartlepool, Thirsk and Whitby	3
No 3	Harrogate, Darlington and West Hartlepool	2
No 4	Port Clarence and Ferryhill	2
Railcars		
No 1	Pelaw, Newcastle, Ferryhill, Whitby, Goathland	2
No 2	Port Clarence, Battersby, Guisborough, Ferryhill	2
No 3	Port Clarence, Ferryhill	2

During the summer Stockton shed was responsible for some workings along the Yorkshire coast to Scarborough and latterly used A5s, A6s and A8 4-6-2Ts, L1 2-6-4Ts and LM 4MT 2-6-0s.

In 1930 Stockton's allocation of engines dropped from 47 to 19 due to the closure of Stockton Marshalling Yard and the allocation of train working to other sheds. Some of the more interesting transfers resulting from this were:

J21 979 to Kirkby Stephen to replace D23 1107 broken up.

Q6 2248 and 2255 to Springhead, 2225/45/84/6 to Selby and Q7 624/6/8/39 to Selby, to allow Q10 engines to be placed in store.

T1 1657/8, the former to Bullcroft for Warmsworth pilot, and the latter to York.

J23 2453 to Pickering (displacing J21 1809 to York) and 2459 to York.

Stockton Yard was reopened during World War II to handle the greatly increased freight traffic, so that in 1947 Stockton shed had more engines than it had in 1923! After the war the shed became responsible for a number of braked freight trains, chiefly to York, and for this traffic acquired eleven B1 4-6-0 engines: 61018 'Gnu', 61030 'Nyala', 61032 'Stembok', 61034 'Chiru', 61037 'Jairou', 61173, 61189 'Sir William Gray', 61214/20/75 and 61303.

Allocations for 1923, 1933, 1947 and 1954 were:

	1923	1933	1947	1954
A7 4-6-2T	2	-	2	-
B1 4-6-0	-	-	-	11
B16 4-6-0	-	-	5	-
D22 4-4-0	-	1	-	-
F8 2-4-2T	2	1	-	-
G5 0-4-4T	5	4	5	3
398 0-6-0	1	-	-	-
J21 0-6-0	13	4	4	-
J22 0-6-0	1	-	-	-
J24 0-6-0	2	2	-	-
J25 0-6-0	1	-	-	-
J26 0-6-0	-	2	2	3
J27 0-6-0	2	-	10	2
J71 0-6-0T	1	-	1	1
J72 0-6-0T	2	2	-	-
J77 0-6-0T	3	3	3	3

K1 2-6-0	-	-	-	6
N8 0-6-2T	2	-	-	-
Q5 0-8-0	1	1	15	-
Q6 0-8-0	7	-	-	-
Q7 0-8-0	-	4	-	-
T1 4-8-0T	-	-	1	3
Y10-4-0T	-	-	1	1
Y3 0-4-0T	-	1	-	-
WD 2-8-0	-	-	-	12
	45	25	49	45

Engines at closure 14 June 1959:

B1 4-6-0: 61030/2/4, 61173, 61220, 61303   J26 0-6-0: 65747/73
J27 0-6-0: 65787/8,65853/84   J71 0-6-0T: 68260
J72 0-6-0T: 68696   J94 0-6-0T: 68049
K1 2-6-0: 62001/3/41/2/7/65   L1 2-6-4T: 67754/66
WD 2-8-0: 90082,90155/72/84,90377,90430 2MT 2-6-0: 46478
J50 0-6-0T: 68892   TOTAL 31

HAVERTON HILL

This four-road double-ended shed was authorised in November 1896 and a tender of £5,783 (later amended to £5,849 3s 1d) was accepted in June 1897. The building was to a standard pattern evolved in the 1870s with round topped doors, later modified to accommodate square topped doors which could be built with a varying number of roads, such as Bridlington (three roads), Haverton Hill (four roads), Stockton and Scarborough (both eight roads).

Although primarily a freight engine shed it did provide an engine to work the passenger service between Billingham and Port Clarence. In 1923 the engine left the shed at 5.15am and did not return until 10.39pm, operated by three sets of men who worked 4.30am to 12.30pm, 11.30am to 7.30pm, and 4.0pm to midnight. A Class F8 2-4-2T was provided to work the service. On Saturdays a fresh engine was turned out at 12.27pm and on Sundays two turns were rostered but both could be covered by one engine: one set of men booked on at 7.30am to work between Billingham and Port Clarence from 8.34am to 9.54am, and another set started work at 4.40pm and ran, in addition, as far as Hartlepool before ending their Sunday on the 9.40pm from Port Clarence to Billingham. By 1939 the shed had lost its passenger turns. *169*

The 1923, 1939 and 1954 allocations were:

	1923	1939	1954
Class F8 2-4-2T	2	-	-
Class 398 0-6-0	1	-	-
Class J26 0-6-0	7	-	-
Class J27 0-6-0	-	4	7
Class J39 0-6-0	-	4	-
Class K1 2-6-0	-	-	7
Class Q5 0-8-0	4	11	-
Class Q6 0-8-0	-	-	6
	14	19	20

The shed was closed on 13 June 1959 and the majority of the engines transferred to the new shed at Thornaby. They were:

B1 4-6-0 61018/21/4/37,61255
Q6 0-8-0 63341/3/4/7/61/7/74/82,63407/16/32/43/6
WD 2-8-0 90086,90397,90479.

The shed was demolished in June 1965.

CHAPTER X

Darlington, Kirkby Stephen

Darlington (Bank Top)

The position at Darlington is often confused, particularly after the amalgamation of the North Eastern Railway and the Stockton & Darlington Railway, as it is not always clear to which shed reference is being made.

North of the present shed and adjacent to the site of the Stockton & Darlington level crossing over the east coast main line is a building known as the Great North of England shed and, of course, the Great North of England Railway opened the section between Darlington and York in 1841. Unfortunately it is not known if this is the building referred to in the York, Newcastle & Berwick Railway Minute of September 1853, when it was 'resolved that the engine shed be taken down and rebuilt in a more convenient situation so as to allow the necessary accommodation for wagons'. On 11 November 1853 plans for this move were approved and four weeks later a tender of £1,150 was accepted.

On 23 December 1859 Mr Fletcher reported that 'an engine set away from the shed at Darlington without any driver; it was stopped at Ricknal Bridge. It is believed that the engine was interfered with by trespassers and it is recommended that a wall be immediately erected at the end of Green Street with a lodge in which a man can be stationed'. Green Street still leads to the shed entrance and countless enthusiasts must have passed along it since Mr Fletcher made his report more than a century ago. Most of the small houses have now been demolished but in 'the good old days' it was the practice for enginemen coming off duty to empty their 'bait-tins' as they walked along the street and the unwanted scraps were eagerly seized upon by the local children.

On 21 October 1864 it was decided to build a new circular shed for eighteen engines and on 2 December this was approved at an estimated cost of £6,000. A turntable was ordered in February 1865 at a cost of £365 and in April a tender of £7,829 was accepted. In 1906 the 42ft 3in turntable in the roundhouse was replaced by one of similar size from the shed yard, and the latter was replaced by a new 'table of 60ft diameter purchased from Messrs Cowans Sheldon & Co for £569. By 1947 (probably when extensive alterations were carried out in 1938/9) the turntable in the roundhouse had been enlarged to 45ft and this was still in use when the shed closed. Similarly the 60ft 'table in the shed yard had been replaced by a 70ft turntable capable of turning Pacifics.

Readers who visited Darlington shed in the 1930s will recall the decrepit building which sufficed as the main locomotive shed until 1939, when the new seven-road double-ended shed was built. The old building had originally been a wagon repair shop until 1885, when the work was transferred to Shildon 'Thereby leaving the wagon shop available for stabling passenger engines which will have to be transferred from North Road on completion of the new Central Station' — later known as Bank Top station. Those readers who possess photographs from the late W.H. Whitworth's collection can see the old shed in the background of a number of his photographs. In recent years a diesel railcar depot has been built adjacent to the steam shed but on the opposite side of the main line.

The engines stationed at Darlington in 1923, 1939 and 1954 were as follows:

	1923	1939	1954
A3 4-6-2	-	-	2
A5 4-6-2T	-	-	10
A8 4-6-2T	-	12	-
B1 4-6-0	-	-	15
B15 4-6-0	1	-	-
B16 4-6-0	2	4	-
C6 4-4-2	-	8	-
D20 4-4-0	7	-	-
D23 4-4-0	1	-	-

E4 2-4-0	-	2	-
E5 2-4-0	6	-	-
G5 0-4-4T	1	-	4
H1 4-4-4T	7	-	-
398 0-6-0	6	-	-
J21 0-6-0	10	13	7
J22 0-6-0	4	-	-
J24 0-6-0	7	2	-
J25 0-6-0	5	17	4
J26 0-6-0	1	1	-
J27 0-6-0	-	7	-
J39 0-6-0	-	8	-
J71 0-6-0T	9	11	7
J72 0-6-0T	8	3	5
J77 0-6-0T	1	5	4
J94 0-6-0T	-	-	10
K1 2-6-0	-	-	13
L1 2-6-4T	-	-	3
N9 0-6-2T	2	5	-
Q5 0-8-0	-	17	-
Q6 0-8-0	2	-	-
Q7 0-8-0	-	3	-
X1 2-2-4T	1	-	-
Y1 0-4-0T	-	-	1
Y7 0-4-0T	-	1	-
LM 2MT 2-6-0	-	-	2
LM 4MT 2-6-0	-	-	4
LM 4MTT 2-6-4T	-	-	3
BR 3MT 2-6-0	-	-	3
BR 4MT 2-6-0	-	-	1
	81	119	98

Although situated on the main line Darlington shed had few
workings north and south; most of its workings were to the east
and west and the introduction of diesel railcars on the services to
Saltburn and on the Stainmore line was the beginning of the end.
The number of steam locomotives allocated to the shed was
gradually run down until at closure to steam on 27 March 1966
there were only ten engines remaining. Of these 4MT 2-6-0 43050
and 43055, and K1 2-6-0 62001/8/41/4/5 were transferred to
West Hartlepool and J27 0-6-0 65859 to South Blyth. The two
east coast pilots — engines standing by to replace a failed engine
on main line trains — were withdrawn on the same day. These

were A1 4-6-2 60124 and 60145.

In the *1923 Passenger Engine Working* book Bank Top shed had passenger workings to both York and Newcastle, but only one through working from Newcastle to York, which was actually on a parcels train, and the shed had no turn covering York to Newcastle. The local workings to Saltburn, Tebay, Blackhill and Richmond required ten engines daily, of which two were single-manned, seven were double manned, and one required three sets of men to cover the day. In addition there was one main line pilot covering from 1.45pm to 11am (treble manned), and one covering 9.30am to 4.30pm (double manned): to complete their day the crew on the late turn of the latter worked the 5.2pm to Saltburn and the 7.47pm return. At this period the main line pilots were Class D20 4-4-0s, perhaps better known as the NER Class R engines.

With the introduction of the non-stop Flying Scotsman on 1 May 1928 larger engines were required to stand pilot at Darlington and at this time new D49 4-4-0s were displacing C7 4-4-2 engines from various sheds. These in turn were used to free C6 4-4-2s for Darlington; thus 702 was transferred from York to Darlington, and 705 from Gateshead to Darlington on 2 April 1928, followed by 697 and 703 from Tweedmouth on 30 April. The latter pair had been displaced by C7 729 (ex Leeds) and 736 (ex Gateshead). The earlier pair allowed D20 4-4-0 2016 and 2110 to be transferred to York. After World War II Class C7 Atlantics were used as stand-by engines but at the end of 1948 the first Gresley Pacifics arrived at Darlington in the shape of 60070 'Gladiateur' and 60076 'Galopin'. These Pacifics were changed regularly until finally replaced by the two A1 engines which were there when the shed closed.

When passing Bank Top shed there were usually some ex-works locomotives to be seen and in later days these spotless engines stood out amongst the home based engines. On the whole, however, Darlington engines were kept in quite clean condition, in marked contrast to some of the engines at other sheds. The works yard could not be seen from the main line but only from the Bishop Auckland and Barnard Castle branches.

The shed was closed on 27 March 1966 and a year later the old roundhouse and the new coaling plant were demolished. However, the straight-shed remained in use for diesel multiple unit railcars from the diesel depot on the other side of the main line, and for a year or two also accommodated a long withdrawn J21 0-6-0 until it was purchased for preservation. Another engine which spent many years at Darlington was an unidentified Kitson tram locomotive. This appears on photographs taken in the 1920s and 1930s and its long sojourn was due to a dispute between the LNER and the owner, a local scrap merchant.

NORTHALLERTON

This shed was sandwiched between the low level Leeds Northern lines and the high level east coast main line, and because of the wind screen on the west side of the station it was difficult to see from a main line train unless one knew just where and when to look. It was a small shed, its primary duty being the provision of tank engines for the passenger traffic on the Wensleydale branch, and also stone traffic off the same branch to the ironworks on Tees-side. To handle the passenger traffic Northallerton for many years maintained a stud of the useful Fletcher BTP 0-4-4Ts but by 1923 these had given way to F8 2-4-2Ts and these were eventually replaced by G5 0-4-4Ts. However, towards the end of the life of the passenger services on the Wensleydale branch to Hawes and Garsdale the trains were worked by D20 4-4-0 62347 and 62359, and J21 0-6-0 65038. On rare occasions Northallerton provided an engine to assist a lame duck on the main line but this rescue was usually performed by Darlington engines.

An unusual engine for Northallerton in 1930 was D17/1 4-4-0 1636, sent there to work the milk traffic on the Hawes branch. To release 1636 from Darlington, C6 4-4-2 701 was transferred from Gateshead to York, to allow D20 4-4-0 1672 to be transferred from York to Darlington. On 8 October 1932 1636 was transferred to Alnmouth to replace 1625 of the same class, withdrawn five days earlier, but no replacement for 1636 was provided at Northallerton.

An odd feature of the shed was that there was no turntable in the shed yard. The turntable, together with the coaling facilities, were provided at the north end of the main line station on the higher level.

The allocation was:

	1923	1939	1954
D20 4-4-0	-	-	2
F8 2-4-2T	5	-	-
G5 0-4-4T	-	3	2
J21 0-6-0	-	1	1
J24 0-6-0	2	-	-
J25 0-6-0	2	-	3
J26 0-6-0	-	2	-
J39 0-6-0	-	-	3
J73 0-6-0T	-	-	1
K1 2-6-0	-	-	1
Y3 0-4-0T	-	1	-
	9	7	13

In 1923 and 1938 Northallerton had only two passenger duties: in 1923 one engine was manned by two sets, each of which worked a return trip to Hawes. The other engine worked trips to Ripon and Leyburn with one set only. In 1938 roughly the same applied, although duty No 1 had each of its trips extended to Garsdale, and No 2 worked a return trip to Hawes.

In 1949 matters were a little more complicated. A G5 was rostered for No 1 duty and the first set worked to Garsdale and back. The second set worked the 2.3pm Northallerton-Hawes as far as Leeming Bar, where they changed engines with Leyburn men, returning to Northallerton on the Leyburn engine working the 12.55pm ex Garsdale. Still with the Leyburn engine they then worked the 4.10pm to Garsdale and back. The engines changed back again at Leeming Bar the following day.

Duty No 2 was rostered for a D20 4-4-0 and involved working the 7.20am to West Hartlepool, then running light to Middlesbrough to work the 11.55am to Northallerton. The second set of men worked the 3.40pm Northallerton to Stockton and the 4.53pm forward to West Hartlepool, returning on the 6.45pm from West Hartlepool.

Duty No 3, again for a G5 engine, was double manned plus 3½ hrs coverage by a set of relief men and involved passenger station pilot and dairy shunting between the hours of 5.30am and noon and 3.0pm and 11.15pm.

The first reference to a shed is dated 24 April 1857 and it deals with the provision of a building at the Low Station, for which a tender of £244 18s 0d was accepted. In 1881 a new shed to accommodate two engines was authorised, and in 1886 an extension costing £213 7s 0d was agreed to. Perhaps it should be mentioned that platforms were provided on the former Leeds Northern lines on the low level until the Northallerton-Melmerby line was doubled in 1901. Until then there was no connection between the Leeds Northern lines and the main lines south of the station and consequently trains for Melmerby had to start from the low level platforms — the Low Station. In conjunction with an emergency route put in to by-pass the high level station in the event of bomb damage in World War II the low level platforms were reinstated but were again removed a few years after the war finished.

The shed was closed on 3 March 1963 and the five remaining engines (Ki 2-6-0 62044 and 62064, and 2MT 2-6-0 78010, 78011 and 78014) were sent to Darlington. The buildings were demolished in November 1964.

BARNARD CASTLE

The shed at Barnard Castle was authorised on 26 October 1864 at an estimated cost of £450 and it was, presumably, opened in the following year. On 22 September 1874 it is recorded that the shed was to be lengthened to take two more engines but in the following month the engineer reported that the building could not be lengthened and that any extension must be made alongside. Authority was given for this and plans were submitted in November 1874, quoting an estimated cost of £800. On 11 January 1875 a tender was accepted but it was reported that the contractor declined to sign as he had miscalculated to the sum of £34. He was, however, allowed to amend his tender by £30 and this was then accepted at the figure of £837 11s 9d. The extension was not built parallel to the original building so that in the completed two road shed the roads were at about 10deg to one another.

In 1923 the allocation comprised three Class 901 2-4-0s, one E5 2-4-0, one J21 0-6-0, and two N9 0-6-2Ts. As the 2-4-0 engines were withdrawn they were replaced by D23 4-4-0s, and as these were scrapped further examples were transferred to Barnard Castle to end their days, until finally the supply dried up and other replacements had to be found. Thus on 22 March 1933 former Great Northern 4-4-0 4313 was transferred from Starbeck to Barnard Castle to join D23 223 and 337:223 was withdrawn in the following month and replaced by another D3, 4075, whilst when 337 went on its last trip to Darlington Works in August 1933 it was replaced by 4349. In July 1933 4313 moved on (to Hull) and in October 1933 4349 was transferred to Kirkby Stephen and replaced at Barnard Castle by 4347 of the same class.

In November 1935 4075 was transferred to Hull and 4347 to Selby and replaced by a single ex Great Eastern 2-4-0, 7463. When Barnard Castle shed closed on 3 May 1937, 7463 moved to Darlington. Of the goods engines the two N9 0-6-2Ts (1641 and 1642) and the J22 0-6-0 (which had replaced the J21 0-6-0) were transferred away in June 1928 when the freight working in the area was taken over by Darlington and West Auckland sheds.

The building has now been demolished.

In 1923 Barnard Castle shed was unusual in that it was responsible for the same number of turns on a Sunday as it was on a weekday, namely three! The first working on a weekday (Mondays and Saturdays excepted) was the 6.45am workmens' train from Barnard Castle to Hulands Quarry platform, consisting of one coach only. The coach was then left at Bowes for the day and the engine returned light to Barnard Castle to work the 7.30am to Darlington and the 9.5am Darlington-Saltburn. It arrived back at Barnard Castle at 1.18pm and after spending the afternoon on the shed it worked the 6.14pm to Darlington and the 7.40pm return with a second set of men. Duty No 2 involved (Saturdays excepted) the 2.43pm to Durham, 6.30pm Durham-Waterhouses and return, 7.19pm empty to Leamside, light engine back to Durham, and finally the 7.58pm Durham-Barnard Castle. On Saturdays the working was the 2.43pm through to Sunderland and the 7.0pm return.

Duty No 3 involved taking over from No 1 at Barnard Castle and working the 12.38pm ex Darlington forward to Tebay at 1.25pm. The return was at 4.30pm from Tebay, arriving back at Barnard Castle at 6.8pm and giving way to No 1 duty engine on the 6.14pm forward to Darlington. On Sundays, although three turns were rostered, they could be worked by two engines. The trains were the 7.15am to Darlington and the 8.45am Darlington-Barnard Castle-Middleton in Teesdale, with the engine then running light back to its home shed. At 5.5pm the second set of men took the engine light to Middleton to work the 5.35pm to Barnard Castle and Darlington, returning at 8.15pm from Darlington. The other engine worked through to Penrith on empty stock, returning from Penrith at 3.45pm on a passenger train, although the main purpose of the train was to convey milk from the Eden Valley farms.

RICHMOND

There is in existence a well-known photograph of a 2-2-2 tender engine standing on a train in Richmond station in the 1860s. It is not know if this engine was then stationed at Richmond or Darlington, but it is a fact that at that time the North Eastern had very few tank engines suitable for use on their numerous branch passenger trains. It was not until Edward Fletcher introduced his famous BTP 0-4-4T in 1874 that it became obvious that a small tank engine was far more suitable for a meandering country branch than the old tender engines used hitherto. Later the North Eastern Class A 2-4-2Ts and Class 0 0-4-4Ts took over and it was one of the latter that was stationed at Richmond in 1922 when the duties involved four return trips to Darlington Mondays to Fridays and five on Saturdays, utilising two sets of men. In December 1929, 2089 was replaced by F8 469 from Hawes Junction and this engine stayed at Richmond until the shed closed on 30 December 1933, whereupon it returned to Hawes Junction. Henceforward the branch was worked from the Darlington end, by Sentinel steam railcars on some turns and by various classes of tank engine on others. Favourites at one time were the A5 4-6-2Ts but A8s also appeared, together with V1 2-6-2Ts.

It appears that the shed was constructed at the same time as the station buildings as no separate tender for the construction of the shed has been located. The earliest refence is dated 4 June 1869, when it was decided to convert part of the shed to a stable for four horses, at a cost of £45. The attractive stone built shed, together with the pumping house, remained standing after closure and may probably still be there.

HAWES JUNCTION

In May 1881 the Midland Railway offered to rent the small engine shed at Hawes Junction to the North Eastern Railway at £2 per engine per month plus 3d per tank of water. To enable them to terminate their last train up the valley at Hawes Junction the NER decided to accept the offer and the Agreement came into force on 1 June 1881. In addition to the shed the NER was also offered the tenancy of three cottages at 3s per week each.

The normal engine stationed at Hawes Junction was a BTP 0-4-4T and all went well until one night in October 1917 when the shed caught fire — with BTP 207 inside. All the paint was burned off 207 and even the wooden buffer-beams disappeared in the fire, but after a visit to Darlington Works the engine ran for another three years before being scrapped.

For a period in 1923 a Class 398 0-6-0 was stationed at Hawes but this was replaced by a Class A 2-4-2T and an engine of this class remained at the shed until May 1935. Until 19 December 1929 the engine was 469, but from that date it was exchanged for 423, of the same class, from Richmond. When 423 was withdrawn in December 1933 it was replaced by 469, which became spare at that very time by the closure of Richmond shed. On 30 May 1935 469 was transferred from Hawes to Tyne Dock and replaced by a G5 0-4-4T, 435 from Ferryhill.

As an economy measure the service between Northallerton and Hawes Junction was cut back to Leyburn from 17 February 1939 but the shed (as Garsdale) was not officially closed until 1 May 1939. Even so the engine — G5 435 — was not transferred to Leyburn (on paper at least) until 17 June 1939.

For many years the working at Hawes Junction had remained the same: the first set of men worked to Northallerton and back in the morning, and the second set performed the same run in the afternoon.

It would appear that the shed destroyed in 1917 was replaced, presumably at the expense of the NER, but no record of this has yet been located.

MIDDLETON IN TEESDALE

For its size this shed had a large variety of engines at one time or another. For instance in a period of nine years the shed housed engines from the designs of six railway companies — North Eastern, Hull & Barnsley, Great Northern, Great Central, Great Eastern, and London & North Eastern! For many years, of course, Middleton relied on North Eastern engines — Class 901s and 1463 2-4-0s in 1924 and 1925, followed by D23 4-4-0 217 until 18 December 1930. On that date 217 was transferred to Barnard Castle to replace an engine of the same class which had been withdrawn from service and it was replaced at Middleton by former Hull & Barnsley J23 0-6-0 2514. After a spell of six months the HBR engine moved on to Darlington on 15 June 1931 and 217 returned to Middleton, but only for a very short time as it was withdrawn from traffic on 8 August 1931. This time the replacement was a former Great Northern, 4-4-0, 4354 of Class D3 and this engine lasted until 14 July 1936 when it was transferred to Hull and replaced by a former Great Eastern engine, this time 7416 of Class E4. Although on paper 7416 remained at Middleton until 30 July 1938 it was moved away earlier and for a while a V1 2-6-2T was on loan, although actually the engine was changed at Gateshead daily. With the lifting of restrictions on Class A8 on the Middleton branch No 1524 was moved to Middleton on 30 July 1938, replaced by 1525 of the same class on 22 March 1939, and this in turn was replaced by A5 4-6-2T 1766 on 20 May 1939.

Eventually the motive power became stabilised when G5 0-4-4T 1764 replaced 1766 on 11 September 1939 and this engine remained at Middleton (later as 7309 and 67309) until June 1952, when it was transferred to Heaton. Henceforward Middleton was supplied with a G5 or J21 engine from Darlington until dieselisation came along and the shed was closed from 16 September 1957 — the building was demolished in the summer of 1961.

The line to Middleton was opened in May 1868 and on 2 January 1869 an estimate of £194 19s 4d was submitted for a shed. However, the Secretary of the Tees Valley Railway reported that there was an old shed at Shildon which might answer the purpose and he was instructed to ask Mr Bouch 'what he would take for same'. Estimates for the removal of the shed and its reconstruction at Middleton were also to be obtained.

Apparently the suggestion fell through because on 31 March

1869 five tenders for the erection of a new shed were considered. These ranged from £190 to £230 but the lowest was not accepted: instead Mr Hepworth, who had submitted the second lowest tender, was asked if he would accept £196 (the amount estimated by the company's engineer) and to this he agreed. The shed was presumably opened later the same year and it continued to house steam locomotives for eighty-eight years.

Two sets of men were usually stationed at Middleton: in 1923 the first set worked to Sunderland and back and the second set to Bishop Auckland and back. In 1939 both sets worked to Newcastle and back.

Kirkby Stephen

When the South Durham & Lancashire Union Railway was opened in 1861 it was worked from the outset by the Stockton & Darlington Railway, and for their use a shed for two engines was built at Kirkby Stephen. It was doubled in size in 1865 and in the following year further extensions were authorised at an estimated cost of £1,847, when six engines were stationed there with accommodation for only four.

The line from Barnard Castle to Kirkby Stephen, which climbed over Stainmore Summit, was a most difficult line to operate because of the long gradients and the wild exposed moorland it traversed. Reaching a height of 1,370ft above sea level at Stainmore meant that the line was very prone to blockage by snow and on some occasions trains have been snowed up for weeks. Actually, for many years Kirkby Stepehn did not play a very great part in working the line as the mineral trains were worked through to Tebay or Cockermouth by Shildon engines, and also by Tebay engines working eastwards, leaving Kirkby to work the branch passenger services to Penrith and Tebay. With the shorter hours for footplate crews, however, it became necessary for the mineral trains to be re-engined at Kirkby and the shed thus became responsible for working the mineral trains west of Kirkby and also gained a larger share in the passenger traffic to Darlington.

The earliest known allocation of engines to Kirkby is dated January 1885, when there were twelve engines stationed there:

Class 38 4-4-0: 426

Class BTP   0-4-4T: 591,623, 1020
Class 1068 2-4-0: 1066
Class 1001 0-6-0: 1176/8/9/81/2/4, 1225

Because of weight restrictions imposed on Belah Viaduct about 1914 the size of engines allowed on the line was limited and for many years the passenger services were worked by 2-4-0 engines of classes 901 (Fletcher) and 1463 (Tennant). As these were withdrawn in the 1920s they were replaced by the smallest type of Worsdell 4-4-0 of Class D23. In turn these were replaced by former Great Northern Railway 4-4-0 engines of Class D3, followed by the E4 2-4-0s of former Great Eastern Railway design. Next came the J21 0-6-0 engines – an old design but a class which performed admirably in spite of their age – and these remained until the LMS and BR types were introduced.

The J21s were doubly useful in that they could also take a share in working the freight and mineral trains, helping out the ageing J24 and J25 0-6-0s. Until 1914 NER T and T1 0-8-0 (LNER Q5) engines worked extensively on the mineral turns but because of the restrictions imposed over Belah Viaduct they had to be withdrawn from the line and all trains 'over the top' had to be 0-6-0 hauled. In 1929 a Q5 engine was required at Kirkby Stephen to work to Tebay and the Engineer gave permission for the engine to travel over Deepdale and Belah Viaducts provided that the boiler was empty, part of the motion dismantled, and the tender run separated from the engine by wagons. In this manner 443 was transferred from Shildon to Kirkby Stephen on 4 November 1929 but on 6 January 1931 it was replaced by 2118 of the same class so that 443 could enter Darlington Works. A second Q5 engine was required at Kirkby Stephen in 1931 and 444 joined 2118 on 18 November 1931. When one of the Q5 engines had to go to Darlington works it was the practice to replace it at Kirkby Stephen by another of the class recently ex works, so that over the years Kirkby had a constantly changing pair of 0-8-0 locomotives. Engines sent in this way included 645, 646, 715 and 1032, and 444 went there for a second stint on 21 May 1941 but remained only six months as it was transferred to Darlington on 17 November 1941. No 2118, also there for its second stint, was the last of the class at Kirkby and remained there until 30

March 1942.

After World War II Kirkby relied on 0-6-0 engines until 1955, when on 3 April, Q6 63355 and 63373 were transferred to Kirkby to work to Tebay. The two engines were used to double-head certain mineral trains and whilst returning to Kirkby on a train of empties on 20 May 1955, both engines running tender first, they were derailed and ran down an embankment. The class was immediately banned from the line and nothing more than six-coupled engines allowed.

In 1922 Kirkby Stephen only had one passenger turn. This was manned by three sets of men and involved a Kirkby-Tebay-Darlington-Penrith-Kirkby diagram. The engine spent five hours at Darlington, 9.57am to 2.57pm, and during that time was employed on pilot duties. By 1939 the single turn had developed into three turns, each double manned:

No 1 E4 or J21 engine Kirkby-Darlington-Appleby-Kirkby-Penrith-Kirkby

No 2 E4 or J21 engine Kirkby-Darlington-Tebay-Darlington-Kirkby

No 3 G5 engine Kirkby-Penrith-Kirkby-Tebay-Kirkby-Penrith-Kirkby-Penrith-Kirkby

The engines allocated to Kirkby Stephen were:

	1923	1939	1947	1954
901 2-4-0	1	-	-	-
E5 2-4-0	3	-	-	-
E4 2-4-0	-	4	-	-
G5 0-4-4T	-	1	-	-
398 0-6-0	5	-	-	-
J21 0-6-0	2	4	5	3
J24 0-6-0	2	-	-	-
J25 0-6-0	-	5	6	4
Q5 0-8-0	-	2	-	-
LM 2MT 2-6-0	-	-	-	7
BR 2MT 2-6-0	-	-	-	4
	13	16	11	18

One class not mentioned in the above table is the former

Great Northern 4-4-0 which became LNER D3. Although these engines started working over Stainmore in 1930 it was not until 5 October 1933 that Kirkby Stepehn received 4349 from Barnard Castle and when this engine departed for Botanic Gardens on 11 November 1935 it was replaced at Kirkby by E4 2-4-0 7411. Kirkby subsequently acquired 7408, 7416, 7478 and 7496 of the same class but they were transferred away in 1940-42, 7478 being the last to go on 9 April 1942.

After the departure of the E4 engines the passenger services over Stainmore were taken over by the J21 0-6-0s — a design which first appeared in 1886 and these gallant engines fought their way over Stainmore until the LMS pattern of 2MT 2-6-0s appeared in 1951. In 1954 the passenger services were taken over by the new 3MT 2-6-2T 82026-9.

In British Railways' days the freight and mineral traffic was taken over by an influx of new 2-6-0 engines and the lifting to some extent of the weight restrictions on Belah Viaduct enabled 4MT 2-6-0 engines to be shedded at Kirkby Stephen. Thus on 1 February 1958 Kirkby had:

2MT 2-6-0	46470/2, 78013/7/8/9
4MT 2-6-0	76020/2/3/47/8/51/2

Because of adjustments to the Regional boundaries Kirkby Stephen was transferred to the London Midland Region from 1 February 1958 and the engines above were transferred on loan to the LMR from that date, becoming a permanent transfer on 23 February 1958. On becoming LMR stock the engines were gradually transferred to other depots in readiness for closure of the shed but a newcomer was 2MT 2-6-0 46458. This engine managed to survive at Kirkby Stephen until the shed closed in November 1961.

PENRITH

This shed was erected by the London & North Western Railway for the Cockermouth,Keswick & Penrith Railway and there was an understanding that the North Eastern should be allowed to use the shed for temporary purposes. The Stockton & Darlington Railway was one of the joint owners of the CK&P and when, as successors to the Stockton & Darlington Railway, the NER

(Stockton & Darlington Section) applied to stable some engines there in 1866 they received numerous excuses as to why this was not possible and, in fact, they did not gain a foothold until 1873. This necessitated an extension to the shed (at an estimated cost of £760) and the CK&P agreed to pay a rental equal to 6 per cent of this sum, namely £45 per annum, of which the NER paid £20.

At Grouping the Penrith engine was a Class 901 2-4-0: when this was withdrawn in 1925 it was replaced by a Tennant 2-4-0, which in turn lasted for a year before it was replaced by G5 0-4-4T 1916. This engine continued to work the four daily return trips between Penrith and Kirkby Stephen until January 1935 when, during a re-allocation of engines in the Darlington district, Penrith received GN 4-4-0 4077 in its place, whilst 1916 joined 1334 of the same class at Kirkby. In 1935 with the influx of Great Eastern 2-4-0s to the Stainmore line Penrith received E4 7408 in place of 4077 and continued to use 7408 until 31 December 1936, when it was replaced by 7411. A year later 7416 replaced 7411 and remained at Penrith until the LNER engine was withdrawn from 1 May 1939. For some reason the engine was not transferred to Kirkby Stephen until 17 June. The shed continued to house London Midland engines but until the diesel railcars came along on the Stainmore route the North Eastern Region engine merely used the turning and watering facilities.

CHAPTER XI

Whitby, Malton, Scarborough, Selby

Whitby

Although no Minute covering it has been discovered it seems certain that the first shed at Whitby was erected by the York & North Midland Railway in 1847, when it commenced using steam locomotives between the foot of Goathland Incline and Whitby, replacing the horse-drawn vehicles of the Whitby & Pickering Railway.

In August 1865 it was recommended that plans be prepared for a new shed to hold eight engines and Mr Harrison and Mr Fletcher were instructed to make a report on the accommodation required. In February 1867 Mr Harrison submitted a report, with the suggestion that the expense of a new shed might be avoided if the existing building was extended to hold four additional engines, and this was approved. A tender of £1,570 3s 0d was accepted in March 1867, and work must have gone ahead rapidly because in May there was an objection to the height of the extension, lodged under a restrictive covenant. Mr Prosser, the architect, was instructed to stop work and to modify the plans so that the building came within the specified height, and this delayed the opening of the shed until the end of 1868. No further major alterations appear to have taken place, although the shed was extensively repaired in 1903 and a dividing wall removed.

Whitby shed at one time was a busy little centre and was responsible for train working over the four routes radiating from this ancient town;

To Saltburn via Loftus
To Middlesbrough via Battersby
To Malton via Pickering
To Scarborough via Robin Hoods Bay

Latterly the workings were in the hands of tank engines but for many years 4-4-0 locomotives were employed, particularly on the line to Malton. This practice started in 1864 with Edward Fletcher's famous Whitby Bogies - a short wheelbase 4-4-0 specially designed for negotiating the sinuous curves through Newton Dale. Later the McDonnell Class 38 4-4-0s played a large part in the workings and until early LNER days the T. W. Worsdell Class G 4-4-0s (the Waterburys) were used. These were followed by various classes of tank engines, from the F8 2-4-2T, through the G5 0-4-4T, A6 4-6-2T, A8 4-6-2T, BR 4MT 2-6-4T, and LMR 4MT 2-6-4T. The handy G5 engines had the longest span and worked, albeit occasionally, right into the 1950s.

In the 1930s, particularly in the summer months, Whitby had to rely on former Hull & Barnsley 0-6-0s, displaced from their home ground by larger engines. The first to arrive at Whitby was 2476, transferred there from Springhead on 7 July 1930: No 2440 from Cudworth followed exactly two weeks later. Two more, both from York and supposedly for the summer season only, followed in July 1931 - 2459 and 2522, and two years later 2469 from Springhead replaced 2440 when the latter was withdrawn. Finally, in June and July 1934 2460 from Springhead and 2477 from Cudworth arrived. In addition to 2440, 2459 was withdrawn in 1933, and in July 1936 2469 was transferred to Dairycoates to release J21 981 to go to Darlington while the others, 2460, 2476, 2477 and 2522, remained at Whitby until the purge of Hull & Barnsley 0-6-0 engines in 1937 and 1938. These engines normally worked passenger services to Malton, with certain trains extended to York and Leeds in the summer months.

Allocations were as follows:

	1923	1933	1939	1947	1954
A6 4-6-2T	5	6	5	-	-
A8 4-6-2T	-	-	3	1	6
F8 2-4-2T	5	-	-	-	-
G5 0-4-4T	3	4	3	5	2
J22 0-6-0	3	-	-	-	-

J23 0-6-0	-	4	-	-	-
J24 0-6-0	1	2	2	3	-
J25 0-6-0	1	-	-	-	3
J27 0-6-0	-	-	1	-	-

In the winter months they were normally employed on goods workings.

By 1939 Whitby shed was responsible for five turns all requiring two sets of men, taking them to Middlesbrough, Scarborough, Malton and Ferryhill and in addition there was the single manned Grosmont pilot. The summer workings to Leeds, already mentioned in connection with the J23 0-6-0, meant that the Whitby engine stayed overnight in Leeds as the men returned with a Leeds engine. The next day Leeds men worked the Whitby engine back and returned to Leeds with the engine the Whitby men had used the previous day. This turn, together with excursions to the coast, brought various types of 4-4-0 engines to Whitby and examples confirmed are D17/1,D20, D21 and D49. However perhaps the most unusual class to visit Whitby shed was a Great Northern Atlantic of Class C1.

In 1955 Whitby received five BR Standard 2-6-4Ts new from Brighton Works: these put in some very good work on passenger trains in the area, although it must be admitted that they were not well loaded and in the winter months could be seen hauling trains of between two and four non-corridor bogie coaches. They were later replaced by three earlier tank engines with the same wheel arrangement, 42083/4/5, and these, together with 3MT 2-6-0 77004 and 77013, were the last engines to be stationed at Whitby when the shed closed on 6 April 1959. The shed building was subsequently used as a fish packing warehouse!

A plan dated 29 September 1900 shows a proposed single square roundhouse to be built at Ruswarp, the first station out of Whitby on the Grosmont line. This was to replace the shed at Whitby, where it was impossible to extend, but the scheme fell through.

PICKERING

Pickering is one of the few country sheds which remain standing in spite of having been closed since 6 April 1959. For years it relied on BTP 0-4-4T to work its services but by 1923 these had been replaced by two G5 0-4-4Ts, with a J22 0-6-0 for the goods turn, which was mainly shunting at Pickering. One G5 was transferred away in 1928 and the J22(491) was withdrawn for scrapping on 23 January 1929. In 1928 Pickering received one of the first two double-geared Sentinel locomotives purchased by the LNER (No 81) and this was used for the local shunting. This was fitted with vacuum brake and the idea of having a Y3 stationed at Pickering was so that it could work a passenger train to Scarborough in the event of the Sentinel steam railcar being unable to take up the working. Incidentally, No 90 of the same class, also vacuum brake fitted, was stationed at York as a spare to replace No 81 if required. No trace of either of these locomotives ever being used in such an emergency has come to light but one of them did carry out trials between Pickering and Seamer on one (or possibly two) coaches. No 81 was replaced by 192 in September 1942 and this Sentinel engine remained until withdrawn from service in December 1952.

In February 1930 it was decided that an 0-6-0 engine was necessary at Pickering and J21 1809 moved from Normanton. However, this was replaced by the former Hull & Barnsley Railway 0-6-0 2453 six months later. After complaints by the enginemen of having to run tender first Pickering received N8 0-6-2T 218 on 30 August 1934 but further complaints were made that a superheated engine was necessary for use on the Alne turn and in November 1934 218 was exchanged with 76 (superheated) from Hull. By this time there was only one G5 at Pickering and on 31 July 1935 this engine, together with the HBR 0-6-0 2453, were transferred to Malton. During 1936 N8 864 was at Pickering when 76 was under repair. On 22 January 1938 76 was transferred to York and N9 1645 from Tweedmouth took its place at Pickering. This was one of the class which for some reason did not receive larger tanks generally fitted to North Eastern 0-6-2Ts in the early years of the century. After a year at its country home 1645 was transferred to York to work the Derwent Valley Light Railway and 76 returned to Pickering.

The next move was on 16 November 1940 when Pickering received D20 4-4-0 1232 from York in exchange for 76. Due to rearrangement of duties brought about by World War II G5 0-4-4T 1755 and 1888 were transferred from Malton to Pickering in December 1941 and a few weeks later 1232 departed for Darlington shed. One G5 (1888) returned to Malton at the end of June 1942 and 1755 followed at an unknown date when the engines at Pickering were reduced to one Sentinel.

In 1948 certain duties were restored and D49 62774 'The Staintondale' arrived at Pickering for a stay of three years but in September 1951 it was replaced by D20 4-4-0 62343 which stayed until February 1953, being replaced by G5 67308. The G5 was withdrawn on 22 November 1955. Henceforward engines were supplied by Malton shed until Pickering closed in 1959.

The date of the original shed building at Pickering is not known but in October 1874 it was decided to extend the shed to take two engines instead of one and this was completed in 1876 at a cost of £604 2s 6d. The building remained in this form until closure.

At Grouping Pickering covered two passenger duties, each manned by an early and late set of men. No 1 commenced by working the 7.15am to York and back and the second set worked the 3.55pm to Pilmoor and back. No 2 worked the 7.10am to Scarborough and back and then, except on Thursdays, acted as goods pilot from 10.0am to 3.0pm and the second set of men then worked the same engine on the 4.20pm to Scarborough and back. On Thursdays, market day in Scarborough, the early set worked an additional trip to Scarborough and back at 10.10am instead of performing shunting duties in the goods yard. This extra trip necessitated them being paid forty minutes overtime each Thursday.

In the summer of 1939 the N8 76 worked the 7.25am to York and back, the 12.30pm goods to Kirkby Moorside and back, and finally the 4.2pm to Alne and back, to give the last service of the day to York via a connection with a southbound slow on the main line.

In 1949 the D49 62774 'The Staintondale' started off in the same way by working the 7.10am to York and the 10.35am back. The same engine, with the second set of men, then worked a goods to Kirkby Moorside and back. On Mondays the next job was a Class D goods to Goathland Summit, returning engine and van to Pickering to work the 5.32pm to York but on other days there was no booked working after returning from Kirkby Moorside until 5.32pm to York. On this train the Pickering men worked only as far as Coxwold, where they changed footplates with the York men working the 5.55pm York to Pickering. The Pickering men then worked back home on the York engine, which stayed overnight at Pickering and was exchanged at Coxwold on the following evening. On Mondays, Wednesdays and Fridays the Pickering engine was worked to York by the York men, who then worked the 8.35pm passenger train to Normanton, returning to York on the 12.10am parcels on Tuesday, Thursday and Saturday mornings. The Pickering engine then worked the 7.25am to Pickering and back with the first set of York men, before setting out on the 5.55pm York-Pickering, still on Tuesdays, Thursdays and Saturdays, with the crews exchanging footplates again at Coxwold.

Malton

The shed was not actually in Malton but at Norton, on the East Riding side of the River Derwent, whereas Malton is in the North Riding. A tender for its construction was accepted in August 1853 at a figure of £435. In 1865 plans were prepared for an extension to the building to provide additional accommodation for six engines but in the following year a new shed was proposed, to cost £6,817. However, in February 1867 it was suggested that the shed should be extended rather than provide a new shed as accommodation was required for only two further engines. Consequently plans for an extension costing £800 were approved. In 1870 it was decided that the engine shed, turntable and coke shed should be lighted by gas, and a crane and tubs be provided for coaling engines; this method of coaling was employed until the shed closed on 15 April 1963.

At one time Malton was an important railway centre with branches to Whitby.Driffield and Pilmoor from the York-Scarborough. Malton never seems to have worked a York-Scarborough passenger train (except in an emergency) and the engines normally worked the branches, together with a few goods trains between Malton and York. To cover these services there were nine daily goods duties and four daily passenger turns. The latter were all manned by two sets of men and in 1923 were:

No 1 Two return trips to Whitby

No 2 Three return trips to Gilling and one to Driffield
No 3 Two return trips to Driffield and one to Gilling
No 4 One return trip to Whitby.

Each engine was used for shunting duties during its lay-over at
Malton or Whitby. In fact No 4 engine was back at Malton at
9.13am (after working the 5.38am 'mail' to Whitby) and acted as
goods pilot until 7.30pm , and it was then relieved until 9.0pm
by the engine of No 2 turn after it had arrived back from
Gilling at 7.15pm. The goods traffic was so heavy that an
additional goods pilot was provided between 12 noon and 2.30pm
(4.0pm on Tuesday market days).

By the summer of 1951 the number of turns at Malton was
down to one, manned by two sets on Mondays—Thursdays, and
three on Fridays and Saturdays. By this time the Gilling and
Driffield branches had been closed to passenger traffic, as had
the Pickering-Scarborough service which Malton had worked for
some years after taking it over from Pickering. The remaining
duty involved working the 4.55am 'mail' to Whitby each day,
returning on the 9.20am from Whitby, and later in the day the
4.0pm to Whitby and the 6.50pm return. The additional set of
men required on Fridays and Saturdays was because on these
two days the 9.20am from Whitby was extended to York and the
4.0pm from Malton started back at York at 3.25pm. Malton men
were also responsible for assisting the Scarborough to Newcastle
and Glasgow trains between Malton station and Scarborough
Road junction. These trains needed to reverse at Malton to gain
the Gilling-Pilmoor line and the complete train (with train engine
in rear) was hauled by a Malton engine between station and
Scarborough Road. The train engine then took over again for the
journey, with the Malton engine usually giving a helping hand on
the climb to cross the Scarborough line and the River Derwent.
In the reverse direction the Malton pilot coupled on the rear end
of the train from the north and hauled it into Malton station
where the train engine was then in the correct position for working
forward to Scarborough.

Malton shed provided an emergency engine on summer Saturdays
when traffic to and from the coast was at its heaviest. Frequently
an engine was borrowed from York or Selby for this purpose as
Malton itself had no suitable express passenger engine, although

when they got some J39 0-6-0 engines in the 1950 s these could be used in an emergency.

The J39 engines, in conjunction with the J27 0-6-0s were responsible for the freight workings, the most important of which was for a long time the morning mineral train to Thirsk conveying limestone from quarries on the Driffield branch. Frequently two trains were run and over the years Malton acquired various classes of engines for this job — at one time or another they had an A7 4-6-2T, a Q5 0-8-0, and WD 2-8-0 and before these the ex North Eastern P and P1 0-6-0 were used. Perhaps Malton's most notable engine was the Stockton & Darlington pattern long-boilered 0-6-0 1275, built by Dübs in 1874. This was the only one of the class to remain in service when the LNER was formed but it was withdrawn soon afterwards and left Malton in February 1923. It eventually found a home in the Railway Museum at York and ran under its own steam in the 1925 Centenary Procession.

With dieselisation and the decline in traffic it was finally decided to close Malton shed and this became effective on 15 April 1963.

Allocations in 1922, 1932, 1939 and 1954 were:

	1922	1933	1939	1954
A7 4-6-2T	-	1	-	-
A8 4-6-2T	-	-	-	1
D2 4-4-0	-	2	-	-
D23 4-4-0	1	-	-	-
F8 2-4-2T	4	3	-	-
G5 0-4-4T	1	3	5	3
398 0-6-0	1	-	-	-
J22 0-6-0	6	-	-	-
J23 0-6-0	-	5	-	-
J24 0-6-0	-	1	5	-
J25 0-6-0	-	-	-	5
J26 0-6-0	-	1	2	-
J39 0-6-0	-	-	-	4
N8 0-6-2T	1	1	-	-
Q5 0-8-0	-	-	1	-
Y1 0-4-0T	-	1	1	-
	14	18	14	13

The A7 engine, 1136, was transferred from Hull in June 1927 specifically for Burdale Quarry traffic and it was sent to Leeds on 3 October 1933. N8 860 was also transferred to Leeds, in July 1932. The five former Hull & Barnsley 0-6-0s (LNER J23) were transferred to Malton in 1928/29 and comprised 2447/54/5/70 and 2515. Together with the Whitby engines of the same class they put in a lot of work on trains between Malton and Whitby. The Q5 0-8-0 was 647, transferred from Selby in March 1938. Another unusual engine for Malton was F4 2-4-2T 7578 (later 7155): this was one of three engines of Great Eastern design transferred to the North Eastern Area in 1945/6. Malton received 7578 in October 1946 (from Dairycoates) and after renumbering it 7155 in December 1946 it remained at Malton until withdrawn in August 1951. It was normally used on shunting work whilst at Malton but it was seen at Scarborough on one occasion after having replaced an engine which had failed at Malton.

Two further strangers at Malton were J36 0-6-0 9172 and 9604, transferred from the Scottish Area on 31 January 1940 'to replace engines sent to the Great Western Railway'. Actually no Malton engines were sent to the GWR but the provision of the two J36s allowed J24 0-6-0 1821 and 1826 to be transferred from Malton to North Blyth to replace two J25s sent to the GWR.

The engines stationed at Malton at the time of closure were: 2MT 2-6-2T 41251;3MT 2-6-2T 82027/8/9;2MT 2-6-0 46413/73; J27 0-6-0 65844/9/88, all of which were transferred to York, except for 46413 which went to Goole. The last turn worked by Malton shed was the afternoon return trip to Whitby worked by 4MT 2-6-0 43055 on 13 April 1963. The shed has since been demolished and the site levelled.

In 1899 plans were prepared for a single square roundhouse on the opposite side of the York-Scarborough line to the original shed but this scheme was not proceeded with.

Scarborough

Scarborough shed, with the York line on one side and the York road on the other, has always been a popular venue for anyone interested in locomotives. Because of its position it was possible to see everything that was going on in the yard, and also to observe the trains passing in and out of Central and Londesborough Road stations. Thus there are quite a number of photographs in existence of engines standing outside the shed and these photographs date back to the 1890s. The building in the background is usually the third shed - an eight road dead-end building completed in 1890 and demolished in 1966. This building stood at the west end of the yard: at the east end was a rectangular roundhouse, tucked in between the main line and the road. Because of its cramped position it was impossible to have all the roads of equal length and the turntable had to be placed off centre in the shed. Thus there were only thirteen roads long enough to accommodate engines and as two of these were access roads the shed provided only limited accommodation. It was no wonder, therefore, that within a few years of being built the locomotive superintendent was recommending the erection of another shed, which eventually materialised as the straight shed already mentioned.

The original shed at Scarborough was opened with the line in 1845 and it was a small two-road building which was demolished in 1906 or 1907 to make way for Londesborough Road excursion station. It had not been used for locomotive purposes since 1882, when the roundhouse was opened, and, in fact, it had latterly been in use as a warehouse. Fortunately, following their practice of photographing almost everything of interest, the NER took a photograph of the old York & Midland shed before it was demolished.

The roundhouse was authorised in 1879 at an estimated cost of £5,393 for the shed and £2,976 for the engineering work, and on 11 March 1880 a tender of £4,330 8s 6d was accepted for the building: work was completed in 1882, when it was reported that the scheme had cost £187 13s 0d more than the authorised expenditure. The turntable came from Ianson, Son & Co of Darlington at a cost of £335.

After the opening of the straight shed the roundhouse fell into disuse for locomotives in traffic and it was used for storing locomotives, especially during the winter months. By removing their tenders engines of up to class V2 could be housed. A hoist was provided for engines under repair but this had been out of use for many years prior to the closure of the shed in 1963.

When the straight shed was built it was constructed on made-up ground: in the 1950s the walls at the east end of the building had to be shored up because of subsidence and eventually half the building had to be demolished. A new wall was provided on the south side of the remaining portion, converting the shed into a four-road building, with the four southerly roads remaining in place but open to the elements.

The shed was closed as a steam depot from 20 May 1963 and the last engines departed two days earlier, with 82027 hauling 41265 and 80117. For another four years the turning and watering facilities were used by engines working in on excursions and Saturdays Only trains but now the turntable and water cranes have been removed, the shed roads lifted, and the yard is a scene of dereliction. The roundhouse still stands, with most of its windows smashed, and the silent clock stands as a reminder of busier days.

A turntable, coaling, and watering facilities were also provided at Gallows Close carriage sidings situated adjacent to the Whitby line between Scarborough and Scalby. However, coal was available only on summer Saturdays and Sundays, and on the three Bank Holiday Mondays at Easter, Whitsuntide, and August. These sidings were provided in connection with the opening of Londesborough Road station in 1908, so that trains could unload their passengers at the excursion station and then run forward to the carriage sidings without blocking the tracks leading to Central station. The engine could stand for the day at Gallows Close and in the evening work its return train empty to Londesborough Road station, load up and be ready for away in a matter of minutes. This greatly relieved the pressure on the shed facilities but the practice was discontinued in the 1950s.

The first locomotives to work a train to Scarborough are known: they were the York & North Midland Railway 'Hudson', an 0-6-0 built by Robert Stephenson & Co in 1845, and 'Lion', a 0-4-2 built by Stephenson's in 1841. They worked the inaugural train on 7 July 1845, hauling a train of thirty-five coaches. However, it is not known what engines were actually stationed at Scarborough, although early photographs taken in the 1870s show 2-2-2 and 2-4-0 locomotives on the York and Hull lines. The former, with its 42 level and easy miles, was just suited to the ageing engines at

York shed, as E. L. Ahrons so well describes.

Scarborough shed later received engines displaced from the main line by new engines, such as Fletcher 901s and Tennant 1463 2-4-0s, Class G 2-4-0s (later rebuilt as 4-4-0), Class I and J 4-2-2s, and Class F, Q and R 4-4-0s. The Class J 'singles' were, pre-1914, responsible for working the 75min non-stop Leeds-Scarborough train — the fastest time ever achieved over the 67½ miles. When the working was reintroduced in 1922 Class R engines from Leeds shed took over the working until it ceased in 1929.

In LNER days the D49 'Hunt' class engines were Scarborough's pride and joy. In 1934 222 'The Berkeley', 226 'The Bilsdale', 258 'The Cattistock', 274 'The Craven', 279 'The Cotswold', and 353 ' The Derwent' arrived new from Darlington Works, and with two regular sets of men to each engine they put in some extremely good work on the Leeds expresses.

In May and June 1939, when a reallocation of engines took place, Scarborough lost D49 258 but received in its place six Class C6 Atlantics — 699 and 704 from Gateshead and 532, 649, 698 and 701 from York. This increased the allocation to twenty-four engines and one railcar. Of these, fifteen were passenger tender engines and then there were two B16 4-6-0s which were often used on passenger workings, although one was used daily on the mineral empties to Gascoigne Wood and the loaded return working. During the war, when traffic was lighter, some of the D20 engines returned to Scarborough, until in March 1945 when the whole of Scarborough's allocation of engines (by now down to twelve) was changed. Transferred away were J21 582 and 976, and D49 274 to York; J21 1574 and D49 336 to Leeds; D20 2011, 2018, 2019 and 2021 to Selby; and A6 688, 689 and 691 to Starbeck. Received in exchange were C7 706, 720, 728, 729, 732 and 737 from York, and 2207 and 2211 from Hull, together with A8 1502 and 1527 from Starbeck, and 1526 and 1530 from Selby. As the C7 engines were steadily withdrawn others were transferred to take their place, namely 716, 722, 2166, 2167, 2169, 2204 and 2208: the last to remain at Scarborough was 2207 which (as 2992) was withdrawn on 1 November 1948, the penultimate engine of the famous Class Z Atlantics.

As the Atlantics were withdrawn in 1948 D49s came back again — 62746, 62749, 62751, 62755, 62769, 62770, and 62774. Some were soon transferred away again but 62751 'The Albrighton', 62769 'The Oakley', and 62770 'The Puckeridge', together with 62726 'The Meynell', 62739 'The Badsworth', and 62756 'The Brocklesby' became the regular allocation of top link engines. They put in some ten years work on the Leeds and Hull lines until the time came for their last journey to Darlington. On 25 January 1959 BR 5MT 4-6-0s 73167-70 were transferred to Scarborough and according to the footplate crews these were the best engines that ever worked from the shed. When they arrived they were in a bad way after a spell of neglect at York, and the local fitters had just about got them all pulled round and running sweetly when they were transferred away after only six months on the coast. On 14 June 1959 the BR engines were replaced by B1 4-6-0 61068, 61304 and 61305 and these three remained until March 1960, when they too were moved on. This time there was no replacement as the passenger services were all worked by railcars, leaving Scarborough with a miscellaneous collection of small engines for minor freight duties, local pilot work, and stand-by.

The coast line to Whitby, Middlesbrough and Saltburn saw very little change in motive power. From its opening in 1885 the passenger services were worked by BTP 0-4-4Ts of Fletcher design, followed for many years by the Class O with the same wheel arrangement but designed by Wilson Worsdell. The Class W 4-6-0T of 1907/8 were specially built for the line but were rebuilt as 4-6-2Ts to give increased bunker capacity and even then they did not appear regularly on the line until the 1920s, when they worked almost every train.

In 1933 the northern terminus of the service was changed from Saltburn to Middlesbrough and, with the increased popularity of 'holiday runabout tickets', the traffic increased enormously, so much so that the existing engines were unable to cope. Class J39 0-6-0s were hurriedly pressed into use from the Middlesbrough end but Scarborough received some of the A8 4-6-2Ts as they were rebuilt from 4-4-4Ts at Darlington Works. During the war they were transferred away to depots where they would be of more use but 1502, 1526, 1527 and 1530 brought the class back to Scarborough in March 1945. Until 1958, when the coast line was dieselised, they put in some good work over the hilly Whitby and Middlesbrough road, assisted latterly by 42084 and 42085.

In the 1930s J21 582, 1516 and 1573 were used as the passenger station pilots, with a Sentinel shunter in the goods yard. When these were transferred away the shunting was often performed by the A6 tanks and various train engines. In September 1946, however, Scarborough received two ex WD J94 0-6-0STs 8016 and 8017 for goods shunting — 8016 departed in just less than a year but 8017 stayed until replaced by the new J72 69016 in January 1950. This popular little engine remained at Scarborough until December 1958 when it was exchanged for 68739 of the same class from York. When 68739 went for scrapping in August 1959 it was replaced by 3FT 47403 — an unexpected class for Scarborough. This also went for scrap after two years work and subsequently shunting was carried out by any available engine — often 82027, 77004, 77013, or 40117 — until the first Drewry shunter (D2151) commenced work on 15 October 1962. Since then one, two, or sometimes, three Drewry shunters have been stabled at Scarborough, and on one occasion a 350hp diesel-electric shunter was in use.

In October 1968 a female learner driver rammed the level crossing gates at Haxby just as the 9.0am York-Scarborough dmu was approaching. The train struck the gates, injuring the driver and putting the diesel set out of action. This was due to be split at Scarborough to form the 10.15 and 11.05 to York. By borrowing part of a Hull set it was possible to run the 10.15 as a railcar but the 11.05 was formed of a Drewry shunter propelling a flat wagon and hauling three coaches. This odd calvalcade took an hour to reach Malton instead of the normal 30min or so but there it was relieved by a larger locomotive sent out from York.

	1923	1932	1939	1959
E5 2-4-0	2	-	-	-
D22 4-4-0	4	1	-	-
D23 4-4-0	3	-	-	-
D17/2 4-4-0	6	5	1	-
BTP 0-4-4T	1	-	-	-
G5 0-4-4T	2	-	-	-
A6 4-6-2T	2	2	2	-
J22 0-6-0	3	-	-	-
J25 0-6-0	2	-	-	-
B15 4-6-0	1	-	-	-
Q5 0-8-0	1	-	-	-
Y3 0-4-0T	-	2	-	-
D20 4-4-0	-	7	3	-

B16 4-6-0	-	1	2	1
J23 0-6-0	-	1	-	. -
J26 0-6-0	-	1	-	-
J24 0-6-0	-	1	-	-
A8 4-6-2T	-	-	3	3*
C6 4-4-2	-	-	6	-
D49 4-4-0	-	-	5	5*
J21 0-6-0	-	-	2	-
12 cyl. Sentinel railcar	-	-	1	-
BR 5MT 4-6-0	-	-	-	4
BR 3MT 2-6-2T	-	-	-	2
J72 0-6-0T	-	-	-	1
	27	21	24	16
				+1 RC

*= In store

Selby

The first roundhouse was erected at Selby in 1871 and had eighteen stalls and two access roads, grouped round a 42ft turntable. In November 1896 it was reported that there were forty-six engines allocated to Selby and a second roundhouse was authorised at an estimated cost of £14,980. This was opened in 1898 and consisted of two access roads and twenty two stalls round a 50ft turntable. Not surprisingly the two buildings, which adjoined one another, were known as the Old Shed and the New Shed.

In 1908 the two petrol-electric bogie railcars 3170 and 3171 were transferred to Selby to work the Cawood branch and in 1912 a single-road lean-to shed was erected at the rear of the coal stage to house these two vehicles. The drivers of the two petrol-electric cars were not drawn from the normal footplate crews but were men specially trained for the job and they were transferred from Scarborough to Selby with the cars in 1908. When the Cawood branch service was reduced in 1915 one driver, George William Lidguard, was transferred to Hull Dairycoates shed where he took up the post of Mechanical Coaling Plant Attendant from December 4. The other driver, Alfred Julius Kelsey, was transferred to the Hull Dock Engineer's Department as an electrician shopman in the Alfred Street workshops on 7 September 1916. Driver Lidguard actually started his working life with the Hull Dock Company in 1891 and was later transferred to the NER Dock Engineer's

Department as a labourer.

In 1923 the Leyland bus fitted with rail wheels (Bus No 110, later renumbered 130Y in the *Coaching Stock List*) was displaced at York by a new petrol car and the Leyland was transferred to Selby to work to Goole and on the Cawood branch. This vehicle was also stabled in the railcar shed adjacent to the coal stage, until early one dark November morning in 1926, when someone decided to see if there was any petrol in the tank — but he used a paraffin torch lamp with a naked flame to do so! The burning bus was manhandled out of the shed without damaging the building but the efforts of the hurriedly called Selby Volunteer Fire Brigade were of no avail and the vehicle was a total loss.

After the North Eastern Railway had taken over the Cawood, Wistow & Selby Light Railway they disposed of the sole engine owned by the company — 0-6-0ST 'Cawood' — and used Class H2 (later LNER J79) 407 on the branch, as well as Class E 0-6-0T (LNER J71) 296 and 1197, all of which were fitted with Westinghouse brake equipment. With the standardisation of the vacuum brake on the LNER the Westinghouse fitted engines became redundant and in April 1929 vacuum fitted engines 495 and 1157, also Class J71, were transferred to Selby to operate the branch for the last nine months during which it had a passenger service. Class J71, J72 and J77 0-6-0T engines continued to operate the goods service on the branch for many years, although before this too was withdrawn on 2 May 1960 204hp diesel locomotives had taken over.

In 1922/3 Selby shed had five passenger turns, all of which were manned by two sets of men:

1. Selby-Leeds-Bridlington-Selby
2. Selby-Leeds-Wetherby-Leeds-Selby-Leeds-Selby
3. Selby-Bridlington-Selby-Leeds-Church Fenton-Selby
4. Selby-York-Selby-Goole-Selby-Burton Salmon-Selby-Goole-Selby-Goole-Selby
5. Selby-Cawood-Selby-Cawood-Selby (On Mondays two additional return trips to Cawood and one return trip to Cliff Common)

Prior to World War I Selby had an engine outstationed at the Lancashire & Yorkshire shed at Low Moor (Bradford) for working Halifax-Hull trains between Selby and Halifax. There was in 1913

only one set of men at Low Moor and their eleven-hour day was
filled by working the following roster:

	arr.	dep.
Halifax	-	8.43am
Selby	9.57am	10.30am
York	11.02am	11.45am
Selby	12.13pm	4.12pm
Halifax	5.25pm	-

Engine utilised for shunting at Selby between arrival at 12.13pm
and departure at 4.12pm. For this turn a Tennant 2-4-0, a
McDonnell 4-4-0, or a Class F 4-4-0 was usually provided.

From the Allocation table it will be seen that the shed had
between the wars more than twenty mineral engines which were
used for collecting coal from the Castleford, Normanton and
Pontefract area collieries and working it to the marshalling yard at
Gascoigne Wood, in readiness for forwarding to Hull for shipment.
The two T1 4-8-0Ts — later replaced by two Q1 0-8-0Ts — were
used for hump shunting at Gascoigne Wood yard.

With the introduction of 04 2-8-0 engines on the Hull & Barnsley
line coal trains the former Hull & Barnsley 0-8-0s became redundant
and on 2 November 1929 2499 and 2509 were transferred to Selby
for trials. Although the men did not like the Hull & Barnsley 'Tinies'
they received a further six on 18 November, thus allowing six Q6
0-8-0s to be transferred to Dairycoates to free six more 04s for
Springhead. Trouble with the 'Tinies' led to four Q6s being sent to
Selby from Stockton in July 1930, followed by four Q7s, also
from Stockton, in November 1930, thus allowing the eight Q10
HBR engines to be placed in store. As a last fling 2503 was sent
from Hull to Selby on 29 December 1930 in exchange for 2511 so
that improved sanding arrangements could be tested during use at
Selby. A start was made on withdrawing the Hull & Barnsley
engines in May 1931 and they were all withdrawn before the year
was out.

Selby was also the home for a few of the Sentinel steam
railcars and on 9 June 1929 one of these achieved notoriety when
it was in collision with a Leeds-London excursion train after the
railcar had run past signals at danger at Marshgate Junction,
Doncaster. The car was 220 'Waterwitch' and it was working a
rather unusual diagram which operated on Sundays only. This

involved working light to Doncaster and then a passenger train from Doncaster to Staddlethorpe to give a connection into a Leeds-Hull train. The car worked back to Doncaster as a slow passenger train and then returned light to Selby. The same working took place again in the evening but in this case the Staddlethorpe-Doncaster working also gave a connection out of a train from Hull. It was on the morning working from Staddlethorpe to Doncaster that the accident occurred — the car was broken in two at the articulated joint and although the passenger compartment remained more or less intact at the top of an embankment the engine and boiler compartment was thrown down the embankment and damaged beyond repair.

In 1939 Selby had seven passenger turns, each manned by two sets of men who worked as far as Bridlington, Hull, Leeds, Doncaster, Wetherby, Castleford and Pontefract. Three turns were booked for D20 4-4-0 engines and one for a J21 0-6-0. The latter worked the 4.45am light engine to Doncaster and then the 6.0am workmens' train from Doncaster to Brough (for Blackburn Aircraft workpeople), returning as far as Goole with the empty stock and th men travelling back home as passengers to Selby after a four hour wait at Goole. The second set travelled to Goole by the 11.13am ex Selby and after a six hour wait worked the 6.30pm goods back home: their actual footplate working time was 43 min irrespective of the time spent preparing the engine at Goole! On Saturdays in summer there were four turns to Scarborough and at one time Selby used to borrow B16 4-6-0s from York for these jobs but in British Railways' days it was decided to utilise Selby's own engines in pairs. The engines used in the 1950s were D20 and D49 4-4-0, and 4MT 2-6- 0, and these could be seen paired in any combination Without a doubt the most impressive sight was a couple of D20s loping along in fine style on the 11.20am Scarborough-Liverpool or the opposite working.

A mechanical coaling plant was authorised for Selby on 19 February 1931.

Allocations in 1923, 1939 and 1954 were:

	1923	1939	1954
A7 4-6-2T	1	-	-
B16 4-6-0	1	-	1
D17/1 4-4-0	-	2	-

D20 4-4-0	-	-	6
D22 4-4-0	5	3	-
E5 2-4-0	1	-	-
G5 0-4-4T	-	-	2
G6 0-4-4T	2	-	-
398 0-6-0	1	-	-
J21 0-6-0	3	2	-
J24 0-6-0	3	2	-
J25 0-6-0	11	11	3
J26 0-6-0	1	1	-
J27 0-6-0	4	5	8
J39 0-6-0	-	-	3
J71 0-6-0T	2	2	-
J73 0-6-0T	-	-	3
J77 0-6-0T	-	-	3
N8 0-6-2T	3	3	-
N10 0-6-2T	1	-	-
Q1 0-8-0T	-	-	2
Q5 0-8-0	2	4	-
Q6 0-8-0	14	11	12
Q7 0-8-0	-	3	-
T1 4-8-0T	1	2	-
Y1 0-4-0T	-	-	2
Y3 0-4-0T	-	1	1
WD 2-8-0	-	-	1
LM 4MT 2-6-0	-	-	6
BR 4MT	-	-	1
	56	52	54

PART THREE
Additional Sheds

CHAPTER XII

Miscellaneous sheds

Sheds closed since 1900
DARLINGTON (NORTH ROAD)

The Stockton & Darlington Railway — the world's first steam
worked public railway — remained an independent line until 1863,
when it was absorbed by the North Eastern Railway, itself formed
only nine years earlier by the amalgamation of other companies.
Thus the Stockton & Darlington had its own shed in Darlington,
some distance away from Bank Top shed, and whilst the latter
served the lines running north and south, the Stockton &
Darlington shed served the lines running east and west. By far the
greatest number of Stockton & Darlington locomotives were
stationed at Shildon and Darlington was of minor importance until
the new North Road locomotive works were opened in 1863.

On 17 December 1847 a report was called for with regard to an
engine shed at Darlington and in January 1848 John Dixon and
John Graham submitted the following:

'We are of the opinion that the best place for a new engine shed
is on the Darlington branch near Appleton's Corn Warehouse. If
the present shed is still retained there only wants standage for two
more engines but the shed is in an inconvenient situation for
getting coke. We think it would be better to concentrate the engine
sheds and have only one, say for four engines, with convenient
apparatus for storing and filling the coke into the tenders.'

Only five days later it was ordered that 'plans be prepared for a
shed at Darlington for six or eight engines, with proper coke depot,
furnace and sand drying place, with water laid on'. On 3 March 1848

plans for the new shed were submitted, and a week later the estimated cost was submitted, although the actual figure is not quoted in the Minute.

From the report of 21 January 1848 it is obvious that there was already a small shed at Darlington and according to a report of 1854 there was still only accommodation for three engines. Taking these two together it would seem that nothing was done in 1848 in spite of the preparation of the plans mentioned above.

The next move was in January 1855, when Mr Bouch reported that additional engine shed accommodation was urgently needed, and the only proof that a further shed was actually built rests on John Dixon's letter of 1859 which states that there was accommodation at Darlington for twelve engines. However, on 5 October 1860 the board authorised the erection of a new shed ' near the junction of the line leading into the new engine works at Darlington, of a size to hold twelve engines. The present shed is to be allowed to stand until the new one is finished, and then the board will consider how far it may be made available for any other purpose'. In February 1861 it was stated that the new shed would cost £1,800 plus £150 for sand store and drying store.

For some years after its amalgamation with the North Eastern Railway the Stockton & Darlington section continued as before, with the locomotive department nominally in charge of Mr Fletcher at Gateshead, although the former chief, William Bouch, was the man who ran the section until his death in 1876. Thus although the following two sheds were actually authorised after the NER had taken over they have always been regarded as Stockton & Darlington depots.

On 10 February 1864 it was noted that passenger engines were to be stationed at Darlington shed and that new lines and a turntable would be required. By 1867 the position was again desperate 'as 18 engines are unprovided for and another 12 are on order'. A roundhouse was authorised at a cost of £4,756 17s 0d and this was opened in 1868, when authority for excess expenditure of £343 3s 0d had to be obtained. Only seven years later another roundhouse was suggested and when plans were submitted in August 1875 the estimated cost was £8,105. This shed was opened in 1877.

Both these roundhouses were situated in the yard of North Road locomotive works and until 4 April 1903 they were used by

Running Department engines. In 1887, with the opening of the new line from Oak Tree Junction to enable trains to and from the Stockton & Darlington line to Middlesbrough and Saltburn to use the south end of Bank Top station a number of the engines at North Road were transferred to Bank Top, and from 4 April 1903 the two circular sheds ceased to be used for working engines and housed only engines for and after overhaul at the works. Both sheds were demolished about 1933 when improvements were made to the layout of the Works Yard.

On the opening of the second roundhouse in 1877 the straight shed authorised in 1861 was converted to the engine paint shop and it remained in use for this purpose until the new paint shop at Stooperdale was opened in 1911. It subsequently became the electric power house, and in British Railway's days the diesel test house. On 17 August 1908 the building was badly damaged at the west end when Class U 0-6-2T 1138, hauling two Class P3 0-6-0 engines, collided with Class E1 0-6-0T and knocked the latter broadside into the paint shop. A corner of the building was demolished and the new brickwork can be seen to this day.

There is a plan and an illustration of the two roundhouses in the *Railway Magazine* for August 1903, and also a photograph of the interior of the paint shop referred to above.

The NER had certain locomotives which were allocated to service stock for shunting duties at their various works and those allocated to North Road consisted of Class E 0-6-0T 263 and two Class H 0-4-0Ts 129 and 898. The same arrangement persisted under the LNER until August 1926 and 129 was actually lettered on the tank side LNER DARLINGTON WORKS. In 1926 the engines were transferred to running stock but remained employed on the same duties. No 898 was the first of the class to be withdrawn from service in April 1929 but it had been replaced by one of the LNER-built members of the class 982 from Heaton – in January 1929. As the locomotives going through the works got larger and heavier a more powerful engine was needed to haul 'dead' engines up the gradient out of the yard and by 1939 the works pilots were all J71 0-6-0Ts-168,492,1103 and 1142. Later J72, J77 and J94 tanks were used, and the final pilot was a 204hp diesel locomotive.

Electric locomotive No 13, built in 1922 for the proposed main line electrification between York and Newcastle, was also allocated to North Road and except for an occasional run over the Newport-Shildon line in its early days it spent its time reclining in the Stooperdale paint shop. In 1935 it was joined by the redundant Shildon electric locomotives Nos 3-12 inclusive. Also allocated to North Road was the counter-pressure locomotive 761, used for testing new and rebuilt locomotives in conjunction with the dynamometer car. With the advent of the Testing Plant at Rugby the locomotive was based there but it was broken up at Crewe in 1951, under its new number 1699.

LEYBURN

This shed also appears to date from the opening of the line in 1856, as the only official reference located is to the erection of two cottages for the engine men in 1866. It was closed as a wartime measure on 1 November 1915 and not reopened until 17 February 1939, when the last train up the valley terminated at Leyburn instead of Garsdale as hitherto. The Garsdale engine G5 0-4-4T 435 was transferred to Leyburn on 17 June 1939.

After the war the branch was in financial trouble for some years until British Railways decided to close the line from 26 April 1954. At that time Leyburn still housed a G5 for the branch services (67345) and a Sentinel locomotive for local shunting (68159) both of which were transferred away on 2 May 1954.

There were two sets of men at Leyburn and in 1939 the first set commenced at 6.17am in readiness for working the 7.17am to Northallerton. After shunting at Northallerton they worked the 10.48am to Garsdale, returning as far as Leyburn where they were relieved by the late shift men at 2.14pm. The second set continued with the engine and train to Northallerton, where they took loco duties and spent the remainder of the time shunting before returning to Leyburn on the 8.14pm from Northallerton. This was extended to Hawes and back to Leyburn on Saturdays.

Under this roster the Leyburn men kept their own engine all day, but the 1949 engine diagrams show that a Northallerton engine spent alternate nights at Leyburn, with the Leyburn engine spending alternate nights at Northallerton. Leyburn men worked the 7.52am to Northallerton and then the 9.45 am to Garsdale. They returned from Garsdale at 12.55 pm and at Leeming Bar changed over with

Northallerton men working the 2.3 pm Northallerton to Garsdale. On arriving at Leyburn the first set were relieved by the late turn men who then worked the Northallerton engines on the Hawes, the 4.0 pm Hawes — Northallerton and the 9.15 pm Northallerton to Leyburn.

MARKET WEIGHTON

This shed was another that was opened with the branch it served, namely that from York on 4 October 1847. The branch from Selby was opened on 1 August 1848 and Market Weighton remained a terminus for these two lines until 1 May 1865, when the long awaited extension to Beverley was opened. On 18 April 1890 the final link was inserted,to Driffield, by the Scarborough, Bridlington & West Riding Junction Railway and this was worked by the North Eastern from the outset.

Unfortunately no records have survived of the Market Weighton engine's working prior to the opening of this final section, but undoubtedly in the early days the engine worked between Market Weighton and York, if not also to Selby. By 1908 the engine was employed on the following duty:

	arr	dep
Market Weighton	-	7.54 am
Driffield	8.25 am	9.48 am
Selby	11.5 am	12.53 pm MX
Market Weighton	1.38 pm	-
Selby	-	2.33 pm MO
Market Weighton	3.18 pm	-

At most other NER sheds where there was only one engine it was the practice to have two sets of men alternating on early and late shifts, but at Market Weighton there was only one set of men, who worked 7.0 am to 5.0 pm, together with the usual one cleaner for lighting-up and relief duties.

The shed, which was situated adjacent to the station, had a 50ft turntable. It was closed as a wartime measure on 1 March 1917, never to re-open.

NEW BRIDGE STREET

This two road shed served the Blyth & Tyne passenger services out of New Bridge Street station at Newcastle and at the time of closure in 1902 there were ten engines and thirty-six men stationed there. Due to the alterations brought about by the construction of the connecting line between New Bridge Street and Manors the shed was replaced by a new shed at South Gosforth and the building demolished. Unfortunately no records of the engines stationed at New Bridge Street in its latter days have survived but in Blyth & Tyne days it is known that some of the company's 2-4-0 engines were shedded there.

PORT CLARENCE

On 7 April 1881 it was suggested that a new shed for nine engines should be provided at Port Clarence and it was recommended that a portion of the shed then standing at Clarence Junction, Stockton, should be removed and erected at Port Clarence to form the shed, the estimated cost being £300. Very little more is known about this shed although it must have been in operation by early 1882 as a Driver J. Worthy was transferred to Port Clarence on 17 February 1882. By 1898 seven engines were stationed at Port Clarence and presumably the shed catered for freight and mineral traffic on the north bank of the River Tees, although it seems very odd that it was not closed when Haverton Hill opened in 1898. Unfortunately the date when the shed closed has not yet been located, the latest reference to it being in November 1914 when Class 476 0-6-0ST 479 was withdrawn, and in January 1915, when Class 398 0-6-0 886 was withdrawn, both from Port Clarence.

From inspection on the site it looks as if the shed building may have been a segment of a roundhouse rather similar to that at Wear Valley Junction.

SEAHAM

This small two-road shed was built by the Londonderry Railway and taken over with the locomotive stock and the line to Sunderland in 1900. About this time there were 7 engines and 27 men at Seaham shed and the duties worked were solely to Sunderland. Later some of the trains were extended northwards to South Shields and, in fact, Londonderry engines had previously worked through to South Shields on excursions, hauling their own stock.

Of the 13 engines taken over from the Londonderry Railway 10 were renumbered into the North Eastern duplicate list, indicating a short expectation of life, but the 3 engines renumbered into capital stock remained in service until 1906: these were 0-6-0 1335, 2-4-0T 1113 and 0-4-4T 1712. It is not known what type of engine the North Eastern used to replace the Londonderry engines but they would probably be BTP 0-4-4Ts or Class A 2-4-2Ts for the local passenger services and Class 398 for the goods and mineral services.

No doubt because of its proximity to Sunderland it was decided to close the shed from 1 October 1913. The shed stood until the 1960s, latterly in use as a banana warehouse.

SOUTH GOSFORTH

Since the original series on North Eastern Sheds was compiled for the Stephenson Locomotive Society *Journal* further information has come to light regarding the shed at South Gosforth. This was not built for stabling the Ponteland branch engine, as I had been told, but it actually replaced the shed at New Bridge Street and housed the engines working the former Blyth & Tyne line services.

The shed at New Bridge Street was demolished in connection with the extension southwards of the Blyth & Tyne line to join the main line at Manors and drawings have been located of a 'Proposed shed at South Gosforth', dated 18 September 1901. Presumably these were the drawings produced to the Locomotive Committee on 31 October 1901, when a shed to cost £480 was approved. The relevant Minute confirms that the building was to replace the shed at New Bridge Street 'which is to be pulled down for the construction of the Manors-New Bridge Street railway'. In fact the locomotive foreman at New Bridge Street later moved to South Gosforth in the same capacity.

From NER footplate staff records it is obvious that New Bridge Street closed 19 December 1902 as certain drivers and firemen were transferred to South Gosforth from that date. It is odd that accommodation for the engines and men could not be found at nearby Heaton shed, especially in view of the impending third rail electrification, which made some of the engines redundant after a short time. Again from staff records it appears as if South Gosforth shed closed on 1 August 1904, when the men were transferred to Heaton.

As the drawings show a corrugated iron structure perhaps it was intended that the shed should be only a temporary measure, but a life of less than two years is very short for a North Eastern shed! The building was 150ft long by 31ft wide, which would be sufficient to accommodate eight BTPs or Class 0 0-4-4Ts, or six 2-4-0 tender engines, such as Class 901 or 1440, on the Newbiggin and Morpeth services.

SPROUSTON

This was the only true North Eastern Railway shed in Scotland although for many years the company rented a building at Edinburgh from the North British Railway. Actually the service on this Tweed-side branch ran as far as Kelso but to have the engine and coaches stabled on their own property the North Eastern decided to house them at Sprouston.

The first shed was erected in 1863 at a cost of £50: it was a second-hand wooden structure from the Newcastle & Carlisle Railway. On 14 October 1881 it was blown down in a gale and a single-road brick building was erected in 1882 to replace it.

The shed was apparently closed on 14 July 1916 as a wartime economy measure and from that date the first train from Kelso to Berwick was altered to start from Coldstream, with the engine and stock running out empty from Tweedmouth. At night, what had been the last train from Tweedmouth to Kelso was diverted on to the Wooler line and terminated at Alnwick. However, the NER staff records quote two sets of men as being transferred to Sprouston on 14 July 1916 but it is considered that this must have been a clerical error and that the men were actually being transferred away from Sprouston.

The building stood until the 1960s and during World War II housed the GWR 'City of Truro' from York Railway Museum.

TEBAY

A reference dated 2 November 1860 states that the South Durham & Lancashire Union Railway was providing a shed for two engines at Tebay, presumably included in the contract for the construction of the line and stations. However, the company was taken over by the Stockton & Darlington Railway in 1862 and on 17 January 1866 a shed for six engines was authorised at a cost of £1,250. Three months later the estimated cost was increased to £1,972 'due to the enlargement of the project'. It is possible that the shed was closed in the early 1870s, judging by a Minute of 15 October 1875 which states 'eight engines are to be stationed at Tebay (all that can be accommodated in the present engine shed) and sixteen houses will be needed for drivers, firemen and guards. The LNWR to be approached to give up some of the joint houses'. It is assumed that this Minute refers to the re-opening of the shed.

Mr J.W. Armstrong, whose family had a long connection with the shed, states that it was re-opened in 1878 with 0-6-0s 1032, 1177/ 80/6, 1212/22/4/78. These were later replaced by eight Class B compound 0-6-2Ts, and eventually − for a matter of months − by four Class T1 0-8-0s.

The forthcoming closure of the shed was announced to the staff in October 1902, and on the 23rd a petition against the proposed closure was submitted to the directors of the NER but this proved to be unavailing and on 31 October 1902 the shed closed for good. The building remained standing for many years, gradually falling into decay, until only the walls remained, but even these have now been removed. However, the site of the shed is still plainly visible (or was, when last visited). One of the shed pits was not filled in so that until the end of the line the engines working the Blackpool trains could receive attention over the pit before taking up their return working.

Sheds mainly closed before 1900 (information incomplete)
BATTERSBY

This three-road shed was demolished in December 1965 after seventy years of disuse as a locomotive depot. The first reference to the shed is one dated 17 December 1874, when it was proposed that a shed for eight engines, together with thirty cottages, should be built at Ingleby. At the meeting of the Locomotive & Stores Committee on 8 April 1875 tenders were requested and at the next meeting on 6 May a tender of £2,500 1s 4d was accepted. No exact date of opening has been located but a Minute of 27 September 1877 refers to 'the new shed recently opened at Ingleby' and about the same time there is a reference to the shed costing £350 1s 3d more than the contract price.

The shed was closed after a few years, no doubt because of a decline in the iron ore traffic, as the main duties of the engines allocated to the shed were to haul the train-loads of ore descending the famous Ingleby Incline from the ironstone mines and drifts at East and West Rosedale. However, the shed re-opened on 1 January 1889 but finally closed on 30 November 1895, when there were four engines stationed there.

After that the shed was used for a variety of purposes: in 1906 eight condemned engines were stored in the building awaiting sale or scrapping, and in 1917 it accommodated six dining saloons. These comprised ECJ 190 and 191, First Class diners built at Doncaster in 1914; ECJ 192 and 193, Third Class diners also built at Doncaster in 1914; and Great Northern & North Eastern Joint diners 26 and 28, built at Doncaster in 1907. The GN/NE Joint vehicles were 12-wheelers and the others we 8-wheelers. In the 1920s the building was used as a miniature rifle range by the staff in the district, and in the 1930s it carried a large notice TO LET. In World War II it was used as a store but then remained empty for many years before being demolished in 1965.

BECK HOLE

A photograph exists of the ruins of an engine shed at the foot of the famous Goathland Incline. This was presumably provided in 1847, when locomotives started working between the foot of the Incline and Whitby, and it must have fallen into disuse when the Incline was replaced by the Deviation line in 1865, thus allowing locomotives to work throughout between Malton and Whitby.

BEDALE

An engine shed was authorised in July 1852, when Bedale was the terminus of the branch from Northallerton. No further details are known.

BOROUGHBRIDGE

No reference to the building of this shed has been located and it would seem that it was included in the Contract for the construction of the line and buildings when the branch was built in 1847, especially as there was no shed at the junction with the main line at Pillmoor (sic). The branch was extended in 1875 to join the York-Harrogate line at Knaresborough, but for another eleven years the first and last trains on the branch commenced and terminated at

Boroughbridge. From 1 July 1886, however, the service was altered so that all trains were worked by Starbeck shed and it seems fairly safe to assume that Boroughbridge shed was closed from that date. An undated diagram in York Museum shows the building converted into a goods shed and in this form it remained, adjacent to the old passenger station, until the line closed in October 1964.

BROTTON

The Appendix to the Working Timetable dated 1 January 1906 refers to a 45ft turntable 'outside the engine shed at Brotton', but no definite information on this shed has been located. Certainly Class L 0-6-0T 544 was allocated to Brotton in 1915 for hauling a naval gun mounted on a 45 ton trolley wagon but this is believed to have been stabled in the open.

BRUSSELTON BANK FOOT (Shildon)

The only justification for including this shed is a Minute of 1 December 1869 authorising 'the wooden engine shed at Slapewath to be removed to Brusselton Bank Foot'. Being a second-hand wooden erection it has no doubt long since disappeared.

CARR HOUSE (Consett)

In 1854 there was one engine stationed at Carr House, with no shed. Early in 1855 Mr Bouch reported that accommodation for locomotives was urgently needed at Carr House which was, of course, at the most northerly point of the Stockton & Darlington Railway. This portion of the line had originally been part of the Stanhope & Tyne Railroad and in 1855 Hownes Gill had not been bridged: consequently traffic was still being worked down one side of the ravine and up the other.

On 1 October 1856 it was reported that an engine shed had not yet been built at Carr House because 'its erection was postponed until the coal was worked underneath'. Some six weeks later the go-ahead was given but then it was decided not to build a new shed but to convert the boiler house instead. Unfortunately no more is known of the project.

CASTLE EDEN

The Hartlepool Dock & Railway Co discussed building a shed here at a meeting held on 21 December 1855, but it was decided to proceed only with some sidings and a reservoir. Six months later it was recommended that the engine shed should be commenced at once and on 20 June 1856 a tender of £548 9s 6d was accepted.

Footplate staff records quote various drivers and firemen as being stationed at Castle Eden shed but final reference located is dated 7 March 1873 when the shed was reported as being 'out of repair: referred to Mr Prosser for a report'. At the next monthly meeting it was reported that the shed was being repaired but how long it remained in use is not known.

CASTLETON

The Working Timetable for 1865 (prior to the opening of the Castleton-Grosmont section) shows the first train on the North Yorkshire & Cleveland Branch as commencing at Castleton and the last train terminating there. No doubt a small shed was provided.

CLIFTON

A small shed was erected here by the Eden Valley Railway for the opening of the line in 1862. Presumably it became redundant when the trains were extended to Penrith over the new link to join with the LNWR main line at Eden Valley Junction, from 1 August 1863.

COCKERMOUTH

In 1875 the North Eastern Railway wrote to the Cockermouth, Keswick & Penrith company regarding the stabling of two NER engines at Cockermouth, but the outcome is unknown. Certainly a shed was built at Cockermouth and it is believed to have been used by North Eastern locomotives until about 1900. The building is still standing and was latterly used as the goods shed, although it is now privately occupied.

COLD ROWLEY

When the Stockton & Darlington Railway took over the southern portion of the Stanhope & Tyne Railroad in 1845 Mr Bouch had already prepared a report on the line; and in it he detailed the various winding engines and suggested which sections could be converted to locomotive haulage. One of these sections terminated at Hownes

Gill and an engine shed at nearby Cold Rowley was approved on 20 August 1845; only two weeks later it was reported that 'the laying of the track into the new Engine House at Cold Rowley Flats is in progress'. Because of the speed of construction this could have been a wooden shed, or perhaps an existing building converted. It appears to have been replaced in 1854, when a shed was authorised 'at or near Hownes Gill which, in future, may be appropriated as a labourer's cottage'. This shed no doubt disappeare when Hownes Gill viaduct was opened on 1 July 1858 and Waskerle engines could work through to Consett and Carr House.

CRIMPLE JUNCTION

An undated NER drawing shows a small single road shed in the V of the junction but no details are known.

DURHAM (Gilesgate)

See DURHAM in main section.

EPPLEBY

The position regarding this shed is confused to say the least. It was situated on the Forcett Railway (opened in October 1866) which was worked by the North Eastern from the outset, but the shed was used (latterly at least) by the locomotives owned by the Forcett Quarry Co. As the Forcett Railway came into LNER ownership under the Railways Act of 1921 the engines had to use LNER (later British Railways) lines to reach their work at the quarries. Presumably the shed was taken over by the LNER and rented or sold to the quarry company, unless it was excluded from the take-over in the first place. Research in the British Railways Archives at York has failed to provide the answer.

Special instructions were in force to ensure that an NER, LNER or BR freight train approaching Eppleby from Forcett Junction did not come into collision with a quarry company's engine proceeding to or from the shed.

The shed was a substantial stone building but a brick extension had been added at the western end. It accommodated a single track

FROSTERLEY

The line to Frosterley was opened in August 1847 but apparently the engine shed was not provided at that date as a report by John Dixon and John Graham, dated 21 January 1848, records that 'the passenger shed will serve for engine accommodation through the winter'. A wooden shed must have been erected shortly afterwards because by January 1854 plans were prepared 'for a substitute for the present wooden engine shed at Frosterley'. There is also a reference to the proposed shed providing shelter for 'turnpike road coaches as well as railway coaches detained during the night'. A year later, on 2 January 1855, Mr Bouch was still pressing for a new shed at Frosterley and presumably this was eventually authorised. However, no further reference has been found and it could have been the wooden shed of about 1850 which on 29 November 1865 was authorised to be moved to the new terminus at Stanhope, which had been reached by the railway three years earlier.

HALTWHISTLE

On 28 June 1872 it is recorded that 'plans be prepared for a shed for one engine at Haltwhistle in lieu of the old shed at Haydon Bridge.' In the following month plans were submitted and on 6 September a tender for £650 3s 11d was accepted. On 28 January 1875 it was reported that work on the shed had ceased because the contractor was in financial difficulties. As there was little work remaining to be done the NER decided to complete the job themselves. There is now no trace of the shed and it is not known when it was closed.

HAYDON BRIDGE

From the above item on Haltwhistle shed it will be seen that at one time there was a shed at Haydon Bridge. No other reference to this shed has been found but the Working Timetable for 1870 shows a morning train commencing and an evening train terminating at Haydon Bridge.

HULL (Drypool)

The only known reference is dated 8 June 1866 and this is a Minute stating 'the old engine shed at Drypool to be taken down and re-erected as a goods warehouse at Lockington at a cost of £79'. (See also HULL [Victoria]).

HULL (Paragon)

On 20 January 1848 a shed adjoining the new station then in course of construction was authorised and a tender of £2,100 was accepted. A new shed was authorised in 1865, when a tender of £594 16s 7d was accepted, and in January 1867 extra expenditure of £826 6s 0d was authorised 'due to the building having been considerably enlarged, and the erection of a chimney'. On 13 August 1874 a tender of £11,092 11s 8d was accepted for a further shed to hold twenty engines and this was completed at the end of 1876.

In 1897 the general manager reported that the site would be required for extensions to Paragon Station and that a new shed would have to be built at Botanic Gardens. As soon as the latter was completed the North Eastern advertised for tenders for the demolition of the shed at Paragon station and on 2 May 1901 accepted one at a figure of £384 8s 6d. The shed was on the north side of the station.

HULL (Victoria)

The Hull & Holderness Railway used the Victoria Station of the North Eastern and in February 1858 they decided to erect a shed for their new engine. A tender of £140 was accepted in May but nothing more is known of this building. However, it seems almost certain that the shed referred to at Drypool was one and the same building, for in 1862 the Hull & Holderness was taken over by the North Eastern and in 1864 the Withernsea trains were extended into Paragon station. Thus the building would become redundant and it seems highly probable that this is the shed re-erected at Lockington.

KNARESBOROUGH

This shed undoubtedly originated with the East & West Yorkshire Junction Railway but the first known NER reference is dated June 1856 and concerns the insufficiency of accommodation. Authority was then given for the shed to be doubled in size; it was situated at what later became known as Goods Junction, where the Boroughbridge branch eventually diverged from the York line.

Nothing further transpired until October 1874, when Mr Fletcher reported that an engine shed would be required at Knaresborough to accommodate the engines working the Knaresborough-Pilmoor line, of which the section between Knaresborough and Boroughbridge was approaching completion. A shed for two engines was authorised together with a new turntable, and in January 1875 expenditure of £895 and £410 respectively was granted. However, on 25 January 1875 it was decided to cancel the whole scheme and to station the engines at Starbeck, where two additional cottages were to be built.

LEEDS (Holbeck)

This, the site of the headquarters of the Leeds Northern Railway locomotive department, was retained for locomotive purposes until 1904, when it was superseded by the new shed at Neville Hill on the eastern outskirts of the city. At the time of closure there were two roundhouses and a semi-circular shed. One of these sheds had been built in 1864 at a cost of £5,888, whilst another dated from 1873. This had been authorised in November 1871 at a cost of £8,500 and a tender was accepted on 9 February at £8,694: this was probably the roundhouse nearest to Central station, with inverted-V roofs over the stalls. One side of the building was adjacent to the Leeds & Liverpool Canal and the North Eastern agreed to pay £1 per annum for seventeen windows and three doors which overlooked and opened upon the Canal Company's property. If the 1864 shed was the circular shed abutting on to the main road to Bradford, then the half-roundhouse cannot be accounted for, although it seems that this was actually used by the works rather than by engines in daily use.

The shed adjacent to the main road is divided into two parts: a smaller section fronting the main road is used as a garage and filling station, whilst the larger part of the building (together with the other roundhouse some distance away) is occupied by Thos. Marshall & Sons Ltd, manufacturers of dustbins and other galvanised articles. In March 1909, 586 sq yd of the building were let to the West Riding Territorial Force Association at £80 a year for use as a drill hall.

LEEDS (Hunslet)

York & North Midland Railway trains at first used the Hunslet Lane terminus of the North Midland Railway and a reference dated 19 December 1849 mentiones three Y & NM engines at the 'Engine House in Hunslet Lane'. Nothing further is known of this shed although Y & NM trains continued to use the North Midland route to Leeds Wellington station until 1869, when the Church Fenton-Micklefield cut-off was opened and they moved across to the adjacent New station.

LEEDS (Marsh Lane)

The Leeds & Selby Railway had a locomotive shed here and it seems likely that a shed was in use until replaced by the shed at New Station in 1871, or probabaly later. It is suggested that the buildings on the south side of the line at the west end of Marsh Lane (or Richmond Hill) tunnel have some connections with this shed but this has not been confirmed.

LEEDS (New Station)

This shed was built in connection with the extension of the line from Marsh Lane to the New Station. The station was constructed jointly with the London & North Western Railway and it was expected that the LNWR would share the expense of the shed but on 14 January 1870 they advised the North Eastern that they did not wish to join in. Consequently the NER decided to go ahead on their own, a tender of £5, 892 was accepted, and the shed was opened in 1871.

The building was disused by 1908, when it was decided to install a 60ft turntable from Cowans Sheldon in the yard adjacent to the shed, and it is believed that the building was demolished a few years later. However, the yard continued in use for locomotive purposes until the 1950s.

LEEMING BAR

The *Working Timetable* for 1865 shows an 'Empty Engine' running from Leeming Bar to Bedale each morning in time to work the first train to Northallerton, and a similar return working each evening after the arrival at Bedale of the last train from Northallerton. From this it is assumed that there was a shed at Leeming Bar and that the shed authorised for Bedale in July 1852 was not proceeded with.

LOW FELL

In 1902 the North Eastern was actively considering building a large engine shed at Low Fell 'in lieu of the existing shed at Gateshead, which is too small and the accommodation at which will be further diminished by the construction of the new bridge over the Tyne'. At that time Gateshead possessed 117 engines with accommodation under cover for 75, and it was estimated that the cost of light engine running between Low Fell and Newcastle Central station would be £2,485 3s 10d a year. For some reason not yet discovered the whole scheme was dropped and Gateshead shed retained.

MONKWEARMOUTH

It is almost certain that there was a shed on the north bank of the River Wear before the line was extended across the river in 1879. The only twentieth century reference is to a turntable 'outside the engine shed at Monkwearmouth Goods'.

NEWCASTLE (Central)

A plan of Newcastle Central Station in Vol VIII of the *Railway Magazine* (p14) shows two sheds built on the outer wall on the south side of the station. An 1859 plan in Vol LXXX of the same publication (p162) shows one building still in existence (although not specified as an engine shed), and a new shed is shown at the south-western end of the station, above Forth Street. The latter building survived long enough to appear in the back-ground of certain locomotive photographs taken in the 1880s and it presumably disappeared in the alterations and extensions which took place in the early 1890s. It had only two roads.

NEWCASTLE (Forth)

Three separate shed buildings are shown on a plan of Newcastle dated 1870. They were situated about half a mile to the west of Central station and were, no doubt, used by locomotives working between Newcastle and Carlisle. The only official reference located is dated 17 May 1872 and refers to the submission of tenders for the purchase and removal of the old engine stable at Forth Banks. A tender of £106 was accepted.

NORMANBY JETTY

Nothing is known of this shed except for a decision to remove the old engine shed and to adapt the site for extension to the warrant store. Normanby Jetty was, of course, the riverside terminus of the Cleveland Railway, a mineral line carrying iron ore from the Cleveland Hills to the south bank of the River Tees so that it could be shipped across the river to the ironworks on the north bank. The line was opened in 1861 and taken over by the North Eastern in 1865.

PILMOOR

A shed was to have been constructed at Pillmoor (sic) in 1853 in conjunction with the branch to Malton but the idea was not proceeded with.

REDCAR

The Stockton & Darlington Railway extended its line beyond Middlesbrough to Redcar on 4 June 1846 and a shed at Redcar was authorised in August 1847 at a cost of £404 19s 0d. In September 1863 it was decided to remove the shed to Saltburn, the new terminus of the line, but it is not clear if this was actually carried out or if a new shed was built at Saltburn.

RIPON

In December 1863 a plan and estimate for a shed at Ripon were prepared and in January 1864 it was reported that a shed could be built for £300. Approval was given and the job was put out to tender but later the same month Mr Fletcher reported that as a turntable costing £600 would be required it would raise the cost of the project to the £1,000 mark and consequently the scheme was abandoned.

SELBY

There was a small single road shed adjacent to the junction of the Cawood, Wistow & Selby Light Railway with the North Eastern. This was used for a short time by the Light Railway Company's engine 'Cawood' but this was taken over by the North Eastern in 1900 and disposed of in June 1901. From this time the North Eastern worked the Light Railway with their own locomotives from Selby shed and the former Light Railway shed became redundant. It was used for a number of purposes, including a locomotive-mens'

Mutual Improvement classroom, until demolished at the end of 1963.

SHINCLIFFE

No official reference has been found to an engine shed located at Shincliffe - the Durham terminus of the Durham & Sunderland Railway. Until about 1860 the line was rope worked by haulage engines but after the introduction of locomotives it is possible to see from the Working Timetable that an engine must have been stationed at the Shincliffe end as the first train on the branch was the 7.40 am from Shincliffe, and the last was the 6.30 pm from Sunderland (Hendon).

No date of closure is known but it could not have been later than 1893 when the terminus was changed from Shincliffe to Durham Elvet.

SLAPEWATH

The only reference is to the removal of a wooden engine shed from Slapewath to Brusselton Bank Foot in 1870, authorised at a cost of £200. Slapewath was in the centre of the Cleveland iron-stone mining area and a number of branches radiated to various mines at this point.

SPENNYMOOR

In 1870 a number of engines stood overnight in the open at Spennymoor and although a shed was authorised it was later decided to build it at Byers Green. There is in existence an old photograph of c 1865 which shows an engine and one coach emerging from a shed at Spennymoor station. However, it is not clear whether this was an engine shed, a carriage shed, or both, probably provided to house the rolling stock used on the service to Ferryhill.

STELLA GILL

An engine shed and eight cottages were authorised in 1857 and on 23 October the Minutes record the conditional acceptance of a tender 'if the firm submitting the highest tender (£1,060) would reduce the amount to that of the lowest tender (£964 18s 1d)'. Why the firm submitting the highest tender should receive preference is not recorded, and neither is the firm's reply.

In 1872 a house for the locomotive foreman was built for £303 15s 3d, but apart from its appearance on maps of c 1895 nothing more is known of the shed. Presumably its usefulness declined considerably when the locomotive line between South Pelaw Junction and Annfield Plain was opened since previously all trains west of Stella Gill had been rope worked via the Stanhope & Tyne Inclines.

SUNDERLAND (Hendon)

This shed, still standing at the junction of the Durham & Sunderland and Newcastle & Darlington Junction lines at Hendon, is one of the most obscure North Eastern sheds. Nothing at all has been discovered of its history. The only item gleaned from NER records is the fact that new lighting was authorised in September 1891.

It seems probable that it must have been built to house the engines working the Sunderland (Fawcett Street) to Durham passenger services, and the goods traffic to and from the docks, but this is only conjecture and awaits confirmation.

THIRSK TOWN

Little is known about the shed at Thirsk Town of the Leeds & Thirsk Railway. James Gow was appointed locomotive superintendent on 29 February 1847 at a salary of £250 per annum and on 29 August 1847 a temporary shed was authorised, followed on 21 February 1848 by the engineer's report that a shed to hold four engines had been completed. A quantity of machinery for repairing locomotives was delivered to Thirsk about this time but this was later moved to Leeds, presumably when the repair shops at Holbeck were completed.

Passenger services from Thirsk Town disappeared from the public timetable after December 1855 but a single passenger train appears in the working timetable from 1 March 1866, leaving Thirsk Town at 6.30am and forming the 7.0am to Leeds. The last down passenger train terminated at Thirsk Junction at 9.25pm and thus it is impossible to tell whether the engine was stationed at Thirsk Town or Thirsk Junction.

There is in existence a photograph of 2-4-0 312, which is reputed to have been taken at Thirsk Town. This appears to have been taken in the 1880s and, of course, the station remained open for goods traffic until 3 October 1966.

CHAPTER XIII

Sheds taken over by NER

Hull & Barnsley Railway Sheds
SPRINGHEAD

The Hull & Barnsley Railway handed over to the North Eastern Railway on 1 April 1922 181 locomotives, but before the LNER was formed on 1 January 1923 43 of these had been condemned. Thus an urgent injection of NER locomotives was necessary to keep the Hull & Barnsley operating and on 6 December 1923, the date of the earliest known allocation list,there were 49 former North Eastern locomotives at work on the Hull & Barnsley section, of which 26 were at Springhead shed. They were mainly freight and shunting engines but did include two 4-4-0s and one 2-4-2T for passenger workings.

At that date Springhead's allocation consisted of 122 engines and there were 96 former Hull & Barnsley engines stationed there. As the HBR services were modified under LNER management the North Eastern locomotives were gradually removed and the last of eleven Q6s departed on 24 May 1927; and the last three N9s on 31 May 1927; the last Q5 on 4 June 1927; and the last J27 on 28 July 1928. For a year Springhead had to rely on Hull & Barnsley types but on 27 September 1929 a new era commenced with the introduction of 04 2-8-0 6581 and 6613 for trials on the Hull & Barnsley section, in an attempt to cut out the double heading of mineral trains necessary with the native 0-6-0s. This idea was successful and within a year Springhead had nineteen 04 engines.

The Hull & Barnsley Class B(J23) 0-6-0s had been steadily decreasing in numbers because of withdrawals and transfers as use was found for these engines off their native section after six had been transferred to York on 12 March 1927. Eventually they were scattered all over the North Eastern Area, at sheds such as Scarborough,Whitby,Malton,Shildon,Darlington,York,Middleton-in-Teesdale, Pickering, West Hartlepool, Heaton, Middlesbrough and Normanton. This distribution was accelerated by the introduction of the 04 engines, so that by 31 December 1932 the number of J23 0-6-0s at Springhead was down to 8 compared with the 34 of 1923.

Also displaced were the Class A(Q10) 0-8-0s and in October and November 1929 examples of the class were sent to Dairycoates, Selby,Borough Gardens and Tyne Dock for trials. Eventually only two were left at Springhead (2498 and 2502): 2500/1/3/10/2 were at Dairycoates and 2499,2504-9/11 at Selby. The latter transfer displaced six Q6 0-8-0s from Selby to Dairycoates, allowing a further six 04 2-8-0s to move from Dairycoates to Springhead.

By January 1939 there were only ten former Hull & Barnsley engines left at Springhead, all N12 0-6-2Ts; which together with two J21 0-6-0s and fifteen 04s completed the allocation of 27 locomotives. Early in 1940 a start was made in transferring the 04s to Darlington, Heaton and West Hartlepool to work extra coal traffic to the south occasioned by the war and they were replaced at Springhead by Q6 0-8-0s from Dairycoates and West Hartlepool. However, under the reallocation scheme of March 1943 Springhead lost its 0-8-0s and received in their place ten former North Eastern Atlantics – 295,649/99,702/3/5/42,1753/76/94, together with J24 0-6-0 1892, J25 0-6-0 1723,1976,2056 and 2139, N8 0-6-2T 267, 345, 445 and 1104, and N11 0-6-2T 2481/2 (from Cudworth).

In March 1944 Austerity 2-8-0s arrived at Springhead before being sent overseas and the last departed in Feburary 1945. As a replacement 01 and 04 2-8-0s were transferred back from West Hartlepool.

After the war some of the WD Austerity engines returned and, in fact, they were mainstay of the traffic until the shed closed. Other classes which appeared in post war years were A7 4-6-2Ts, J73 0-6-0Ts and 350hp diesel-electric shunters.

The shed was closed to steam on 15 December 1958, but the remaining steam engines were transferred away on 30 November 1958. They were: J73 0-6-0T 68360/1; BR 3MT 2-6-0 77000/10;

WD Austerity 2-8-0 90011,90233,90352/78,90427/82,90503/11/
86,90623/77/88. The shed continued in use for diesel locomotive
and railcar maintenance until July 1961.

During the 1939-45 war one of the GWR Dean 0-6-0s sold to
the War Department spent some time at Springhead, and attention
was also given to American 2-8-0s and 0-6-Ts.

The last Hull & Barnsley engine stationed at Springhead appears
to have been N13 69119, which was transferred to Neville Hill in
September 1953. This engine, together with 69117, was withdrawn
on 5 July 1955 and they were outlived by only one other Hull &
Barnsley engine, namely 69114 withdrawn on 22 October 1956.

The allocation over the years was as follows:

	1923	1932	1939	1950
A7 4-6-2T	-	-	-	4
D22 4-4-0	2	-	-	-
D24 4-4-0	5	-	-	-
F8 2-4-2T	1	-	-	-
J21 0-6-0	-	-	2	-
J23 0-6-0	34	12	-	-
J25 0-6-0	-	-	-	3
J27 0-6-0	3	-	-	-
J28 0-6-0	19	15	-	-
J75 0-6-2T	10	6	-	-
N8 0-6-2T	1	-	-	-
N9 0-6-2T	4	-	-	-
N11 0-6-2T	4	-	-	-
N12 0-6-2T	1	2	-	-
N13 0-6-2T	8	9	10	4
01 2-8-0	-	-	-	7
04 2-8-0	-	20	15	3
Q5 0-8-0	6	-	-	-
Q6 0-8-0	9	-	-	-
Q10 0-8-0	15	-	-	-
Y3 0-4-0T	-	1	-	-
WD 2-8-0	-	-	-	7
	122	65	27	28

Springhead shed was responsible for five passenger duties at the
time of Grouping on 1 January 1923.

No 1   6.10am South Howden and return, then Locomotive Pilot
        until 12.30pm: three return trips to South Howden and

	North Cave (four on Saturdays) commencing with the 1.5pm Hull to South Howden. This was manned by two sets of men on Mondays-Fridays and three on Saturdays.
No 2	6.50am Hull-Cudworth and return.
No 3	Pilot from 6.30am;8.30am to North Cave and return; pilot 9.45am to 1.45pm
No 4	2.55pm Hull to Cudworth and return.
No 5	7.15pm Hull-South Howden and return, and 9.25pm Hull-North Cave and return (+10.40pm Hull-North Cave and return on Saturdays only).

ALEXANDRA DOCK

The shed at Alexandra Dock, Hull, had to be supplied with North Eastern locomotives soon after the NER/HBR amalgamation, and by 6 December 1923, out of the 29 engines at Alexandra Dock, only 6 were from the Hull & Barnsley Railway stock. The NER engines comprised three types of 0-6-0Ts, J71,J74 and J76, and J72 followed in 1925;there were also 7 ex NER design Y7 0-4-0Ts. The J74s and J76s had disappeared by the end of 1931 and until the introduction of the 350hp diesel-electric locomotives in 1953 the bulk of the work was performed by J71 and J72 0-6-0Ts with, at times, J73s and J77s with the same wheel arrangement. The last two Y7 0-4-0Ts at Alexandra Dock moved to Dairycoates on 11 June 1939 as part of a plan to have only J72, J73 and J77 engines at the Dock shed, and the various J71 engines moved away at about the same time. Thus by September 1941 the allocation comprised:

J72: 462,516/24/71/4/6,1715/21/42/4,2317
J73: 549 and 550
J77: 145,199,614,948,1340/1,1433/61   *TOTAL* 21

However, a Hull & Barnsley engine returned to Alexandra Dock from May 1949 to November 1950 and it was the last to be stationed there – 69119.

The first diesel-electric locomotive 12114 was transferred to Alexandra Dock in October 1953 and eventually all the shunting was performed by 204hp or 350hp diesel locomotives.

The locomotives at Alexandra Dock were transferred to Dairycoates on 27 October 1963, but Alexandra Dock was retained as a signing-on point for the crews and the locomotives continued to stand overnight on the dock premises.

	1923	1932	1939	1954
J71 0-6-0T	7	6	9	-
J72 0-6-0T	-	3	6	9
J73 0-6-0T	-	-	4	2
J74 0-6-0T	8	-	-	-
J75 0-6-0T	3	3	-	-
J76 0-6-0T	1	-	-	-
J77 0-6-0T	-	-	7	-
J80 0-6-0T	3	-	-	-
Y7 0-4-0T	7	4	2	-
350hp diesel	-	-	-	8
	29	16	28	19

CUDWORTH

On 6 December 1923 Cudworth had an allocation of thirty engines, but in less than twenty years this had been reduced to six! All thirty were Hull & Barnsley types but in 1924 a former North Eastern Class A (LNER F8) 2-4-2T was transferred to Cudworth to work the passenger service on the Wath branch. This engine, No 262, spent the summer of 1925 back at York but returned to Cudworth on 2 October. No similar transfer for the summer of 1926 has been noted but from 20 April 1927 to 3 October 1927 262 was at Malton. The passenger service to Wath was withdrawn on 6 April 1929 and 262 was transferred away for the last time on 15 May, when it departed for Scarborough.

The working involved the engine first running light to Kirk Smeaton at 6.0am to work the 7.10am to Wath, and the engine continued to work the service all day until the last train, the 7.10pm Wath to Kirk Smeaton after which the engine returned light to Cudworth. Three sets of men were required on this, Cudworth's only passenger turn (in 1923); the first set travelled out with the light engine and were relieved at 10.15. They then travelled home 'on first available up train from Kirk Smeaton', which would probably be a coal empties. The second set travelled to Kirk Smeaton on the 9.55am Cudworth-Hull train, but ended their duty at Wath when relieved by the third set. The latter men travelled by the 3.55pm passenger train from Cudworth to Wath(Midland) and walked to the Hull & Barnsley station, and the second set returned the same way by the 4.41pm from Wath(Midland).

   The engines used on the mineral trains from the Cudworth end were the HBR Class B 0-6-0 engines but withdrawal commenced in April 1925 and Cudworth's allocation gradually dropped. In addition the 0-6-0s were often required in pairs on the mineral trains and to save the need for double-heading some of the famous 04 2-8-0s of Great Central design were transferred to Cudworth, commencing with 6576 on 5 October 1929, closely followed by 6549, 6577 and 6578. This also allowed Cudworth's only two 0-8-0s to be sent to Hull on 23 October 1929 (No 2500) and 18 November 1929 (No 2508).

   By March 1932 the allocation was: J23 2438/9/45/51/2/6/61/2/4/5/6/7/8/77; N11 0-6-2T 2481; N12 0-6-2T 2483/4/7/9/90 N13 0-6-2T 2415; J75 0-6-0T 2525/6/7; J28 0-6-0 2414; 04 2-8-0 6549/76/7/8. On 9 May 1934, when the Hull & Barnsley 0-6-0s were getting low in numbers at Cudworth, the locomotive running superintendent at York issued an instruction that two former North Eastern classes were to be tried out at Cudworth These were both 0-6-0 classes and two of each type were sent, J21 875 and 1558, both belonging to West Hartlepool but sent from store at Gateshead Works, and J25 2038 of Shildon and 2136 of Darlington, both sent from store at Darlington. On 29 June 1934 it was decided to return the two J21 engines and to replace them at Cudworth with two more J25s — 25 ex Wear Valley Junction and 1990 from Darlington. The loan of 2038 and 2136 was made permanent from the same day. Four weeks later the four remaining Hull & Barnsley 0-6-0s at Cudworth were transferred away, 2445/56/62 to Hull and 2477 to Whitby.

   The J28 0-6-0 2414 was transferred away in July 1933, and in January 1934 N13 2415 and J75 2525/6/7 departed, all to Hull, leaving only two classes of HBR engines at Cudworth, both of which were 0-6-2Ts, 2483/4/7/9/90 of Class N12 and 2481 of Class N11. On 27 July 1936 2490 was transferred to York in exchange for 2485 of the same class, the reason being that a vacuum brake fitted engine was required at York. However, on 19 October 1936 2490 returned to Cudworth and sent in its place was 2483 'to work the D.V.L.Rly. (at the request of the D.V.L.Rly)'. Only eleven days later 2490 went to Hull in exchange for 2488. Nos 2484 and 2487 were transferred to the Southern Area in March 1936 and 2489 was withdrawn in February 1937, leaving 2488 as the only one of its class at Cudworth. Rather than have one N11 and one N12 at Cudworth, 2488 was exchanged for 2482 of Class N11 on 2 August 1937 and this date is of note in being that of the last true Hull & Barnsley engine at Cudworth since although 2481 and 2482 remained at Cudworth until March 1943, they were not of Hull & Barnsley design, even though they were purchased by the HBR.

Of the four J25 0-6-0s already mentioned, 25 and 2038 were exchanged for J21 875 from Dairycoates on 26 July 1935, and the other two departed for Hull in 1936. However, 2072 arrived at Cudworth early in 1935 and once again, to save having a single example of two classes at a shed, J21 875 was replaced by J25 1970 in August 1937. A couple of J21s returned to Cudworth in June 1939 when, under the re-allocation scheme 1970 and 2072 were sent to Darlington, and replaced by 613 and 1516.

On 6 July 1940 A7 4-6-2T 1114 and 1195 were moved from Dairycoates to Cudworth to release 04 6549 for West Hartlepool and 6611 for Heaton, the official reason being the 'extra coal traffic in the north'. Another newcomer, a few weeks earlier was Q6 0-8-0 2250, moved from Dairycoates on 25 March.

Thus Cudworth's allocation became: A7 4-6-2T 1114/95; J21 0-6-0 613 and 1516; N11 0-6-2T 2481/2; 04 2-8-0 6576/9,6616; and Q6 0-8-0 2250. The engines were employed on the following duties:

Class A7	One on 8-0am Upton; one spare. Single shifted.
Class N11	One on double-shifted pilot 5.30am - 9.45pm. One spare.
Class J21	One on 10.45am Upton mineral. Single shifted. One away 'on loan'.
Class 04	One on 5.30am Hickleton mineral. Double-shifted. One on 6.30am Wath mineral. do One on 7.0am Brodsworth mineral. do
Class Q6	On 9-0am Denaby mineral. Single shifted.

At this time (1942) there was some discussion with regard to using some of the Cudworth engines on duties worked by nearby LMS Royston shed when the Cudworth engines had spare time available. For instance it was suggested that one A7 could work a Royston 9.0pm to 5.0am daily shunting turn; that the Q6 could work a trip to Grimesthorpe, and that a J21 could work a trip on the Wharncliffe branch. However, it is not known if this arrangement actually came into force as this was six years before nationalisation, but it may have been implemented because of the war effort.

In March 1943 there was a mass reallocation of locomotives in the North Eastern Area and Cudworth lost all its locomotives except the two A7 4-6-2Ts. In place of Q6 2250, J21 613, N11 2481/2, and 04 6576/9,6614 the shed received J25 459, 1993 and 2080, and C6 4-4-2 696 and 697. The last two were most inappropriate for a shed handling only mineral and heavy freight work!

In March 1944 more suitable power arrived in the shape of Q6 2251/78/87, but 2278 was exchanged for 2246 two months later. In October 1944 696 and 697 departed for Hull Dairycoates. The three Q6s left in September 1946 and were replaced by Q5 772 and 3311. Thus in January 1947 the allocation was J25 5667, 5703/14, Q5 3311/32, and A7 9771/89. By the end of 1951 all the above had been transferred away and replaced by 04 2-8-0 63620/67,63751/4,63845/9/57;63620 and 63667 were transferred away in 1951 and replaced by 63772 and it was these six engines — 63751/4/72 and 63845/9/57 which were transferred to Royston shed when Cudworth closed on 30 July 1951.

	1923	1933	1939	1947	1950
A7 4-6-2T	-	-	-	2	-
J23 0-6-0	19	13	-	-	-
J25 0-6-0	-	-	2	3	2
J28 0-6-0	1	1	-	-	-
J75 0-6-0T	3	3	-	-	-
N11 0-6-2T	1	1	2	-	-
N12 0-6-2T	4	5	-	-	-
N13 0-6-2T	2	1	-	-	-
04 2-8-0	-	4	10	-	4
Q5 0-8-0	-	-	-	2	-
	30	28	14	7	6

BULLCROFT

The Hull & Barnsley sheds were taken over by the North Eastern

Railway on 1 April 1922 but the earliest allocation list known is dated 6 December 1923, when Bullcroft had one Class B 0-6-0 and three Class F2 0-6-2Ts. Early in 1925 two F2s were transferred away and replaced by another Class B and a North Eastern A7 4-6-2T. The next move was on 12 September 1928 when one of the 0-6-0s (2436) was withdrawn and not replaced. Next came the first transfer of an 04 2-8-0 to Bullcroft — 6611 from York on 29 October 1929, displacing A7 1174 to York a few months later.

On 9 July 1930 T1 4-8-0T 1657 was transferred from Stockton to Bullcroft but after only ten days it was replaced by 1658 from York. This engine was for the Warmsworth pilot duty and on 8 December 1930 1660 also moved to Bullcroft as spare for the same duty. However, as a forerunner to closure the Warmsworth duty was taken over by Doncaster shed on 12 October 1931, making the two 4-8-0Ts redundant and they moved to Hull Dairycoates. This left 0-6-0 2469, 0-6-2T 2486, and 2-8-0 6611 at Bullcroft and all were transferred to Springhead when Bullcroft closed on 5 December 1931.

DENABY

Denaby shed was probably at one time responsible for working the passenger service on the branch but this was withdrawn on 1 February 1903 and henceforward the shed housed only one or two freight engines. At 6 December 1923 these comprised one J23 0-6-0 and one N12 0-6-2T. The N12 (2489) was transferred to Hull Dairycoates on 28 May 1927; two days later the staff were moved away, and on 31 May 1927 the shed closed when 0-6-0 2461 was transferred to Cudworth.

North British Railway Sheds taken over by LNER

DUNS

In exchange for Carlisle(London Road) the North Eastern Area of the LNER took over three former North British sheds from the Southern Scottish Area and Duns was one of these. At the time of the takeover Duns still retained two North British 2-4-0s of Class E7, 1245B and 10246: these were both withdrawn in 1925 and replaced by two former North Eastern 4-4-0s of Class D23,

probably 223 and 258 which had just been transferred to
Tweedmouth from Hull. In 1926 two J21 0-6-0s were at Duns, and
in the following year a solitary D23. This was 258 which, in
April 1929, was replaced by an unusual engine for a North Eastern
Area shed – 4739, a former Great Northern Railway 0-6-2T of
Class N2. In July 1934, after five years in the Border country, the
N2 was exchanged for H1 4-4-4T 2160 of Heaton: in May 1936
2160 departed for Darlington Works to be rebuilt to an A8
4-6-2T and in its place Duns received another North British engine
– C15 4-4-2T 9131. This remained until May 1942 and it was
then returned to the Scottish Area in exchange for a North
Eastern engine allocated to the Scottish Area. This was D17/2
4-4-0 1901, which had been at Carlisle (London Road) when that
shed was taken over by the Scottish Area in 1925. No 1901
was withdrawn in June 1945 and it was replaced by another NER
4-4-0, 2028 of Class D20. After nationalisation another North
British engine arrived, but this time a 4-4-0 62448 of Class D32
and this was still at Duns when the shed returned to Scottish
control on 13 June 1948.

In 1939 the working of the Duns engines was confined to the
St Boswells-Duns-Reston-Berwick service, with one afternoon
working (Saturdays excepted) from St Boswells to Kelso and back.
The first set booked on at 5.30am and the second set relieved them
at Duns at 1.35pm as the engine was working the 12.52pm Berwick
to St Boswells.

REEDSMOUTH

Although a North British Railway shed this depot is included
because on 1 August 1924 it was transferred to the North Eastern
Area of the LNER, becoming a sub-shed to Tweedmouth. At the
time of the changeover the engines at Reedsmouth were D51
4-4-0T 1402, J33 0-6-0 9024, and J36 0-6-0 9754 and 9779.
The D51 was replaced by a North Eastern engine in September
1925 when the 4-4-0T went to Cowlairs for scrapping. The
newcomer was a BTP 0-4-4T and this in turn was replaced by
an F8 2-4-4T in 1927. This as No 172 which, when withdrawn for
scrapping in December 1929, was replaced by 1583 of the same
class from Hexham. This was withdrawn in May 1936. In the meantime the J33 9024 had been withdrawn in December 1930 and

replaced by another North Eastern engine, J21 0-6-0 1813. When this was withdrawn in October 1933 9791 of Class J36 from Rothbury joined the others of the class already at Reedsmouth.

9791 went to Blaydon in April 1940 but returned to Reedsmouth 'for snowplough duties' until 1949, when it was again transferred to Blaydon. The other two J36s were sent to the Scottish Area, 9754 in September 1943 and 9779 in 1951. When 9754 departed it was replaced by J21 0-6-0 1588 and this class persisted until the shed closed, at first in company with one or two J36s, and finally two J21s responsible for all the workings. Engines of the class known to have been allocated to Reedsmouth in addition to 1588 (later 5101) were 65033,65042,65105,65111 and 65119. On the closure date of 15 September 1952 the allocation consisted of 65033 and 65119 but 65033 was absent and the last train from Reedsmouth to Scotsgap and back on 13 September was worked by 65042.

In 1939 Reedsmouth was responsible for two passenger duties, one worked by two sets of men and the other by one set. No 1 early turn prepared the engine and left the shed at 7.15am to carry out any necessary shunting before working the 7.53am to Scotsgap: they shunted there before returning to Reedsmouth at 10.34am. On Mondays only they then worked the 11.30am goods to Scotsgap and returned, also on a goods, at 1.15pm; On other days they shunted as required at Reedsmouth after arriving back at 11.3am, until relieved by the second set who booked on at 2.15pm. They had no booked train to work but worked 'as required' and then stabled their own engine and the engine of No 2 passenger turn. No 2 turn men booked on at 11.50am and also worked 'as required' prior to working the 3.37pm to Bellingham, the 4.5pm return, then the 4.15pm to Scotsgap and the 6.22pm return. On Saturdays No 2 turn was combined with No 1 and a new No 2, worked by two sets of men, started off by working an empty train to Kielder, then at 1.29pm to Hexham, followed by the 7.5pm Hexham-Bellingham, 8.10pm Bellingham-Hexham.10.25pm Hexham-Kielder, and then back home with the empty train to Reedsmouth at 11.58pm.

ROTHBURY

This shed in mid-Northumberland was one of the three former

North British sheds transferred to the North Eastern Area of the LNER in 1924. At the time of transfer on 1 August 1924 Rothbury accommodated D51 4-4-0T 1401 and J36 0-6-0 9791: the 4-4-0T was withdrawn in October 1924 and a 2-4-2T of Class F8 was supplied to take its place. The last F8 to be stationed at Rothbury was 1599, which was withdrawn in May 1936 and replaced by G5 0-4-4T 2086 from Heaton. This engine was transferred to Alston on 29 May 1940 and for a while one engine sufficed at Rothbury, until another G5 – 1918 – was transferred there from Heaton on 23 November 1940. This engine, latterly as 67296, was stationed at Rothbury until the branch and shed closed from 15 September 1952. However, at the time of closure 67296 was away under repair and the last passenger trains were worked by 67341 of the same class.

The goods engine, 9791, was transferred to Reedsmouth in October 1933 and replaced by J21 0-6-0 877 from Heaton. This engine remained until it was withdrawn in May 1944 when it was replaced by 1557 of the same class. Finally 5035, another J21, arrived in 1948 and remained until closure, actually working the last goods train to Morpeth on 13 September 1952.

The small single-road shed was approached by a turntable at the end of the station platform.

Appendices

1 Footplate Staff Records

The North Eastern, like many other railway companies, imposed monetary fines or suspension from duty for misdemeanours and offences committed by its staff. The footplate men were liable to be punished for many different types of offences and I have recently been able to inspect the records of many footplate staff dating from 1870 to 1928. Some of the oldest men listed were born in the 1830s and retired as drivers in the present century as seventy was the usual age of retirement on the NER.

Some types of accidents appear time and time again in the records, the most common being (not in order):

1. Running past signals at danger.
2. Leaving behind the guard, brake van, or part of train, or all three.
3. Collisions in shed yards.
4. Derailments due to engine reversing on spring or hold-up points.
5. Engine driven by fireman (often in the absence of the driver) and run into buffers/train/shed wall/turntable pit etc etc.
6. Single line working irregularities.

It is surprising how many engines have finished in the turntable pit, or been derailed moving off a turntable. And what a wonder that more accidents have not resulted from trains running through single line sections without any form of authority - staff, tablet or ticket!

A locomotive short of steam brought a caution or a fine and cases occur where staff were taken to task for smoking on duty or for going to speak to the crew of another locomotive, and a driver was usually held responsible for his engine running hot.

I have listed some of the more unusual happenings. They are given in shed order and represent only a very small fraction of the details examined:

Fireman J.S., Blaydon, 28 February 1919. Brought off footplate. Not being able to maintain pressure on East Coast trains, causing time to be lost.

Fireman W.C., Blaydon, 6 June 1899. Suspended one month. Losing fire pricker off engine on High Level Bridge, it fell through the roof of a house.

Fireman W.E.W., Borough Gardens, 16 December 1921. Cautioned. Putting too much coal on fire of engine, causing it to be extinguished and delaying the train.

Driver T.K., Borough Gardens, 11 March 1920. Cautioned. Stopping his train on the main line at Durham when given a clear run, to allow his fireman to seek refreshments, causing delay to 5.35pm passenger York to Newcastle and his own train.

Driver G.B.D., Darlington, 22 September 1906. Fined 5s (25p). Leaving engine 622 at Clifton and going for a walk causing serious delay to 3.55pm goods from Penrith to Darlington.

Driver J.H.C., Darlington, 23 January 1900. Strong Caution. Not having cleaned firebox front and cab of engine 1575.

Driver J.M., Darlington, 19 September 1904. Suspended 1 week. Allowing an unauthorised person to ride on engine 933 when working 8.52am North Road to Darlington.

Driver J.M., Gateshead, 8 August 1912. Fined 2s 6d (12½p). Allowing an inexperienced fireman to move engine 730, and thus causing it to run into No 1 turntable hole at Gateshead shed.

Driver T.S., Heaton, 13 August 1923. Cautioned. Having steam pressure of engine 2157 too high, causing engine to blow off and bring soot from roof of Sunderland station, damaging passengers' clothing.

Driver J.W.W., Hull, 13 July 1907. Fined 2s 6d (12½p). Using foul language at Everingham station when on footplate of engine 1100 working 11.13am passenger Driffield to Selby.

Driver S.W., Hull, 10 June 1907. Strong caution. Running past signals at danger at Edge Hill, Liverpool, with engine 1622 when working emigrant special.

Driver H.B., Springhead, 13 February 1909. Reduced in rate from
6s 0d (30p) to 5s 6d (27½p) per day.
Being implicated in the case of engine 68, which ran out of Loco
Yard into dead end road near locomotive junction and fell into
Lodge Lane.

Driver A.H.H., Hull, 8 March 1906. Cautioned.
Putting a snickle in the blast pipe of engine 369.

Fireman A.E.G., Hull 4 May 1901. Suspended 1 week.
Neglecting his work and playing dominoes in shunters' lobby at
Hull when on duty.

Driver G.M., Holbeck, 18 August 1886. Suspended for two weeks.
Working goods train Thirsk to Leeds on main line without his
fireman to permit latter to gather mushrooms.

Driver T.K., Holbeck, 11 January 1902. Fined 5s 0d (25p).
Leaving engine 2089 at Hull and going to sleep in L&Y carriage
and being carried to Goole, causing delay to 2.7pm passenger
train Hull to York arranging another man and engine to work the
train.

Driver W.J.N., Holbeck, 8 November 1913. Rewarded £1.
Arranging to stop runaway engine 324 which had been abandoned
by Driver L. and Fireman W. to prevent collision between it and
Diner at Northallerton.

Driver E.F., Leeds, 8 November 1913. Rewarded £3.
Overtaking runaway engine 324 which had been left by Driver L.
and Fireman W. after giving it steam to prevent 3.20pm Diner
Edinburgh to London colliding with it at Northallerton, and
mounting footplate whilst engine was in motion to shut off steam.

Driver W.S., Leeds, 27 November 1911. Commended.
Promptitude in bringing engine to a stand on an unknown man
attempting to commit suicide by throwing himself on the line.

Driver A.W., Leeds, 8 October 1909. Reprimanded.
Taking goods train forward to Masham without Conductor over
road on which he had not been for 7 years, which in some measure
contributed to serious accident — engine 208 running amain down
the bank with Special Goods from Ripon to Masham and through
dead-end at Corporation Siding (65 tons overloaded)

Driver H.W.T., Shildon, 5 September 1910. Cautioned.
Abusing engine 1072 whilst proceeding from Loco Coal Depot to
shed.

Driver W. T., Shildon, 21 March 1910. Suspended one month.
Allowing fireman to place wicket gate on tender of engine 1024
without first questioning him as to whether he had got it honestly
or not.

Driver J. C., South Gosforth, 16 July 1898. Fined 2s 6d (12½p).
Unable to maintain steam in private locomotive and having to
leave it at Plessey through getting ashpan full of ashes.

Fireman R. M., Middlesbrough, 12 July 1899. Suspended 2 weeks.
Practical joking in stating that engine 1684 was amiss and required
changing when such was not the case, another engine being lighted
up and sent from Middlesbrough to Newport.

Driver M. W., Shildon, 5 July 1904. Sharp reprimand.
Leaving engine 1037 in charge of fireman to attend to points.
Fireman lost control down Shildon Lodge Bank and in order to
save engine running off at catch points left it entirely.

Driver T. K., York, 8 May 1896. Fined 6d (2½p).
Taking engine keys home.

Driver T. H., York, 24 November 1919. Commended by O/C RAF.
Promptly going to the assistance of airman in burning aeroplane
at Eryholme whilst working Naval Special.

2 Autocars and Railcars

Mention has been made in the text to the BTP 0-4-4 engines which worked the 'autocars', or push-and-pull trains, throughout the North Eastern system. By Grouping the original total of 124 engines had fallen to 46, some of which were approaching their half century. Thus it was obvious that their days were numbered and it is strange that no G5 engines were fitted with push-and-pull gear at that time to replace them. Although the North Eastern was interested in petrol engined vehicles for branch lines only two such vehicles were produced after World War I and it was apparent that a light cheap to run vehicle was required for branch lines, especially as bus competition was beginning to be felt.

In 1925 the LNER purchased two Sentinel steam railcars for use in the Southern Area, and two years later a couple were obtained for use in the North Eastern Area. These were followed by twenty of similar design in 1928, followed by a single improved two-cylinder car, and six and twelve cylinder vehicles. By 1935 57 Sentinel cars were at work in the North Eastern Area, together with five Clayton steam cars and four Armstrong-Whitworth diesel cars.

These railcars were scattered throughout the Area at twenty locomotive sheds and the workings of some of them have been described under their respective sheds. A list of the duties operated by each shed, together with the number of cars available, is given in tabular form. It will be noted that Heaton and Hull Botanic Gardens housed the greatest number of cars but note that because of the unreliability of the Clayton cars there were eleven units to cover a maximum of five duties.

The diesel cars were withdrawn in 1939 and the last Sentinel cars disappeared in 1948, the first year of British Railways: the Clayton cars became extinct in 1937.

The railcars tended to be a nuisance at engine sheds because of the space they required, but fortunately both Botanic Gardens and Heaton had some long sidings where the cars could be stabled. The dirty conditions in and around engine sheds did nothing to enhance their appearance and the cars themselves were liable to make plenty of dirt of their own if not correctly fired. With the doors of their coal bunkers being in the roof they were difficult to coal at some sheds and in any case it meant the fireman going on the roof of the car.

If well maintained and handled by regular crews the Sentinel cars were economical and a pleasure to handle, although the engine compartment got very hot in the summer months. However, if handled by a ham-fisted driver used to 'flogging' a B16 or K3 then the car would soon lay down on him, and although you could raise steam very quickly with a Sentinel you could lose it even faster!

ALLOCATION OF RAILCARS WINTER SERVICE 1935-6

BLYTH		
Sentinel 2-cyl	272	Hero
Sentinel 12-cyl	2291	Phenomena
BRIDLINGTON		
Sentinel 6-cyl	2245	Criterion
DARLINGTON		
Sentinel 6-cyl	2271	Industry
GUISBOROUGH		
Sentinel 12-cyl	2283	Old Blue
HEATON		
Sentinel 2-cyl	2135	Integrity
Sentinel 6-cyl	2198	Times
	2257	Defiance
	2270	Independent
	2276	North Briton
Clayton	287	Royal Sailor
	289	Wellington
	296	Wonder
	2101	Union
	2121	Pilot
Diesel Railbus	294	—————

HULL B.G.

Sentinel 2-cyl	21	Valliant
	22	Brilliant
	26	Tally Ho
	29	Rockingham
	210	Highflyer
	212	Eclipse
	238	Yorkshire Huzzar
	255	Perseverance
	283	Teazle
	263	North Star
	265	Neptune
Sentinel 6-cyl	2242	Cornwallis
Diesel Railcar	224	Lady Hamilton

LEEDS

Sentinel 6-cyl	2133	Cleveland
Diesel Railcar	232	Northumbrian

MALTON

Sentinel 6-cyl	2236	British Queen

MIDDLESBROUGH

Sentinel 12-cyl	2281	Old John Bull
Diesel Railcar	25	Tyneside Venturer

SALTBURN

Sentinel 2-cyl	267	Liberty

SCARBOROUGH

Sentinel 12-cyl	220	Defence

SELBY

Sentinel 2-cyl	273	Trafalgar
	225	True Blue

STARBECK

Sentinel 6-cyl	2200	Surprise
	2268	Emerald
	2279	Norfolk

STOCKTON

Sentinel 6-cyl	2139	Hark Forward
	2231	Swift
	2232	Alexander
	2235	Britannia

SUNDERLAND

Sentinel 6-cyl	2140	Eagle
	2145	Ruby
	2147	Woodpecker
	2151	Umpire
	2238	Celerity

TWEEDMOUTH

Sentinel 6-cyl	2217	Royal Charlotte

TYNE DOCK

Sentinel 2-cyl	237	Rodney
	244	True Briton
	254	Phoenix
Sentinel 6-cyl	2267	Recovery

WEST AUCKLAND

Sentinel 6-cyl	2144	Traveller
	2152	Courrier
	2136	Hope
	2218	Telegraph
	2261	Diligence

WEST HARTLEPOOL

Sentinel 2-cyl	226	Ebor
	250	Rob Roy
	253	Red Rover

WHITBY

Sentinel 6-cyl	2219	New Fly
Sentinel 12-cyl	246	Royal Sovereign
	248	

SHED	SERVICES			CARS ALLOCATED					
	M—F.	Sat	Sun	SENTINEL 2. 6. 12. cylinder			CLAYTON	DIESEL	TOTAL
BLYTH	2	2	1	1	-	1	-	-	2
BRIDLINGTON	1	1	-	-	1	-	-		1
DARLINGTON	1	-	1	-	1	-	-	-	1
GUISBOROUGH	1	-	-	-	-	1	-	-	1
HEATON	4	3	5	1	4	-	5	1	11
HULL B.G.	7	8	3	11	1	-	-	1	13
LEEDS	2	2	-	-	1	-	-	1	2
MALTON	1	1	-	-	1	-	-	-	1
MIDDLESBRO'	2	1	-	-	-	1	-	1	2
SALTBURN	1	1	-	1	-	-	-	-	1
SCARBOROUGH	1	1	-	-	-	1	-	-	1
SELBY	1	1	-	2	-	-	-	-	2
STARBECK	2	2	1	-	3	-	-	-	3
STOCKTON	3	1	-	-	4	-	-	-	4
SUNDERLAND	4	-	4	-	5	-	-	-	5
TWEEDMOUTH	1	1	-	-	1	-	-	-	1
TYNE DOCK	3	2	-	3	1	-	-	-	4
WEST AUCKLAND	3	2	2	-	5	-	-	-	5
WEST HART'PL	2	2	1	3	-	-	-	-	3
WHITBY	2	2	-	-	1	2	-	-	3
	44	33	18	22	29	6	5	4	66

3   List of Turntables 1921

Length of turntables required by various classes of engines:

     55ft 0in Classes 4cc, S, S1, S2, S3, V, Z and WD

     50ft 0in Classes 3cc, R, R1, M, Q and Q1

     46ft 0in Classes F, J and T3

     45ft 0in Classes G, I, T, T1 and T2

     40ft 10in Classes P1 and 1463

     42ft 6in Classes P2, P3, and 38

All other classes can turn on a 40ft 0in turntable.

The following table lists the turntables at the various North Eastern sheds. At some locations the turntable was situated away from the shed (Northallerton,Pickering etc) but they are given here for completeness. There were other turntables, often situated at a station where there was no shed (Hornsea,Withernsea,South Shields etc); where the shed was some distance away (Harrogate, Blackhill etc); or at a goods yard (Gascoigne Wood etc) but these have been omitted.

STATION	NO. OF TABLES	WHERE SITUATED	LENGTH FT	IN
Alnmouth	1	In siding between Aln-wick branch and main line, north of station	42	2
Alston	1	End of platform line	42	4
Barnard Castle	1	Outside engine shed	50	0
Battersby	1	Outside engine shed	42	0
Blaydon	2	Inside engine shed	50	0
Blyth	1	Outside engine shed	50	0

Borough Gardens	2	Inside engine shed	45	0
Borough Gardens	2	Inside engine shed	42	6
Bowes Bridge	1	Siding near engine shed	42	0
Bridlington	1	Loco Yard	50	0
Byers Green	1	Outside engine shed	42	0
Carlisle	1	Inside engine shed	50	0
Carlisle	1	Inside engine shed	45	0
Carlisle	1	Outside engine shed	50	0
Darlington	1	Bank Top Loco Yard	60	0
Darlington	1	Round shed	42	0
Durham	1	Outside engine shed	42	10
Ferryhill	1	Outside engine shed	43	0
Gateshead(Greensfield)	3	Inside engine shed	60	0
Gateshead (Greensfield)	1	Inside engine shed	42	5
Gateshead (Paint Shop)	1	Inside Paint Shop	41	10
Guisborough	1	Outside engine shed	42	0
Hartlepool	1	Outside engine shed	42	0
Heaton Junction	1	Outside engine shed	60	0
Hexham	1	Outside engine shed	42	6
Hull	3	Dairycoates shed	60	0
Hull	3	Dairycoates shed	50	0
Hull	2	Botanic shed-inside	50	0
Hull	1	Botanic shed-outside	50	0
Ilkley	1	Outside engine shed	50	0
Kirkby Stephen	1	Outside engine shed	50	0
Leeds	1	West end of new station(On site of old shed)	60	0
Leeds	1	Holbeck Erecting Shop	42	6
Leeds	4	Neville Hill-inside	55	0
Leeds	1	Neville Hill-outside	55	0
Leyburn	1	Outside engine shed	42	4
Malton	1	Loco Yard	46	0
Market Weighton	1	Loco Yard	50	0
Masham	1	Outside engine shed	42	0
Middlesbrough	3	Inside engine sheds	50	0
Middleton in Teesdale	1	Outside engine shed	45	0
Newport	2	Inside engine shed	50	0
Newport	1	Outside engine shed	44	0
Northallerton	1	Station sidings	42	0
North Blyth	1	Inside engine shed	50	0
Pateley Bridge	1	Loco Yard	42	6
Percy Main	1	Outside engine shed	50	0
Pickering	1	Siding near High Mill Box	50	0
Richmond	1	Outside engine shed	45	0

Location		Description		
Saltburn	1	Outside engine shed	50	0
Scarborough	1	Inside engine shed	44	8
Scarborough	1	Loco Yard	50	0
Scarborough	1	Gallows Close Loco Sidings	60	0
Selby	1	New shed	50	0
Selby	1	Old shed	42	0
Shildon	3	Inside engine shed	50	0
Skinningrove(Carlin How)	1	Outside engine shed	55	0
Stanhope	1	Outside engine shed	45	0
Starbeck	1	Loco Yard	50	0
Stockton	1	Outside engine shed	46	4
Sunderland(South Dock)	1	Inside engine shed	42	0
Sunderland(Hendon)	1	Outside engine shed	42	0
Tebay	1	East end of yard	50	0
Thirsk	1	Loco Yard	60	0
Tweedmouth	1	Outside engine shed	60	0
Tweedmouth	1	Inside engine shed	45	0
Tyne Dock	1	Outside engine shed	60	0
Tyne Dock	2	Inside engine shed	42	2
Tyne Dock	1	Inside engine shed (Under construction replacing 41' 10")	50	0
Wearhead	1	Outside engine shed	45	0
Wear Valley Junction	1	Inside engine shed	50	0
West Auckland(Fieldon Junction)	1	Inside engine shed	50	0
West Hartlepool	1	Inside engine shed	42	3
West Hartlepool	1	Inside engine shed	50	0
Whitby	1	Yard sidings Bog Hall Junction	50	0
York	2	New shed, Leeman Rd	60	0
York	1	New shed, Leeman Rd	50	0
York	1	New shed, Leeman Rd	45	0
York	2	Old sheds	42	0
York	1	Midland shed	45	0
York	1	Queen St New shed	60	0

4 Coaling Depots 1921

Alnmouth
Alnwick
Alston
Annfield Plain
Barnard Castle
Blaydon
Borough Gardens
Bowes Bridge
Bradford(Mid)
Byers Green(Todhills)
Carlisle
Carlin How
Darlington(Bank Top)
Darlington(Hope Town)
Durham
Ferryhill
Forth Junction
Gateshead
Hartlepool

Haverton Hill
Heaton Junction
Hexham
Hull(Dairycoates)
Hull(Botanic Gardens)
Ilkley(Mid)
Kirkby Stephen
Leeds(Neville Hill)
Malton
Masham
Middlesbrough
Newport
Normanton(Mid)
Northallerton
North Blyth
Percy Main
Pickering
Rosedale

Saltburn
Scarborough
Selby
Shildon
South Blyth
South Dock
Starbeck
Stockton
Thirsk
Tweedmouth
Tyne Dock
Waskerley
Whitby
Wear Valley Junction
West Auckland(Field-
on Junction)
West Hartlepool
York

WATER COLUMNS

In NER days the various locomotive sheds were responsible for the maintenance of the water columns situated in their areas. The supervising shed was indicated on each column by a one, two or three letter abbreviation, followed by a serial number.

5 Shed Codes

North Eastern Railway locomotives did not carry any indication of their home shed, but the headlamps, which were proper to one engine only, often carried the name of the shed as the lamps had to be handed in at the stores when the driver signed off duty, and collected again when he signed on the following day. On some photographs the name of the shed can just be distinguished on the lamp.

In LNER days it was decided to indicate the home shed of every engine by means of an abbreviated form of the name stencilled inside the engine cab and sixty-seven of these codes were used:

Annfield Plain	A'PLAIN	Masham	M'HAM
Alston	ALSTON	Newport	N'PORT
Alnmouth	A'MOUTH	North Road Works	N.R.W.
Alexandra Dock	ALEX DOCK	Northallerton	NALLTN
Borough Gardens	BORO GDNS	North Blyth	N.BLYTH
Bowes Bridge	BS BRIDGE	Normanton	N'TON
Barnard Castle	BD CLE	Percy Main	P.MAIN
Blaydon	B'DON	Pateley Bridge	P.BRIDGE
Blyth	BLYTH	Pelton Level	P.LEVEL
Bridlington	BRID	Penrith	P.RITH
Bullcroft	B'CROFT	Pickering	P.KING
Bradford	B'FORD	Reedsmouth	R'MTH
Carlisle	C'LISLE	Rothbury	R'BURY
Consett	C'SETT	Rosedale	R'DALE
Cudworth	CUDTH	Richmond	R'MOND
Durham	D'HAM	Scarborough	S'BRO
Darlington	D'TON	Starbeck	S'BECK
Denaby	D'BY	Stockton	S'TON
Ferryhill	F'HILL	Saltburn	S'BURN
Gateshead	G'HEAD	Shildon	S'DON
Guisborough	G'BORO	Sunderland	S'LAND
Heaton	H'TON	Stanhope	S'HOPE
Hartlepool	H'POOL	Selby	S'BY
Haverton Hill	H'TON HILL	Springhead	SPHEAD
Hexham	H'HAM	Tweedmouth	T'MTH
Hull Dairycoates	HULL D	Thirsk	THIRSK
Hull Botanic		Tyne Dock	T'DOCK
Gardens	HULL BG	Wear Valley	
Hawes	HAWES	Junction	W V JCT
Ilkley	ILKLEY	West Hartlepool	W H'POOL
Kirkby Stephen	KBY STN	Waskerley	WKLY
Leeds(Neville Hill)	LDS	West Auckland	W AKLD
Middlesbrough	M'BRO	Whitby	WTBY
Middleton-in-	MTON-IN-T	York	YK
Teesdale			
Malton	MLTON		

Late in December 1937 it was suggested that small enamelled plates carrying the name in black letters on a white background should be used, with the plate bolted to the interior of the cab just under the eaves. It was estimated that the plates would cost 1s 0d (5p) each and that it would cost 1s 3d (6p) to drill and tap the holes and to provide fixing bolts, thus making the cost 2s 3d

(11p) per engine and bringing about an economy when compared with the old method of stencilling the name. Plates were ordered to be manufactured for all the sheds in the North Eastern Area, and each shed kept a supply of its own plates in the stores so that they could be affixed to any engine received on transfer from another shed.

The enamelling on the plates did not stand up to the fumes encountered in the engine cabs and after a few years they fell into disuse, although the plates could still be found on a few engines well into the 1950s, usually covered by several coats of paint, which had helped to preserve them.

In March 1940 it was decided that engines at certain sub-sheds should carry the plate of the main shed and the following alterations were made:

SUB-SHED	ENGINES TO CARRY
Alston	GATESHEAD
Bowes Bridge	BOROUGH GARDENS
Duns	TWEEDMOUTH
Durham	SUNDERLAND
Guisborough	MIDDLESBROUGH
Ilkley	LEEDS
Leyburn	NORTHALLERTON
Middleton-in-Teesdale	DARLINGTON
Normanton	YORK
Pateley Bridge	STARBECK
Pelton Level	TYNE DOCK
Pickering	MALTON
Reedsmouth	HEATON
Rothbury	HEATON
Waskerley	CONSETT
Wearhead	WEST AUCKLAND

Early in 1943 it was decided that the shed should be indicated on the front buffer beam and applied by stencil, usually in an abbreviated form. Some sheds appear to have used the old stencils formerly used for putting the names inside the cab, but whereas some sheds used the same abbreviation as used pre-1938 others started to use a different version:

Pre-1938	1943	Pre-1938	1943
HULL BG	BOT GDNS	D'TON	D'GTON
HULL D	HULL DC	LDS	NEV HILL
P.MAIN	PCY MAIN	W AKLD	W'A'LAND

Other sheds began to use the name in full: *BRIDLINGTON, CUDWORTH, HEATON, SELBY, TYNE DOCK, WHITBY* and *YORK*, but some sheds used more than one version: *TYNE DOCK* and *TYNE D.*

This method persisted until the introduction of the British Railways' code, based on the former LMS system. The codes allocated to former North Eastern sheds were originally:

50A	*YORK*	52A	*GATESHEAD*
	Normanton		Bowes Bridge
50B	Leeds	52B	Heaton
	Ilkley	52C	Blaydon
50C	Selby		Hexham
50D	Starbeck		Alston
	Pateley Bridge		Reedmouth
50E	Scarborough	52D	Tweedmouth
50F	Malton		Alnmouth
	Pickering	52E	Percy Main
50G	Whitby	52F	North & South Blyth
			Rothbury
51A	Darlington		
	Middleton-in-Teesdale	53A	*DAIRYCOATES*
51B	Newport	53B	Botanic Gardens
51C	West Hartlepool	53C	Springhead
51D	Middlesbrough		Alexandra Dock
	Guisborough	53D	Bridlington
51E	Stockton	53E	Cudworth
51F	West Auckland		
	Wearhead	54A	*SUNDERLAND*
51G	Haverton Hill		Durham
51H	Kirkby Stephen	54B	Tyne Dock
51J	Northallerton		Pelton Level
	Leyburn	54C	Borough Gardens
51K	Saltburn	54D	Consett

Due to Regional Boundary alterations and other reorganisations some shed codes were subsequently changed:

Blaydon	52C to 52A Sub-shed March 1963
Borough Gardens	54C to 52J October 1958
Consett	54D to 52K October 1958
Durham	54A Sub-shed to 52G Sub-shed October 1958
Heaton	52B to 52A Sub-shed June 1963
Hull (Alex Dock)	53C Sub-shed to 50B Sub-shed January 1960
Hull (Botanic Gardens)	53B to 50C January 1960
Hull (D'Coates)	53A to 50B January 1960
Hull (Springhead)	53C to 50B Sub-shed January 1960
Ilkley	50B Sub-shed to 55F Sub-shed January 1957
Kirkby Stephen	51H to 12E February 1958 and to 12D April 1958
Leeds (Nev Hill)	50B to 55H January 1960
Normanton	20D to 55E January 1957
Pelton Level	54B Sub-shed to 52H Sub-shed October 1958
Penrith	12C to 12B January 1955 and to 12B Sub-shed January 1958
Sunderland	54A to 52G October 1958
Tyne Dock	54B to 52H October 1958

Index to Sheds